"A powerful book that our country needs now more than ever. It's a story of a family, community, and our nation coming together for a rare happy ending where the good guys win. Chris has written must-read for everyone."

— **John Walsh**, victims advocate, host of *In Pursuit with John Walsh*, former host/creator of *America's Most Wanted*, author of *Tears of Rage*

"In this captivating book, Chris Thomas takes us on a fascinating journey of some of his choice life experiences and challenging disappointments. He skillfully presents the lessons, trials, and triumphs that have been so meaningful to him. Knowing him as a gentle, soft-spoken man with a compassionate heart, I can now see how he developed his unique set of personality traits. His journey is a remarkable tale of 'becoming' while engaging with others and their challenges, disappointments, opportunities, and rewarding experiences. I highly recommend this enlightening book."

— **Gail Miller**, philanthropist, former owner of the Utah Jazz; current owner of the Larry H. Miller Group of Companies, author of *Courage to Be You*

"Elizabeth Smart's rescue was a cultural landmark with few equals. Her abduction was a distinctly Utah crime, a tragedy of religious extremism that put an entire community in the national spotlight. In *Unexpected*, Chris Thomas details the behind-the-scenes struggles of the PR campaign he managed to help bring Elizabeth home. His experiences growing up in the LDS faith uniquely prepared him for this task. Through tales of his own childhood, Chris does a remarkable job of explaining the complex nuances of Mormon culture and its service-based traditions. This is an inspiring story of a misunderstood community coming together and pulling off a miracle."

— **Jared Hess**, writer and director, *Napoleon Dynamite*, *Nacho Libre*, and *Gentlemen Broncos*; executive producer and co-director, *Murder Among the Mormons*

"More than two decades after the abduction and rescue of Elizabeth Smart, Chris Thomas has done the unthinkable. After countless media accounts, movies, and millions of already written words, Thomas offers incredible color and context to a story we thought we knew. His behind-the-scenes experiences as family spokesman, coupled with his keen observations on the people, faith, and culture that both raised and found her, make the book hard to put down. Only Thomas could have written this, and you'll be grateful he did."

— **Jason Wright**, *New York Times* best-selling author of *Christmas Jars*

"*Unexpected* is engaging and deeply touching. As a young mother who watched in horror the news of the kidnapping of Elizabeth Smart two decades ago, this glimpse behind the scenes of a grieving family forced into the public eye was heart-wrenching and captivating. Thomas skillfully interweaves the large-scale effort to rescue Elizabeth with his own experiences growing up in a Latter-day Saint community, exposing the humanity in the Smarts' miraculous story and in an American faith."

—**Dr. Jennifer Finlayson-Fife**, therapist, and host of *Conversations with Dr. Jennifer*

"Chris Thomas has a way of seamlessly interweaving his own childhood memories with those he experienced behind the scenes with the Smart family during Elizabeth's abduction. *Unexpected* is a powerful, poignant, and inspirational journey that leaves you with a deeper appreciation for the good of humanity in the face of the unimaginable."

—**Deondra Brown**, musician, *The 5 Browns*; co-founder/president of The Foundation for Survivors of Abuse

"What's it like for every part of your life to come together in a moment of crisis? To feel like you've been uniquely prepared to help another? Chris Thomas knows. In his memoir, he traces experiences as far back as his childhood that made him exactly the right person for what Elizabeth Smart's family needed. Chris is a consummate storyteller, and his different perspective on one of the most famous crime cases of our time is riveting."

—**Neylan McBaine**, author of *Pioneering the Vote*, and founder/editor-in-chief of *The Mormon Women Project*

"Chris Thomas' *Unexpected* is a lyrical plunge into the rich memories of a Utah childhood, and the layers of meaning that accrue when this narrator's coming-of-age conflates with the national tragedy of a missing child. At times funny, at other turns heartbreaking, Thomas' prose weaves a masterful story. This book reads like memory: enchanting, digressive, and above all insightful, with the dreamlike quality of a tale that must be read to be believed."

—**Nicole Stansbury**, author of *Places to Look for a Mother*

"The book is truly unexpected, there are few things that are predictable. While the account of the Elizabeth Smart case was gripping, I was struck by the interplay between Chris and his veteran, alcoholic neighbor. This provided a new degree of appreciation for the brave men and women from other generations who sacrificed so much for our freedom. *Unexpected* offers a thought-provoking journey that will cause you to reflect on your own story and see the threads of those experiences and people who prepared and paved the way for you."

—**Jennie Taylor**, Gold Star widow, founder of the Major Brent Taylor Foundation, co-host of *Relentlessly Resilient*

"Chris Thomas takes readers through the treacherous details of one remarkable year of finding Elizabeth Smart while sharing compelling reasons that growing up in The Church of Jesus Christ of Latter-day Saints prepared him for this journey. Through stories of overcoming in his youth and the agonizing hours spent in Elizabeth's absence, we are inspired and encouraged by love, forgiveness, and the strength of the human spirit."

—**Kristin Andrus**, community champion, activist, chief culture officer to her six children

"*Unexpected* inspired me to be a better person. Chris's insights and stories about faith, family, and work have uplifted and enriched my life."

—**Brilliant Miller**, founder of the School of Good Living, author of *Behind the Drive: 99 Inspiring Stories from the Life of an American Entrepreneur*

"When Old Testament Moses and his tribe were being bitten by fiery serpents in the desert, Moses fashioned a serpent out of brass and put it up on a staff for everyone to see. If they would simply look, they would be healed. Chris Thomas brings all those fiery serpents out into the open for his readers to look at. It is only when we really look and bring those things that bite us high enough into the open for everyone to see that we create healing. Tragedy may visit us all at some point. By looking at all aspects of it and considering what may be there for us to learn, we see things from a higher perspective and perhaps even develop empathy. Empathy swallows up judgment and creates love. Thomas has done just that in his masterful, must-read, *Unexpected*. This is the perfect read for anyone who seeks healing, empathy and higher perspectives from the furnace of trauma."

—**Jeff Olsen**, speaker, best-selling author of *Knowing*

"Chris' journey drawing on the vicissitudes of life demonstrates that combining professional acumen and skill with Christian charity, service, and forgiveness leads not only to an exemplary and rewarding career, but also to the joy of a life well lived."

—**Laurie Wilson**, APR, Fellow PRSA, author of *Strategic Communication for PR, Social Media and Marketing*

"The Elizabeth Smart story captured the nation. Now, Chris Thomas takes us behind the scenes. *Unexpected* is a story of faith, survival, perseverance, and miracles. It is also a deeply felt memoir that weaves together elements from Chris's personal life with his experience coordinating communications between the Smart family, national media, and government leaders. As a senior policy advisor to Senator Orrin Hatch, I worked closely with Chris as he dealt with the enormous pressure of managing the PR response to the search and rescue. His account adds a new dimension to the story we all thought we knew. Reading *Unexpected* is an immersive experience that will leave readers with hope and a deeper sense of gratitude for the goodness of humanity."

—**Melanie H. Bowen**, former state director to Senator Orrin G. Hatch

"I got to know Chris on the PR speaking circuit, as we have often been invited to give keynotes at the same industry conferences. I thought I knew pretty much all there was to know about the PR intricacies of Elizabeth's case. But reading this book was mind-blowing. I had no idea how low the media were willing to go, and how many rabbits Chris pulled out of a hat to protect the Smarts. In fact, I started this book one evening and then blew off the next day of work until I finished it. I'll admit—as intrigued as I was to uncover the unrevealed accounts of Elizabeth's case, I didn't have much interest in Chris' life story, but I quickly found myself sucked into that narrative, too, and then at the end of the book utterly amazed at how his seemingly disparate and highly unusual life experiences combined to mold him into the one person on Earth who could handle the PR groundwork that contributed to this miracle happy ending. I started this book to learn more about public relations, but when I finished it, I had internalized lessons of empathy, forgiveness, inclusion, and faith that go way deeper than words I can summon here."

—**Michael Smart**, CEO, MichaelSMARTPR, PR advisor to companies
such as Aflac, GM, and Lowe's

"Over the years, Chris has generously shared parts of this remarkable story with me, my students, and colleagues. This new book ties that story together, illuminating it with rich, introspective, personal experiences that both shaped and were shaped by his journey. *Unexpected* is a fascinating read and a powerful lesson in overcoming challenges through the power of compassion, empathy, determination, and character."

—**Susan Walton**, APR, Fellow PRSA, PR educator, former director of corporate
communications, Harley-Davidson Motor Company

"What forms a person's core? What refines instincts for quick assessment and decision? What life experiences build compassion, even empathy? How do you find that internal '6th gear' for days, weeks, and months of endless drive and pressure? I thought I had a pretty good understanding of the Elizabeth Smart story. I thought I knew Chris Thomas. But not until now. Not until I understood Chris at his core. What I learned was totally unexpected. This memoire is a great read."

—**Sally Dietlein**, co-founder and artistic director, Hale Centre Theatre

"Sometimes, on the path of life, we find ourselves in singular and extraordinary circumstances prematurely—before we are emotionally, mentally, and professionally prepared for such a task. Chris Thomas' *Unexpected* is precisely that kind of story. Two decades of reflection now witness that his entire young life prepared him to muster the know-how, courage, empathy, and resiliency required to navigate that premature moment, that in reality, wasn't premature at all."

—**J. Scott Featherstone**, author of *Hallelujah: The Story of the Coming Forth
of Handel's Messiah*

UNEXPECTED

UNEXPECTED

The Backstory of Finding Elizabeth Smart and
Growing Up in the Culture of an American Religion

CHRIS THOMAS

Post Hill
PRESS

A POST HILL PRESS BOOK

Unexpected:
The Backstory of Finding Elizabeth Smart and Growing Up
in the Culture of an American Religion
© 2023 by Chris Thomas
All Rights Reserved

ISBN: 978-1-63758-769-0
ISBN (eBook): 978-1-63758-770-6

Cover design by Scott Eggers
Cover photo by Salt Lake Tribune
Interior design and composition by Greg Johnson, Textbook Perfect

Post Hill Press
New York • Nashville
posthillpress.com

Published in the United States of America
1 2 3 4 5 6 7 8 9 10

For my mom, who taught me how to
write and be different.

For my dad, who taught me how to
work and hustle.

For my parents, who together taught me to be
curious and creative.

For my wife, Laura, who had the vision for this book
and continually gifts me her unwavering love and support.

For my children, Harrison, Carter, Grayson, and Willa,
who inspire me daily and remind me the world
is still full of joy and wonderment.

Contents

Foreword

BY ELIZABETH SMART

When I was abducted in 2002, I didn't believe I would live another year, let alone twenty. During those days, I spent countless hours imagining what it would be like to be rescued, how it would happen, and what reuniting with my family would feel like. When it finally did happen, it was a whirlwind of names, places, many tears, and feelings of fear regarding the unknown. Only a few people stand out in my memory from shortly after I was rescued, and Chris Thomas is among them. When I reconnected with my family, I quickly realized I had no idea what life had been like for them on the other side of my story, what they had been through, how extensive the search effort had been, and how highly publicized my case had been during the nine months I was missing.

Even now, when I am stopped at Costco, the airport, or at a park with my kids, it still amazes me how many people were impacted by my story. When I first met Chris, I didn't know what the phrase "public relations" meant. I didn't know people could have such expertise in that area to call it a profession, and ironically, thanks to the last twenty years of friendship with Chris, and the many conversations we've had, I feel I might make a half-decent PR representative myself.

My first memory of Chris takes place in the front entryway of the home in which I grew up. It was the first night I was back. I remember my parents being anxious, in a good way, for me to meet him.

When I finally met Chris face to face, I didn't understand what his role had been in my rescue beyond that he had helped my family in their interactions with the media. I didn't know yet what an ordeal that had been for them. I didn't have an inkling of the good, the bad, and the ugly that my family had experienced while I was gone, but over time I learned that Chris had been there to guide them and had been a steady force for them to lean on. Years later, with a family of my own now, I have never experienced anything like what my family endured while I was gone. Their experience and mine during those months were completely different, and honestly, there is no comparing them, except that they were both extreme beyond what the body and mind can fathom.

The sense I got from Chris when we met was his disbelief that the moment was actually real. His excitement to finally meet me, after his every living and breathing moment had required keeping me at the forefront of media attention, was visible. Funnily enough, I was confused as to why he was so excited to meet me. I didn't feel special. But from that point on, Chris has been a friend, mentor, and sounding board, like a big brother. He has been a part of or supported me in every major life decision and event I have experienced since my rescue.

When I have a question and need input, I call him. He is included in my "favorites" phone list. He has seen me at my best and my worst, and still hasn't washed his hands of me. Chris also knows me well enough to typically guess what I am thinking, and can tell when I'm not happy but trying hard to be polite and gracious. So, what I am getting at is that Chris is a very special person to me. He can often see beyond my panic or emotion and give solid advice as to how I should handle a given situation.

When I have struggled with issues of faith, he has always been someone I can ask questions of, or admit anything to, without fear of judgment. I know that after his advice, I will walk away feeling heard and will have a different perspective than the one I had before.

Chris' book helps us do that very thing. You may come to its pages with one perspective, but I promise you will leave it with another. As Chris retells the story of my kidnapping and rescue, along with his own story of growing up, you will see a beautiful theme of the virtues of learning to love, understand, appreciate, and serve those who are different from ourselves as well as a reminder about how adversity shapes and refines our character.

Over the past twenty years, I have many memories of Chris—some, I'm quite sure, he has no idea about. Since he has asked me to write this foreword, I will be sure to embarrass him with at least one. Very shortly after I was rescued, some incredibly kind and generous clients of Chris' offered my family airfare and the use of their condo in Turtle Bay, Hawaii, on Oahu's North Shore. This was my first trip to Hawaii, and it created an instant love within me for the islands, so much so that my husband and I chose to be married there. Chris helped arrange everything for that first trip (and for the wedding nine years later). He planned all sorts of activities: the beach, a private tour of Pearl Harbor, a submarine ride, the Polynesian Cultural Center, and even surf lessons. Two of my four brothers were included in the surf lessons, along with Chris and myself. I am not naturally athletic. Even after years of running, skiing, and strength training, I'm still hopeless, and it certainly was no different then.

Every time we paddled out, I would fall off my surfboard and get pummeled by the very wave I was trying to catch. I'm not sure how long we spent out there. I was determined, but the whole process was exhausting! After a while, I just lay on my surfboard, trying to find the courage to paddle out and try again. While I was lying there, I searched the water to see if anyone else had caught a wave yet. I saw Chris in the distance, paddling back out, and at that precise moment, a wave washed right over him and pulled his swim shorts down—not all the way off, but far enough down that I caught an eyeful of blinding whiteness, so blinding it could have been confused with the sun. I quickly looked away, not knowing whether to say something or just laugh.

To this day, I haven't shared that memory with Chris. I suppose my reason for sharing it now is that I can genuinely say I know Chris very well. Our friendship has many different facets. And as you read this book, in which Chris offers a very personal glimpse into my family's life, as well as the lives of others, you will come to learn of his brilliance, kindness, empathy, and diligence. But this funny little anecdote will remind you that occasionally he gets caught with his pants down too. You're welcome, Chris.

Introduction

As I write this, it has been nearly twenty years since the afternoon I received a call from a good friend with the news that Elizabeth Smart had been found. Thinking back on those nine months between her abduction on June 5, 2002, and her rescue on March 12, 2003, I have found the process of writing and retrospection to be both illuminating and instructive.

Reflecting on one of the most exhilarating and inspiring experiences of my life, helping find Elizabeth Smart, has been enlightening. I have discovered many things I did not fully realize two decades ago. Most salient to me, however, has been the recognition of one powerful and universal truth. Each one of us has experiences, adversity, and people who come into our lives with the purpose of teaching and preparing us for future challenges and opportunities. We progress in various ways through these, only to be tested and further refined by the next round of experiences and individuals.

My journey in writing *Unexpected* began with my feet pointed down a very different path. During the COVID-19 lockdown, I wrote a draft of a book about growing up next door to an alcoholic neighbor who was a hidden, broken war hero with a secret. In writing the epilogue and listening to several astute observations by my wife, Laura, I discovered there were many connections from those childhood experiences that had pushed me to acquire the exact kind of intuition needed to manage Elizabeth's kidnapping and rescue, and to do it while the world watched. This became the foundation of a new book. I had waited almost twenty years to write it because the approach and direction never felt right—not until these two seemingly disparate periods of my life seemed to collide and begin running parallel to each other in both purpose and theme.

Unexpected combines the backstory of finding Elizabeth Smart with an account of some of my childhood experiences, including growing up next door to one of the unlikeliest teachers in my life. A central theme throughout the book is the culture of The Church of Jesus Christ of Latter-day Saints, which is commonly known as the Mormon Church, or LDS Church. It was never my intention to write in detail about the church and its culture. This changed as a result of the insights and feedback from Marion Roach Smith, a former *New York Times* reporter, commentator on National Public Radio's *All Things Considered*, and the celebrated author of four books. She has been an incredible mentor and instrumental in bringing this memoir to life.

In addition to working with Marion, I have been fortunate to be part of a master class with fellow writers who reside around the United States and in Paris, France. They have had very limited exposure to The Church of Jesus Christ of Latter-day Saints, but in providing feedback to the drafts of several chapters of this book, they have constantly pushed me to explore and explain my church's culture.

As I have looked at my story through that cultural lens, I have come to recognize how when you live inside a certain box, too often you don't fully understand or appreciate it. The culture of The Church of Jesus Christ of Latter-day Saints has played a significant role in the backstory of finding Elizabeth and has created so many facets of who I am and how I was prepared for the unique opportunity of working on the Smart case.

It is interesting to note that the vast majority of memoirs surrounding The Church of Jesus Christ of Latter-day Saints are from people who have left the faith or are critical of it. These stories generally employ a formula of "It's a beautiful religion and culture, but..."

Instead, my story is about how leaning into that culture made a pivotal difference in finding Elizabeth and in my own personal happiness, and how that culture has improved the lives of countless others. At the same time, the book is a straightforward attempt to share the culture without proselytizing or being overtly didactic. Instead of telling you what to feel or believe, I am striving to take you on a journey that will allow you simply to experience the culture through my eyes.

I want to emphatically state how much I love and care about the people I write about in this book, especially my own family and the Smart family. These individuals have played a significant role in my life and mean so much to me. I want them to know that I have worked to be true to the facts and authenticity of my story, while also being as sensitive as possible. I recognize that my perspective and memory of various experiences, places, and people may be different from their recollections. I describe my experiences, including quoting conversations, to the best of my memory. I also want to note that in one instance from my childhood, I use a pseudonym for a character and have changed a few insignificant details to protect the identity of this very private individual.

I also reviewed the four books written about the Elizabeth Smart kidnapping as well as numerous news articles and photos. I quote from these works verbatim in several places, and express my gratitude to the media organizations, publishers, journalists, authors, and others who contributed to them.

I feel it is also important to note that beginning in 2018, The Church of Jesus Christ of Latter-day Saints began making a concerted effort to avoid using the sobriquet "Mormon." Instead, it began recommending that its members use the full name of the church, or "Latter-day Saints" for short, in both speech and written communications. This encouragement was meant to emphasize the church's belief in and cornerstone of Jesus Christ. I have worked to abide by this as much as possible in this book. At the same time, since most of my experiences in finding Elizabeth and during my childhood took place before this change, when the church and culture were commonly referred to as Mormon, I use this moniker in a few instances. Please know that this is not meant to be disrespectful in any way; it is to help provide clarity and simplicity for those of you who, like the members of my master class, are unfamiliar with the faith and its culture.

Finally, I hope my story will provide you with a new perspective and appreciation for the people, efforts, and faith that played a role in finding Elizabeth, as well as for the culture of an American religion that is often maligned, misunderstood, and underappreciated.

CHAPTER 1

Like a Brother

I walk slowly up a steep, winding column of concrete stairs. The area is blanketed in shadows from a flood lamp that temporarily blinds me as I try to climb without stumbling. Muffled voices echo in the background. A cool, dry breeze is moving across the foothills, manifested by small rippling waves in a dozen baby blue ribbons tied to posts and railings. The scent of juniper permeates the air from a forested area a few hundred feet behind the affluent homes on the East Bench neighborhood in Salt Lake City, Utah, a short distance from the canyon that Mormon pioneers traversed when they first entered the Salt Lake Valley.

It's March 12, 2003. And it's nearing eleven o'clock at night, which makes the first thing that comes into focus somewhat puzzling. The French doors to the main entry of 1509 Kristianna Circle are swung wide open. Elizabeth's parents, Ed and Lois Smart, are standing together on an ornate red Oriental rug in the entry. They are visiting with a couple, who are close friends and neighbors, I recognize. Their mood is loose and celebratory. Behind the four adults on the inside staircase, leading to the third level of the 6,600-square-foot home, stand all six of the Smart children—including Elizabeth—adorned in a variety of brightly colored satin pajamas, each standing on a different step.

Seeing all the siblings hanging out together had been unthinkable when the family awoke that morning. There had been no trace of Elizabeth Smart for more than nine months after she had been abducted at knifepoint in the middle of the night from her bedroom. Her younger sister, Mary Katherine, had feigned sleep next to her in the bed while observing the unthinkable crime. Many people, even within the family, had believed Elizabeth's body might never be found.

I step toward the porch, and Elizabeth eyes me with the intensity of a bird of prey. She seems perplexed and a little uneasy, likely wondering who I am and how a stranger like me has passed through two police checks—one in front of the house and the other at the end of the cul-de-sac. She stares me down with serious apprehension. Her brow furrows.

Overcome with emotion at the sight of the Smart family being back together, I am conflicted. I don't want to make a teenager who was in captivity less than twelve hours earlier feel the least bit uncomfortable, and yet part of me wants a small connection with her. We haven't formally met, but she has been at the forefront of my thinking, work, prayers—and at times my very being—for more than nine months. This isn't the first time I've been in this awkward position today, but now the situation is unavoidable.

A trace of perspiration rolls down my back as my mind flashes to earlier that afternoon.

I am sitting at my desk, looking out the window of my company's six-hundred-dollar-per-month office, housed in a dilapidated small business complex called the Diamond Building. Bobi Whitlock, a part-time receptionist shared by half a dozen companies in the complex, pokes her head into my office. Looking at me sheepishly, Bobi informs me that someone on the phone urgently wants to speak with me.

"I'm sorry, but I'm not taking any calls," I tell her.

It's around 2:30 p.m. Just forty-five minutes earlier, the news of Elizabeth's rescue broke, whipping the media into a frenzy.

"I know...b-b-but—"

"It doesn't matter if it's Barbara Walters, Tom Brokaw, or Katie Couric," I say, cutting her off. Later I will learn she had spoken to all three. "Tell them no. We'll let the police and FBI speak to the press first, so we can respond to what they say and clarify any misinformation."

I'm being uncharacteristically intense and aloof, caught up in thought trying to process the events that are unfolding while balancing my excitement at Elizabeth's rescue and the anxiety from the tsunami of media requests and issues that are crashing in front of me. My response catches

Bobi off guard and exacerbates the tension. She watches me as I pick up my phone, speed-dial one of my business partners, and begin to type on my laptop.

I have largely been on sabbatical since Elizabeth's abduction, handing off my duties of managing clients and running The Intrepid Group, a fledgling public relations firm I joined as a partner eighteen months ago, so I could focus on the case. What began as a volunteer engagement to help the Smart family strategize and manage the news media for a couple of weeks has evolved into something much bigger. I have become so immersed in the family, the investigation, and the search for Elizabeth, it nearly consumes me. I work night and day, even holidays and weekends, and have become a close confidant of the family, collaborating with them on so much more than public relations. In fact, Lois Smart regularly refers to me as her fifth son, because I'm around the family and home so often.

Although I'm only thirty years old, working on this case has taken a heavy toll on my physical and emotional health. I have broken four teeth, unaware that I was grinding them due to the daily stress and strain. I am gaining weight and starting to lose my hair. I rarely sleep more than a few hours at a time, suffer from frequent anxiety, and experience occasional migraines as a result of the never-ending pressure.

My marriage has experienced some challenges and neglect. My wife, Laura, and I had celebrated our first anniversary one day before the abduction. She works in advertising and travels a fair amount. While juggling the demands of her career and my constant needs, Laura is also putting the finishing touches on a historic home we moved into in February 2002. Over the past nine and a half months, I've frequently been distracted—and on some occasions, completely absent. Laura does her best, but at the same time it has been a constant challenge for her to navigate the newlywed phase with a husband who struggles to disengage from the case for more than an hour or two at a time.

My parents also got divorced during the period when Elizabeth was missing, after more than thirty years of marriage. It wasn't a complete shock, but it was disappointing and challenging nonetheless. Since I am their oldest child, many of the family responsibilities fall in mine and Laura's laps. This has included my eighteen-year-old sister, Amy, living with us for several months after my mom accepted an assignment to work in India, and my father staying with us frequently as he worked to move and acclimate to southern Utah. This new burden usurps whatever little bandwidth I have left and creates frustration for Laura, who often has to pick up the pieces with my family.

To say I am exhausted is an extreme understatement. But something inexplicable has been propelling me forward and not allowing me to stop.

Bobi steps out of my office, only to return a few minutes later.

"It's someone at the police station," she says. "They need to talk to you urgently. I don't know what you did, but it sounds like you might be in trouble. I think you should take the call."

I jab the flashing button on the phone and lower my voice, trying to sound calm.

"Chris Thomas."

I listen to a few brief, almost cryptic details and am summoned to the police station immediately.

Racing along 300 West (Salt Lake City's downtown streets are plotted on a grid where nearly every address has a set of coordinates for how far east or west and how far north or south a location is from the Latter-day Saint temple), I ignore the incessant vibration of my mobile phone and flip on KSL NewsRadio. The afternoon host, Tim Hughes, is doing his best to juggle reporters and guests while trying to get more information to add to the scant available details about Elizabeth's rescue. He and the others on the air speculate on what might have happened, working to provide some perspective on this Utah news story that is rivaled only by the coverage of the 2002 Olympic Winter Games held in Salt Lake City.

As I turn onto 200 South and pass several antique brick buildings heading toward the modern high-rise towers in the city center, the voice of Ben Winslow, a field reporter I've spent more time with during the past nine months than with many members of my own family, comes on the air. He is outside Salt Lake City's nine-story public safety building, painting a picture of the exact scene unfolding right in front of me. Police cars with flashing sirens are blocking each end of the street in front of the building, closing the road in both directions. Three helicopters are idling loudly overhead. A growing throng of journalists, photographers, and bystanders is congregating in a rectangular area half the size of a football field, cordoned off by yellow police tape. Like tomcats, they wait nonchalantly, as if completely unimpressed by their surroundings. Then, when they see someone coming in or out of the large front doors that keep the frenzied press outside the dilapidated structure, they pounce.

Tightrope-walking around the perimeter, I try to blend in, determined not to become their prey. It works temporarily. Then someone yells my name. Reporters with notebooks and microphones followed by cameras race toward me, aggressively pushing and shoving. Working to keep my balance, I try to ignore the cacophony of questions and focus on the door. It feels as if I'm moving in slow motion, and an eternity passes before I'm able to finally navigate through the chaos and duck under the yellow tape.

At the front desk, I pull out my driver's license, but before the receptionist can check it, an officer intercedes.

"They're waiting for you. Follow me."

We step into an elevator, and when the doors reopen on the sixth floor, I see a teenage girl exiting a room across the hall. She has puffy, sunburned cheeks, tightly braided blonde pigtails, and is wearing a gray blouse that looks like it was sewn from bedsheets. A frayed rope serves as a belt, holding up her dirty, heavily worn, oversized jeans.

The officer stands by my side, neither of us speaking. I try not to stare.

As Elizabeth takes a few steps alone into the hall, she is unexpectedly stopped by Rocky Anderson, Salt Lake City's mayor, who has been a strong advocate for the Smarts. He went to battle multiple times for the family when there was conflict with the leadership of the Salt Lake City Police Department.

Rocky puts his hand out and introduces himself to Elizabeth. He is followed by a few members of his staff and the police department. It's the type of gladhanding that would occur if a local luminary such as Hall of Fame 49ers quarterback Steve Young were to stop by to film a public service announcement.

Elizabeth seems confused and overwhelmed by the commotion. Her eyes dart around the hall, likely looking for someone to rescue her yet again. I am repulsed but ill-equipped to do anything about the situation.

Like a life preserver tossed from shore, Lois finally appears, puts an arm around her teenage daughter's shoulder, and leads her away from the group down the hall. I follow while trying to maintain some space.

Lois, who is slender with perfect posture, short auburn hair, and wears a sleek black blouse with a white neckline, stops suddenly when she spots me.

"Where have you been? They're waiting for you. Ed *really* needs you."

She points across the hall toward a door. I knock on it, and an officer briskly steps out.

"Now, what did John Walsh tell you?" the officer asks, his bravado on full display.

Before I can answer, Ed rushes the door and gets in his face. He gestures in my direction.

"I'll talk with Chris, *alright?* I'm not going to take this any longer. I've put up with your crap and lies for more than nine months. I don't have to do this anymore. Go on, get out of here. Go."

The officer stares Ed down, then moves aside and shuts the door as he exits.

Ed sits and buries his face in his hands. His thinning blonde hair is completely disheveled. The underarms of his white polo shirt are drenched with perspiration. He struggles to speak, becoming emotional. At first I think he's going to cry, but to my surprise, Ed's suddenly overcome with anger.

"After everything they've put us through, they have the gall to do this to Elizabeth?" he says. "They can make my life a living hell, but they have no right to do this to my daughter."

Ed exhales loudly and proceeds to explain what happened after I called him less than an hour ago. I was relaying a message regarding victims' rights from John Walsh, the father of a kidnapped and murdered child and host of the popular television show *America's Most Wanted*.

After Ed hung up the phone with me, "he flew into an absolute rage," according to Lois, and exhibited behavior "that was not typical of my husband." In the book she and Ed wrote, *Bringing Elizabeth Home*, Lois also notes that Ed was yelling at everyone and pounding his fists on the table, demanding that Police Chief Rick Dinse, FBI investigator Chip Burrus, and Mayor Anderson stop interrogating Elizabeth.

A detective tried to calm Ed down by explaining that in order to ensure that the kidnappers, Brian David Mitchell and Wanda Barzee, were convicted, investigators had to get as much information as possible from Elizabeth before her answers could be tainted by family, friends, and the media. This only infuriated Ed more, and he had to be restrained by several officers. That's when I received the call asking me to come to the police station.

Upon hearing about Ed's experience, I call John Walsh, put him on speaker, and explain the situation. John also becomes incensed, and advises Ed that it is within his rights to demand that interviews with Elizabeth cease for the day and that she be allowed to go to the hospital and then home.

We are interrupted by a knock. It is Ed's oldest son, Charles. He walks in with the other Smart children: Andrew, Mary Katherine, Edward Junior, and William. After dropping Lois off at the police station forty minutes prior, Charles had returned to pick up his siblings from school and then drove back downtown.

Mary Katherine rushes past her brother into the middle of the room, asking, "*Where's Elizabeth?*" Wearing a pink T-shirt, the blue-eyed tween with a timid smile puts one of her braided pigtails into her mouth, attempting to soothe herself. I imagine the experience for the kids of not seeing their sister must be like waking up on Christmas morning and finding no presents under the tree.

Mary Katherine and her brothers endure another ten minutes of waiting. Then Ed and Lois finally escort Elizabeth out of an interrogation room. All of her siblings except four-year-old William immediately embrace her. William doesn't recognize Elizabeth and is apprehensive of the roughly dressed stranger, so he recoils and hugs Lois' leg. This draws giggles from Andrew, Mary Katherine, and Edward Junior. Elizabeth seems unsure how to respond.

A central doctrine of The Church of Jesus Christ of Latter-day Saints is that families are eternal. This tenet includes a belief that we will be reunited with our loved ones after death. The Smart family's reunion is so tender, it makes me wonder momentarily if this is what it might be like in the hereafter.

The children talk for a few minutes before we are all whisked toward the elevator by two officers.

Once the door closes, Andrew, who is wearing a blue polo shirt and has a thick bowl cut, begins bragging to Elizabeth that he got straight A's on his last report card.

"Did you cheat or something?" she responds. "Or did the teachers give you extra credit because I was missing?" She cracks a smile as she elbows Andrew. This is the first time I've heard her speak. I thought she might look tormented and as if she were suffering, but Elizabeth is disarming, funny, and a little sassy.

Andrew and Elizabeth banter as if they've never been apart. The interaction underscores the cliché that sibling rivalry never dies.

While the discourse is entertaining, I won't realize until later that evening how important it was for me to witness the family's reunion. Observing this exchange has provided me with crucial insights that will be key to demonstrating Elizabeth's emotional state of mind. It will help to address numerous questions about Stockholm syndrome, a condition that occurs when a hostage or victim demonstrates positive feelings toward, and even cooperates with, a perpetrator. The media will ask whether Elizabeth wanted to be back with her family or not, and if she felt any sympathy toward her captors. There will even be speculation about whether or not Elizabeth was complicit in her own kidnapping.

Several officers lead the family to a secure loading dock at the back of the building, where they assure us Elizabeth will be protected from the public and media. Unfortunately, it is another broken promise amid the many we have experienced in the nine months since the abduction. An Associated Press photographer, who has been tipped off, shoots pictures of Lois and Elizabeth as they step off the loading dock and into the open door of a police van with heavily tinted windows. They are exposed for mere seconds.

The vehicle departs for Primary Children's Hospital with the sound of the camera shutter rapidly clicking in the background. Ed, his other children, and I are overwhelmed watching the scene unfolding in front of us and don't fully comprehend the new reality this represents for them.

The Smart family's lavender Mercedes-Benz station wagon is parked in a lot across the street. Like a valet, I run and retrieve the car and deliver it to the dock while Ed and his children wait. As they drive away, the photographer reemerges, and I hear the sound of his camera shutter again.

Standing on the front porch of the Smart family's home later that night, I find myself at a loss, squirming helplessly under Elizabeth's glare. I had a handful of opportunities to introduce myself at the police station, but I was so put off by the mayor, city, and police staff that I was reticent to do so.

After a long minute or two, Ed notices Elizabeth's reaction.

"Elizabeth, you don't know who this is, do you?"

I feel self-conscious as she looks me over before responding in a matter-of-fact way: "No."

Ed steps toward me, placing his hand on my shoulder.

"This is Chris. He has done more for you than you can imagine. I consider him a brother. You should too."

I try to contain myself, to no avail. I turn away, attempting to conceal the tears raining down my cheeks.

Lying in bed a few hours later, I try to catch some shut-eye, but it's impossible. The events of the day are replaying over and over again in my mind, as if on a loop. My senses are heightened. I can see and feel every minute, every conversation, every detail of the day. The euphoria and overstimulation rival anything I experienced in childhood: Christmas, birthdays, Disneyland.

Many people likely will never fully understand or appreciate the events of March 12, 2003, or those leading up to it. But this day will rank among the most significant of my life.

CHAPTER 2

The Day the Fences Came Down

My mom intentionally stepped in front of the TV, blocking my view of a crucial at-bat. The year was 1983, and I was ten years old, watching a Chicago Cubs game on WGN-TV.

"I didn't know they were taking the fences down today. Christopher, I need you to give the backyard some attention, and quick. It's *embarrassing*."

She paused. The muscles in her face tightened, and the piercing glint of her hazel eyes underscored the urgency of the request.

After Cubs second baseman Ryne Sandberg struck out, I begrudgingly left the comfort of our off-brand brown La-Z-Boy, staggered outside, and surveyed the project. The backyard was a maelstrom of neglect and disorder. The lawn was overgrown in several spots and completely dead in others. Dandelions and tall green and yellow weeds with seedlings that looked like mini corn stalks were growing in a small garden area that hadn't been planted. Red plastic cups, many split into multiple pieces, and discarded peat moss bags from a business venture of mine were piled on the side of our garage. The back side of our home, with its redbrick exterior and rows of uneven cement seams as a result of sloppy masonry, was coated with a thick layer of dirt that had accumulated over several years.

My mom was pregnant with my sister Amy, and my father was working out of state that summer, so I labored alone that afternoon, mowing, weeding, organizing clutter, and spraying down the house at a breakneck pace. As I was finishing, I noticed something I had been oblivious to for hours: Most of the other neighbors were doing the exact same thing.

This had to be the largest and fastest cleanup in neighborhood history. It was akin to cleaning up the living room at lightning speed after realizing an unexpected visitor had just pulled up to the curb.

My family had moved to East Millcreek, a suburb ten miles outside of Salt Lake City, seven years earlier. We lived in the shadow of Mount Olympus, the namesake of the famous landmark on the border between Macedonia and Thessaly, Greece, which we could see in the distance from our backyard. It's still a popular icon in Utah's Wasatch Front region and is especially visible in East Millcreek.

Growing up, I regularly saw T-shirts, coffee mugs, and even bottled water that featured depictions of this majestic structure. Local legend has it that William Wadsworth (W. W.) Hodkinson, the founder of Paramount Pictures and a native Utahn, had drawn a picture of Mount Olympus on a napkin from memory and handed it to an artist, who then created a live-action logo that still brands the beginning of every one of the studio's movies.

Locals believe that Mount Olympus, with an elevation eclipsing nine thousand feet, would be world famous if it were in New York or California. They believe this not just about the Wasatch Mountains but about everything else that is noteworthy in Utah. The pervasive attitude among Utahns is that we are just as smart (if not smarter), more capable, more faithful, and even harder working than other sophisticates in more populated and prominent cities along the East and West Coasts.

While there are many affluent homes at the base of Mount Olympus, the more modest neighborhood where I grew up is a little farther down the road. The street where my family lived, Celeste Way, was like the rest of its largely homogenous community. The neighbors were predominantly middle- to working-class families with stay-at-home moms, and were white and members of The Church of Jesus Christ of Latter-day Saints, or Mormons.

I lived with my parents and three younger siblings in a mecca where religion, culture, and everyday life were inextricably interconnected. The place was close-knit, family-focused, and at times oddly neurotic.

The Church of Jesus Christ of Latter-day Saints organizes its congregations throughout the world geographically, and requires members to attend church services at the same time each week with others living in the same location. Each designated area is generally based on the population density of church members. In some parts of the world, congregations span an area of more than a hundred miles, but in the case of Salt Lake City, the members living in a few square blocks could fill a church building.

My congregation, or "ward," was less than a mile in circumference, and approximately 80 percent of my neighbors attended church with us each Sunday. We met in a tan brick building topped with an iron steeple that stood resolute at the end of my street.

In the 1850s, Joseph Smith, the founder of The Church of Jesus Christ of Latter-day Saints, created the small geographic regions called wards. They were overseen by a bishop in the Mormon settlement of Nauvoo, Illinois, which was one of the largest cities in the United States in its heyday.

When the Mormon pioneers settled what would become the state of Utah, the congregational moniker of "ward" stuck. Over the years, the organizing of wards has created neighborhoods in Salt Lake City that often resemble small towns, where nearly everyone knows and watches out for one another. The ward is typically the epicenter of neighborhood activity, and local lay church leaders function as de facto mayors and town council members. While this structure is not without some challenges, it does create the proverbial "village." It's a place where members of the tribe strengthen one another, provide support in times of need, and help to rear everyone's children. The goal is to help the younger generations become good, kind, God-fearing people who will make meaningful contributions to society and the church, while continuing the legacy of serving beyond their local communities.

In 1983, northern Utah experienced extreme precipitation, coupled with an unseasonably hot summer, which took its toll on the whitewashed wooden fences in my backyard and in those of my neighbors. Many boards had split right down the middle, posts were decaying, and some sections of fencing were leaning heavily—only days away from losing their battle with gravity.

The demise of the fences, which snaked around the backyard of my home and approximately twenty other residences on three surrounding streets, was imminent. When one neighbor asked a contractor for a bid to replace his fence, the contractor saw an opportunity. He provided an estimate for building the fence as a one-off, and then said he would do the work for nearly half the price if all the other homeowners also agreed to have their fences replaced.

The sales pitch traveled quickly along the fence line, from neighbor to neighbor, like wildfire. The general notion was that if we banded together, the project would get done more quickly, there would be uniformity and greater safety, and it would cost a fraction of the price compared to doing it on our own.

While a few of the neighbors needed some cajoling, everyone finally agreed. Contracts were signed, and on an overcast Saturday, a team of workers began demolishing the white fences, exposing all the backyards in the process. While there was an air of excitement surrounding the new fences, most of the neighbors also were a little apprehensive about the disruption the project might cause.

Despite the hard work and good intentions of each neighbor, our backyards were largely pedestrian and unkempt. Unlike with the façades of the homes in the neighborhood, builders had put the absolute minimum into finishing the backs of the houses. There were no shutters, clapboard, or trim around the windows. Landscaping was modest, and because many people worked long hours, they often didn't have enough time or interest in creating a beautiful backyard that would rarely be used, let alone seen.

When the fences came down and exposed our yards, most of the neighbors were in the same embarrassing predicament. Despite our shared circumstances, however, it felt like each of us was uniquely scarred and suffering alone.

This uneasiness might have been somewhat attributable to the residence of one of our neighbors, the Squires family. While the other homes and yards were mostly identical in size, features, and condition, the Squires property was an anomaly.

The home itself was modest and had the same front setback as the six other residences on Celeste Circle. But the property featured a teardrop-shaped backyard that was at least an acre in size and that abutted one-third of the other plots, including my family's.

The property was not only large but well kept. Mary Squires, a single mother, was the quintessential gardener. She had instilled in her six children, who were then in their teens and twenties, an affinity for impeccable gardens, flowers, and shrubbery. And because of its size and location, the

Squires property became Grand Central for what became known as the "backyard neighborhood."

The temporary lack of fences created a few merged acres of grass and trees without boundaries and a newfound freedom for the neighborhood kids.

It didn't take long for children to congregate and begin exploring. That first afternoon without fences, all the kids couldn't help but venture out into their newly expanded backyards. By dusk, night games had commenced.

Silhouettes of small bodies skipped and jumped in the moonlight, and laughs and squeals echoed throughout the new playground. An energy and a feeling of wonderment abounded. It was a mood that likely hadn't been that pronounced since the area was an open field in the late 1950s.

While the children didn't have any inhibitions, the adults—especially the women, who were more conscientious than most of the men—initially avoided venturing out into the backyard neighborhood. It took a few days for their metaphorical fences to come down.

The first interactions occurred when a man who liked to grill saw an opportunity to follow the kids' example, or he simply wanted an excuse to have a barbecue. The aroma of burgers and hot dogs cooking over mesquite charcoal helped spark the first neighborhood gathering in the Squireses' yard.

A long makeshift picnic area consisting of several folding tables, joined under red checkered plastic tablecloths, was soon bedecked with a smorgasbord of potluck dishes. The delicacies included Lit'l Smokies in maple barbecue sauce, tater tot casserole, three-bean chili, and two local staples: green Jell-O with shredded carrots, and funeral potatoes (cheesy hash browns, customarily served following a funeral as part of a meal provided by women from our church for the family of the deceased).

Blankets were spread across the backyard lawns, and each family sat together and ate before eventually making the rounds, visiting old friends and neighbors and becoming acquainted with those who were less familiar.

A new family had just moved to our neighborhood from Alabama, and they had a girl my age. Her name was Annabelle. The barbecue provided the family with the perfect opportunity to meet their new neighbors.

At one point during the evening, without thinking, I found myself a few feet from Annabelle. I was shy but felt the need to be welcoming. I thought, *I should say hello. It would be awkward and rude if I ignored her.*

I was about to introduce myself when I got blindsided.

"Hey, Maynard, glad you found yourself a girlfriend."

My friend Chad Ragland, who lived up the street and called everyone Maynard, couldn't contain his laughter. "I'll leave the two of you alone."

Annabelle gave me a cynical stare as I shrunk and walked away. I headed home and retreated to my room, where I spent the next several hours sulking.

When my mom came downstairs to visit later that evening after putting my two younger siblings to bed, I wanted to hide. Socializing in the backyard neighborhood had made her giddy. My mom's disposition was in stark contrast to how I was feeling.

"Did you have fun tonight?" she asked. "I thought the barbecue was extraordinary. I met people I barely knew who felt like longtime friends by the end of the evening. Did the boys hang out? Was it similar?"

I quickly realized my mom was not aware of the incident with Annabelle. I needed to play it cool to avoid further embarrassment.

"Not really, I don't think.... Ah, Chad and I got bored, so we went skateboarding."

I held a straight face, desperately hoping my mom hadn't seen Chad while I was in exile.

"That's a shame," she said. "It was really something special. It's too bad the new fences will be up in a week. I could really get used to this."

In the days that followed, the backyard neighborhood became a nightly beehive of activity. The adults began congregating, cooking, laughing, and playing, almost as much as the children. It was as if everyone were part of one big extended family.

What at first felt unfamiliar, uncomfortable, and even unwanted had evolved into an unexpected suburban utopia.

While the experience was nirvana for most, it did present a challenge or two. One evening a neighbor forgot about the fences being down and let the family's Rottweiler out. The dog ran through the backyard neighborhood and fatally wounded another neighbor's pet rabbit. When the dog's owners realized what had happened, they quickly ran through the backyard neighborhood, knocked on the door of the family of the dearly departed bunny, and apologized profusely.

The children were devastated, but the family forgave the neighbor and even the dog. Many people believe that the good vibes from the backyard neighborhood had averted what could have been an embittering incident.

The next night the neighbors came together to mourn. A graveyard service was held, complete with a brief eulogy and "Taps" played by one of the kids on a trumpet. The children then helped shovel dirt over the large orange Nike shoebox that housed the bunny's lifeless body. "Ashes to ashes, dust to dust…" they chanted softly.

When construction of the new fences was delayed a week, another barbecue was organized to celebrate. The adults always seemed to be looking for a reason to throw a party.

When the delays continued for weeks, there was less fanfare. Yet at the same time, some neighbors were now hoping the fences would never be resurrected.

While most families frequented the backyard neighborhood on a nightly basis, one man never made an appearance: my next-door neighbor Baker Paxton. He was a mysterious character who kept to himself unless someone, or something, was making noise or trespassing on his front lawn. On those occasions, his apoplectic response was so unnerving, it often would strike fear in children and adults alike.

When the whitewashed wood posts and pickets around Baker's yard came down, we discovered something unusual: The perimeter around the back of his house also was protected by a three-foot-high chain-link fence. This galvanized mesh wire served to keep us out, and in the process, kept him in and away from one of the most enriching and memorable experiences in our neighborhood's history.

Looking back, I often wonder: If that chain-link fence hadn't been such a deterrent for Baker, would we somehow have connected in the felicity of the backyard neighborhood? But the fence did exist. And much like Elizabeth's rescue many years later, growing to understand the old man would not happen quickly or easily.

CHAPTER 3

Lost and Found

A thin trail of white smoke rises from the beef patties sizzling on a large steel grill in front of the church where the Smart family attends services. Members of The Church of Jesus Christ of Latter-day Saints call the box-like building a ward house. It's constructed of off-white bricks, with an iron steeple jutting up the west side, along with various trees and bushes and a large pole, flying the American flag, in front. In June of 2002, this ward house is serving its intended purpose as a place of worship while also doubling as the Elizabeth Smart Search Center.

Karen Hale and her husband, Jon, along with four of their five children, are in constant motion, flipping burgers, toasting buns, assembling meals, and refilling condiments, especially fry sauce (a popular mixture of ketchup, mayo, and horseradish, believed to have originated in Utah), all while making small talk with volunteers. The temperature is a scorching ninety-plus degrees on this summer afternoon, and the heat in the grilling area is almost unbearable.

The extended Hale family owns and operates a handful of Salt Lake-area restaurants, including two Hires Big H drive-ins. Together with dozens of other eating establishments, they are providing food, drinks, and snacks at the front lines of the search for Elizabeth.

Stopping briefly to grab a strawberry-banana smoothie from Jamba at one of the tables where food is regularly delivered outside the ward house,

I am taken aback recognizing how depleted my body is, and something even more striking, noticing Karen working with her family.

I take a sip of the smoothie, which has become my primary form of sustenance, since I am so inundated and distracted I rarely eat anything. Seeing Karen evokes butterflies in my stomach, a lightheadedness, and watery eyes.

This reaction is not uncommon. Working at the search center involves enduring a roller coaster of emotions. I experience both the grief and weight of Elizabeth's abduction, along with deep humility and gratitude from experiencing the very best of humanity selflessly responding to this tragedy.

Less than a week before starting work at the search center, my business partner at the time, Mike Grass, and I were golfing with a client early one morning when we received an urgent call. It was Mike's father, Ray, the outdoors editor for the *Deseret News*, asking us to reach out to his colleague and close friend Tom Smart, the paper's photo editor, whose niece had been abducted.

Brandishing a knife, a stranger had entered the bedroom of Elizabeth and Mary Katherine Smart in the early morning hours of Wednesday, June 5, 2002. He woke up Elizabeth and threatened to kill her if she made a sound. After guiding Elizabeth to get her shoes, the man led her out of the room and down the hall.

Mary Katherine, who was in the bed next to her older sister, feigned sleep. Concerned for the safety of her other family members, she waited for the man to exit with Elizabeth and stayed still for nearly an hour until she felt safe enough to run to her parents' bedroom.

"Elizabeth's gone," she told Ed and Lois Smart. "Somebody has taken her."

Despite Mary Katherine's demonstrative language and behavior, Ed didn't initially believe her. After he asked more questions and inspected the girls' bedroom, reality set in when Mary Katherine said, "You're not going to find her. A man took her. A man with a gun."

Less than ninety minutes later, Tom arrived at Ed and Lois' home and began setting in motion media relations efforts that would result in Elizabeth Smart quickly becoming a household name.

I knew Tom from working with him on several stories for our clients. Additionally, we had recently hired his daughter, Sierra, as a public relations intern, and as a result it wasn't uncommon for Tom to stop by the office to visit if he had a photo assignment in the vicinity.

We offered Tom our help pro bono. He was grateful but initially declined, then enlisted our team a couple of days later when the number of journalists covering Elizabeth's abduction swelled.

Mike and I were happy to help. We pulled in our other partner, Missy Larsen, who had grown up in the Smart family's ward and neighborhood, and we added three other members of our staff.

Mike, Missy, and I believed the assignment would last only for a few days, that Elizabeth would be found alive, we would celebrate, and then we'd go back to our day jobs at the agency. Instead of realizing this pipe dream, my partners and team would return to the office a couple of weeks later to attend to our neglected clients, and I would take a nine-month sabbatical to work for the Smart family (with Mike's and Missy's ongoing help and support).

When I first arrived at the Elizabeth Smart Search Center, Karen Hale was one of the first people I recognized. Several years earlier, I had knocked on doors and participated in "honk and wave" campaigns, successfully helping Karen get elected to the Utah legislature. Our paths had crossed several times since, and with each interaction, my admiration and respect for her grew deeper. Karen, who is a friend of one of Ed Smart's sisters, put her experience editing magazines, hosting radio shows, and working in several public relations capacities to work for the Smarts. The morning of the abduction, she started assisting Tom, who was leading media relations efforts. When we arrived on the scene a few days later, Tom and Karen immediately welcomed our help.

At its peak, the search would include as many as eight people helping with the media full time. We could have used twice this number to manage the sheer flood of calls, interviews, and other requests, while creating and adapting a communication strategy and responses, as well as to monitor volumes of published articles along with hours of daily broadcast coverage. The additional firepower would have helped us better anticipate the needs of the media and be responsive, following the golden rule of media relations: If you make a journalist's job easier and/or pleasant, they will positively reciprocate.

Each day of the search effort begins for my team and me at 3:30 a.m., when we speak with the morning network and cable shows to confirm details. Preparation with Ed, Lois, and extended family members starts around 4:30 a.m., with morning interviews commencing at 5 a.m. and lasting until around 10 a.m. The next hour is spent regrouping and preparing for an 11 a.m. press conference with law enforcement, which is followed by an hour of one-on-one interviews with print media. This overlaps with interviews with the twenty-four-hour cable networks, which go live every fifteen to twenty minutes.

Each cable network provides the opportunity for dozens of interviews throughout the day. Additional local and network radio and television appearances are also happening simultaneously, leading up to a second daily press conference with law enforcement at 4 p.m. The interviews then continue throughout most of the afternoon and evening, ending around 10:30 p.m.

After my team reviews coverage logs and collaborates on communication strategy for the next day, we all get less than three hours of sleep before the alarm sounds and Groundhog Day starts all over again.

Tom has been taking a very open and inclusive approach to working with the press. His media background and connections, combined with his amiable personality and great family support and hustle, help the story of Elizabeth's abduction garner international headlines almost overnight. Tom's philosophy is that the more coverage the family can secure in a diversity of outlets, the more likely they are to reach someone who can help bring Elizabeth home. This works relatively well in the early hours and days, when the story is largely about the plight of the Smarts in trying to find their daughter, and the community's incredible response to help them. About a week later, when the story becomes more accusatory and complicated, this open approach will have some unforeseen consequences, especially with partisan cable media.

Among the volunteer PR group members, I have significant crisis communication experience, including working during college for two years with the head of communications for the Salt Lake Olympic Bid Committee, helping the FBI and Atlanta Olympic Organizing Committee with press briefings following the bombing at the 1996 Games, and later being part of a team that managed a handful of crises at the Salt Lake office of Publicis Dialog, a global public relations firm. As a result, I quickly come to lead the strategy and messaging for the Elizabeth Smart Search Center.

In addition to working to organize the chaos of the media machine by establishing some simple systems and protocols, we also forge an alliance with the public information officers at the Salt Lake City Police Department. This allows us to obtain as much information as they're willing to share. I collaborate with them in a symbiotic manner on messaging and details for the two daily press conferences and the plethora of interviews, to help ensure that the family and investigators don't contradict one another. From this and the information gathered from the family and head of the search center, I draft proactive messaging along with a question-and-answer document. We use these, usually on the fly, to help prepare family members and other spokespersons so they can communicate strategic and consistent messaging.

Although my focus is primarily on strategy and messaging, I am still actively involved in managing the glut of media demands for interviews and information—helping facilitate requests, preparing spokespersons, and then serving as a liaison at each interview.

The pace is frenetic. There are constant questions, issues, deadlines, needs, and problems to be solved. Everyone works at a fever pitch, which is why I am taken aback when I see Karen temporarily step away from the media madness to flip burgers.

Couldn't her family handle the food on their own, since we need her help with the media? I think at first. Then I take another sip of my smoothie and my eyes become moist, as I remember that Karen and Jon's daughter Chelsea passed away eighteen months earlier, following an ATV accident. She was just twenty years old.

Because Karen was an elected official, the story of Chelsea's death received a fair amount of attention and media coverage. Karen and Jon demonstrated dignity, grace, and thoughtfulness throughout the ordeal, and made every effort to honor Chelsea's memory in the months following the tragedy. This included Karen working to introduce and pass legislation that helped streamline organ donations in Utah—and of course, their work with the Smart family, both on the front lines with the media and in doing the little things to help sustain volunteers who were working to find Elizabeth.

As I watch the Hales, I am overcome, realizing that although they recently lost their own daughter and sister, they are doing everything they can to help someone else find theirs.

CHAPTER 4

Baker

His aged and broken body seemed to miraculously transform. The acute arthritis that had swollen his arms, fingers, and sinews suddenly disappeared. The old man was surprisingly quick on his feet. He threw a wobbly right hook, accompanied by a barrage of angry, mostly incomprehensible words that were vile in tone.

Despite being caught off guard by the man's jab and burst of energy (akin to what happens when Popeye eats his spinach), I saw his fist flying toward me just in time. I awkwardly ducked and stumbled. Before I could yell, a mist of whiskey sprayed from his nose and mouth. I breathed it in and gagged, having never tried a drop of alcohol in my fifteen years of life.

The bitter taste and foreign odor, heightened by the electricity of the situation, temporarily stunned me. I was fully aware yet felt paralyzed. For a brief moment, I felt vulnerable to his physical attack, an assault that paled in comparison to the emotions gushing out.

The old man now had both fists in front of him. He shook them up and down. His ability to control his impulses was long gone.

There was likely no one in the world Baker Paxton despised more than me. And the feeling was mutual. He had been my nemesis for more than a dozen years. Despite the fact that we were decades apart in age—he was in his late sixties and I was fifteen—the anger, animosity, and malevolence we both felt from the conflicts that had ensued from our living next door to each other had hit a crescendo.

My mind raced. I tried to process the situation, while my brain kept telling my body to bob and weave. Another fist flew in my direction. I swerved, but not fast enough. This one glanced off my left shoulder. It didn't hurt, but adrenaline might have been masking the pain.

Baker recoiled, then threw another punch. My reflexes kicked in, and I was able to swerve as he tripped and stumbled forward. I stepped to the side, finally creating some space.

I had never really been in a fight. A few times on the playground and in a handful of church basketball games, I had been involved in pushing matches with a few punches thrown, but nothing had escalated.

This time was different. I was in an altercation with an adult, and it seemed far more terrifying. Although I couldn't think clearly, I knew the situation might have serious repercussions. As a news junkie who read the newspaper before delivering it in my neighborhood each morning, I was well versed in current events and familiar with many types of crimes. I had read about violent youth who were sentenced to serve time at the Decker Lake Youth Center, a criminal facility.

As Baker continued to swing at me, I grew increasingly irate. The years of my childhood, which had been filled with threats, verbal abuse, embarrassment, and acrimony, were boiling to the surface. I no longer cared much about the consequences.

He stepped closer and then slipped. I had a clear shot. I felt my body tighten and my fingernails dig into my palms. Then a scene flashed across my mind, a recollection of the first time I encountered Baker. This was followed by the series of events—the years, the arguments, the confrontations—that had led up to this precipice.

I was not quite three years old when we moved to East Millcreek—an age before most people have any type of memories, but the events of that day were unforgettable.

Our house, a modest 1,100-square-foot split-level with green trim, had a double driveway to the west. The home next door had a large nonflowering plum tree that hadn't been pruned in years. Its branches created a canopy over a large circumference of grass, almost spilling over our property line.

While my parents were visiting with some neighbors, I tried to bounce a small rubber ball my dad had helped me purchase from a gumball machine that afternoon at Skaggs Drug Store. As I threw it aimlessly against the driveway, it suddenly bounced on a diagonal trajectory, disappearing next door and landing near the plum tree.

I ran after it, ducking to avoid some low-lying branches. After retrieving the ball, I avoided returning through the rough foliage and instead chose to walk around the back side of the tree. I was just about at the driveway when I heard something unsettling. I turned around.

There stood a man, hunched over, with emaciated, arthritic hands and elongated, swollen elbows that looked like lopsided grapefruits. He wore a stained green T-shirt, baggy navy-blue pants, and tarnished black shoes that looked like something you'd find discarded on the side of the freeway.

He stared at me and then growled, his long nose flaring. His mostly white receding hairline was dotted with sweat, and his face sported a bristly five o'clock shadow.

"Get the hell off my property," he snarled.

Entering into flight mode, I dropped the ball and darted toward my mom, who had just appeared with my father at the end of our driveway. I grabbed her leg and clutched it tightly. Tears ran down my face.

"Get that damn kid off my lawn and teach him to never come over here," Baker ordered my parents. "I will call the police if I ever see him again."

Before my father could respond to the stranger's outburst, the old man turned, walked back across his unkempt yard, and disappeared into the house.

This was my introduction to Baker Paxton.

To say the experience frightened me would be a gross understatement. From that day forward, I was reluctant to go near the old man's property line. I began to have persistent nightmares.

In one of my first dreams, the angry old man took on the form of a demon and cornered me in my bedroom. He snarled, relishing the moment of his capture. I woke up soaked in sweat and screaming inconsolably. Rushing into the room, my mother scooped me up and held me tight.

"Christopher, it was only a dream. You're okay. It wasn't real. I've got you."

In the days, weeks, months, and even years that passed, I kept my distance from Baker. Occasionally I saw him driving his beat-up blue sedan slowly down Celeste Way before parking it in front of his house.

When I was a little older, my friends, siblings, and I would refer to his monstrosity of a vehicle as "the car with a thousand dents." Baker's sedan, a blue Ford Fairlane from the 1960s, had more craters, dings, and divots on its rusted and peeling exterior than any car I have ever seen.

Just as people claim that most dogs look like their owners, in many ways that car matched Baker. It had been through a lot and wasn't particularly pleasant, but it was still running—for what purpose, it likely didn't know.

CHAPTER 5

Word of Wisdom

Lighting a cigarette, a tall female journalist with rectangular tortoise shell glasses takes a drag as she strolls into the foyer of the Arlington Hills ward building.

"Excuse me, miss, there is no smoking in here," says a man in his mid-sixties, rushing toward MSNBC host Ashleigh Banfield.

"I'm sorry, I didn't see any signs." Banfield shrugs her shoulders, grimaces, and walks back out the door.

I witness the encounter while conversing with Ben Winslow, a youthful, iconoclastic reporter with church-owned KSL NewsRadio. He switches gears midsentence.

"Signs? Who needs signs?" he says. "No one smokes inside of a Mormon church. Who smokes inside any church? You can't blame this one on a national journalist not understanding the local culture."

Winslow, who has purple hair and isn't a member of the predominant Utah faith, is animated as he tries to process the awkward exchange. Banfield's faux pas is exacerbated by the tenets of the local culture.

Some members from the Smarts' congregation who are working at the search center are becoming increasingly apprehensive and skeptical of the members of the media. Their concern is being fueled by the inconsiderate actions of a growing throng of reporters, producers, photographers, and talking heads who have parachuted into Salt Lake City for the story du jour, after covering the recent shark attacks in Southern California.

Members of the Arlington Hills ward, and even some of its lay leaders, are questioning why we are going out of our way to accommodate and cooperate with journalists—who can be rude, use coarse language, and have the temerity to smoke cigarettes, "even inside the church."

Despite their unease, I know that dismissing, rejecting, or even isolating the media, especially because some of its members don't subscribe to or appreciate the sociocultural norms of our religion, would be catastrophic. It is imperative to take the high road and maintain strong relationships with the media, especially since the Smart family agrees with the communication team's position that the media is one of our best tools to help find Elizabeth.

Followers of The Church of Jesus Christ of Latter-day Saints abide by a strict health code, known as the Word of Wisdom, which dates back to 1833. It prohibits partaking of any type of drugs, alcohol, or tobacco, and even discourages drinking coffee and black tea. It also calls for members to consume meat sparingly and to eat herbs, fruits, and grains. Until recent years, many people believed that drinking Coca-Cola was taboo because it contains caffeine. In fact, church-run Brigham Young University sold only caffeine-free Coke on its campus for several decades.

Joseph Smith, who founded The Church of Jesus Christ of Latter-day Saints after claiming he'd had a visitation from God the Father and Jesus Christ (and later from an angel, who led him to ancient golden plates that he then translated into the Book of Mormon), received a revelation about the Word of Wisdom after being rebuked by his wife, Emma. She had complained to him after frequently cleaning up chewing tobacco and pipes left by Joseph and other church leaders, who would meet on the floor above a general store where the Smiths were living. Emma asked Joseph to inquire of God regarding tobacco use. He did so and received a far-reaching revelation that has governed the conduct of church members for almost two centuries.

Many in the faith today consider breaking the Word of Wisdom a grievous sin. In fact, in worthiness interviews, necessary to gain admittance to the church's temples, one must answer questions about chastity, honesty, paying tithes, and adhering to the Word of Wisdom.

When I was growing up, those who were seen smoking or drinking beer in public were quickly labeled sinners or rebels and, in many cases, were treated like outcasts by much of the community. This was especially prevalent in East Millcreek during the 1970s and '80s when a high percentage of the population were church members who, at least outwardly, lived the Word of Wisdom.

In teachings about the Word of Wisdom at church, it is often emphasized that one doesn't know whether or not they "have the gene," meaning even one sip of booze could result in becoming an alcoholic. While there may be some truth to this notion, it serves as a deterrent and, in the process, sometimes creates a sense of paranoia.

For those who actually suffer from alcoholism, the level of shame and rejection was, and sometimes still is, exponentially elevated in the local culture. Individuals who struggle with this addiction feel their sense of belonging is often diminished, and they have to navigate an unforgiving labyrinth of judgment, whispers, and insolence.

Those in the church who are beset by the disease might even feel a bit like Hester Prynne in *The Scarlet Letter*, with their demons on public display.

* * *

"It is a danger to the child, to the mother, to the entire neighborhood," Baker slurred as he staggered across the street.

While he likely didn't advocate for abortion, Baker insisted that a certain pregnant woman in our neighborhood couldn't have the baby, being that she was over forty years old. It was a dangerous confluence of irrational thought, emotion, and hard liquor. Baker couldn't provide a solution but was adamant that something had to be done—and now.

The woman, Ruth Hitler, lived with her husband, Doug, and their three daughters across the street from my childhood home. While I don't believe they were directly related to the family line of the former chancellor of the German Reich, carrying his namesake obviously bore its own set of challenges. Baker, who had fought in World War II, was always a little suspicious of the Hitlers. He may have struggled to believe that they weren't related to Adolph, and likely surmised that someone in the family line was culpable for the acts that destroyed countless lives in Europe and around the world.

Ironically, the Hitlers were the kindest, most generous people anyone could ever hope to have as neighbors. All five family members were thoughtful, conscientious overachievers who went out of their way to help others. On several occasions, I was the recipient of their kindness, especially Ruth's.

Beginning around the time I was six years old, Ruth often hired me to weed her garden or shovel snow from her walks. While she didn't necessarily need the help, she likely viewed it as an opportunity to help build me up, connect with me, and be part of the "village" raising the children.

The story I heard repeatedly growing up was that on the day Baker discovered that Ruth was pregnant, he was visibly angry—and inebriated. It was not uncommon for him to become enraged. Like a young child, he would yell, make unreasonable demands, and then after several minutes of protest, angrily stomp back into his house and slam the door. This time, however, it was different. He wasn't backing down.

Ruth tried to reason with Baker, telling him he was intoxicated and that she wasn't upset with him. Baker screamed. Ruth began to sob. After a few minutes, she began to cry hysterically.

A couple of neighbors heard the commotion and came running to Ruth's aid. Unfortunately, their efforts fanned the flame.

"If you…don't…do…do something now…I'll get my gun," Baker ranted. "I'll take care of things. I'll fix it. I'll shoot you."

Baker's anger continued to escalate, his guttural yell increasing in intensity. He combined profanity-laced threats with a string of words that sounded like he was speaking in tongues.

His final comment before he slammed the door was, "I'm going to get…get my g-g-gun."

In a matter of minutes, a cop car with domed red and blue sirens on top and two officers sitting inside sped up Celeste Way. They parked quickly in front of Baker's driveway, and the first officer ran and knocked on Baker's door. He disappeared inside while the other walked across the street and began speaking with the neighbors.

The 1970s were a very different time regarding gun violence. Instead of immediately confiscating Baker's firearms and arresting him, the police asked questions and took notes. They also asked the Hitlers if they wanted to press charges. The Hitlers decided they would think about it.

The fact that the police initially chose not to take any serious action bothered many who lived on the street. The consensus along the fence line was that Baker should have been arrested. His threats not only were troubling and illegal, but they were amplified because they were directed at one of the most beloved neighbors on the block.

A couple of hours later, a small parade of women carrying flowers and baked goods assembled on the Hitlers' front porch. Ruth answered their knock on the door, then stepped out and hugged each of the women.

It was as if Celeste Way had been preserved from the 1950s, and the almost-too-good-to-be-true stereotypes from TV programs like *The Andy Griffith Show* and *Father Knows Best* were still alive.

While the women attended to Ruth, a short and slightly overweight man walked across Baker's lawn and knocked on his door. He quickly disappeared into the home.

The man reemerged on the porch about a half hour later, accompanied by Baker. In a jovial, energetic way, he reassured Baker: "It's going to be okay. I'll talk to everyone. Next time, call me before you say something stupid.... Hey, you're a good guy. You're okay."

The man affectionately hit Baker on the shoulder. The door shut, and he whistled as he walked across the lawn to my driveway, where my father and I were standing taking everything in.

"Hi, I'm Ron Ballard. Could I talk to you for a minute?"

He had a rounded face, thinning hair, a high-pitched voice, and a cheerful disposition that was magnetic. In many ways, Ron seemed to personify the opposite of all things Baker.

"I know you're new to the neighborhood and probably don't know much about Baker. He's a really good man deep down inside. If you knew Baker like I do, you would see it. His drinking is the problem. It creates an enormous fence that, in some way, provides him with a shield but, sadly, doesn't allow people to get to know him."

Ron explained how he and another man named Neal, who lived a few streets up, had become drinking buddies with Baker, even though Baker was more than a decade older than them both. The three would party together on the weekends. Over several months, the weekend get-togethers had expanded to weeknights. While the three men did their best to maintain employment, the frequency and intensity of their drinking was taking a toll on their marriages, families, and health.

"Baker was the voice of reason. One Saturday night, he told me and Neal that he was giving up booze. He claimed he wasn't going to have another drink for the rest of his life, and he was serious. We were both very skeptical, since Baker has had a problem since his twenties. Then Baker challenged us to join him."

Baker informed the duo that in addition to going stone-cold sober, he would be going to church with his wife, Vaunna, and he invited them to attend.

The next day three clean-cut strangers walked into the tan brick ward house on the south end of Celeste Way. Ron told us that they not only attended the services but were actively engaged. Baker even answered questions during Sunday school.

In the days following the church appearance, the trio started walking together in the mornings to burn off their beer bellies. Instead of drinking on the weekends, they got together, along with their wives, for pinochle and dinner dates.

Their healthy, sober routine continued for months. Ron said the three had never been happier, more productive, or more connected to their families. Then one day Baker didn't show up to church. Ron and Neal were so concerned, they left halfway through the service to check on him. Baker wouldn't answer the door or the phone. This continued for days.

"Baker fell off the wagon. He white-knuckled it until he knew Neal and I were safe, and then he gave in. I will never be able to repay him. Baker gave me back my life, my family, my everything."

Ron added that he and Neal had been sober for several years now. They still walked together each morning, attended church on Sundays, and regularly visited Baker.

"You never give up hope, but it's not likely Baker will change. I try to see the good in him and love him regardless. He's a good man."

While it's unlikely that Ron told my father the story as a ploy to get his buy-in regarding the situation with Ruth Hitler, it was the perfect lead-in for his pitch.

"I spoke to Baker about the incident with Ruth. He feels terrible. It was the alcohol talking. I promise you Baker is harmless. If there are any problems or issues, please call me. I will take care of it. Let's not escalate things. Please, as a favor to me, will you forgive him and let this go?"

My dad nodded. It was hard to say no to someone as genuine, kind, and well-meaning as Ron.

After speaking with my father, Ron went door to door like a politician, lobbying each neighbor to give Baker a second chance.

His final visit was to the Hitlers. Ron begged them not to press charges and offered to personally intercede if there were any future issues. The Hitlers agreed, and Ron promised they would never hear a mean word from Baker again.

While this may have been true for the Hitlers, it wasn't necessarily the case for my family. In the months that followed, my father started construction on a garage and art studio at the back of our lot, abutting the border with the Paxtons' property. My dad did the construction work himself, aside from occasionally hiring some of the teenagers in the neighborhood.

Baker protested at every step of the project, constantly yelling, complaining, and calling the county. As a result, the inspectors were thorough and unrelenting. On more than one occasion, my father had to demolish certain sections of the work and start over. As payback, he made as much noise as possible in the process of correcting the issues.

One time I heard my dad confront Baker when he stepped onto our driveway during the project.

"You can shut up," my dad said. "I wouldn't be making this noise if you hadn't complained to the inspectors, who are making things difficult. Keep calling them and I will continue to be as loud as I can. *Enjoy.*"

It took more than a year to complete construction, and the garage created even more conflict with Baker when it was fully operational. My father purchased a secondhand air compressor, an array of industrial power tools, and a modest auto mechanics bay.

A few months later, while driving around scouting yard sales, my dad saw the shell of a 1940 Ford coupe and many of its parts strewn under an apple tree in someone's front yard. He knocked on the door of the home and handed over five hundred dollars to become the proud owner of a project that would take nearly twenty years to complete.

The 1940 Ford looked like a cousin to Baker's car, with plenty of dents and other damage. The biggest differences were its faded pink color and the fact that it didn't run. Hundreds of auto parts were now scattered throughout our carport and new garage.

My father always had a project going, and Baker always had a beef with it. The two men were like oil and water, and to say their relationship was acrimonious would be a gross understatement. Baker was constantly yelling, threatening to call the police, and doing whatever he could to disrupt my dad's work.

While Ron regularly stopped by to say hello, the incidents with Baker occurred either so suddenly that my dad didn't think to call him, or so frequently that he didn't want to bother him. It seemed there was little that could be done.

Most of the time, my father closed the garage door when Baker appeared. He'd put large headphones on and lock the side entrance, then continue to work as Baker pounded on the door or tried to get his attention through the back window. Inside, it was as if nothing unusual was happening and no one was outside.

If my father was tired, or if Baker interrupted him in the middle of an intricate task, he wasn't very forgiving. In these cases, my dad generally ignored him, put on eye and ear protection, connected the grinder to an air hose, stepped into the carport, and went to work on one of the faded red fenders of his antique dream.

Sparks would shoot in all directions. The high-pitched sound of metal grinding metal would echo off the bricks of our home and reverberate against the Paxton home's exterior. My dad would work relentlessly until Baker finally couldn't take it any longer and left.

While it would have been easy for my father to hate Baker, I believe he saw him more as a nuisance. My mother understood my dad's frustration, and at the same time wanted to shield me from the ugliness. She frequently reminded my dad that he set the tone and the example.

When things were tense between my father and Baker, a not-infrequent occurrence, my mom would try to use the situation as a teaching moment. She worked to help me understand the consequences of some of the poor choices Baker had made. She tried to get me to walk in his shoes and recognize his feelings so that I might have a small amount of respect and empathy. My mom hoped I wouldn't be scared by the constant fighting, and that by some miracle I might learn something that would aid me later in life.

CHAPTER 6

Service

The moonlight creates a blurry outline of the simple furniture and pedestrian features in the foyer of the Arlington Hills ward as I fumble around, dropping a pen and several papers, trying to find a light switch. It's nearly three o'clock in the morning. Elizabeth has been missing for more than a week, and I need to access the search center's situation room to blast-fax a statement to the media.

As the fluorescent lights flicker on, I get my bearings. I walk gingerly toward the locked room that houses maps, stacks of reports, radios, phone banks, orange vests, and other equipment, including a fax machine.

As I creep down the hall, a wave of raw emotion unexpectedly crests. The feeling is so overwhelming that I stop and sit on the floor, trying to catch my breath and composure.

I stare at a dozen empty round tables in the cultural hall—a community gathering place in church buildings that features a basketball gym, a stage, and an accompanying kitchen. (The name "cultural hall" is believed to have originated in the 1950s when the London city council initially rejected plans for a ward house in the Hyde Park neighborhood because it included a gymnasium, which wasn't deemed proper for the area. After a city official conferred with the architect and learned that the space would also be used for music, drama, and dining, the room was labeled a cultural hall and the revised plans were approved.)

For the past few days, countless volunteers have filed in and out of the cultural hall signing waivers, putting on orange vests, pinning a round badge with Elizabeth's picture and baby blue ribbons to their shirts, and participating in a twenty-minute orientation before receiving their search assignment.

I have passed by the cultural hall numerous times each day. No matter how overwhelmed I was juggling numerous media requests, developing strategy, collaborating with law enforcement, or trying to solve a never-ending string of issues, the sight of all these willing volunteers stopped me.

Each time, I witnessed something extraordinary. The place was a melting pot of individuals, some who came alone and quickly integrated with other strangers of different ages, religions, ethnicities, and socioeconomic statuses. They quickly put aside any differences and connected in a remarkable way. Fences came down. Each person was driven by a single thought and purpose: to find Elizabeth. In the process, they were opening their hearts and minds and becoming one.

This had been especially evident at the start of each orientation, when someone at the table was asked to offer a prayer. While many uttered a Latter-day Saint invocation (which begins by addressing "Heavenly Father," followed by impromptu dialogue, and then concludes with "in the name of Jesus Christ"), others occasionally recited the Lord's Prayer or even called upon a higher power in Hebrew.

Each time I passed by the cultural hall, I became distracted and engrossed—not so much from the sight of it all, but rather from an inexplicable feeling that overcame me.

Strangely, this feeling has just returned in the dimly lit church building; in fact, it seems even more pronounced as I pause alone near the large, empty room.

Later I'll come to understand that this feeling isn't necessarily new, but rather reminiscent of something I experienced many decades earlier.

* * *

It was a hot spring morning in 1983, and I was ten years old. The chorister of my ward, Dorcus Frewin, was trying to warm up parishioners during the opening hymn at the church on Celeste Way. Aside from the organ pipes behind her, the church was largely pedestrian, with exposed yellow bricks, large and clear windows, and a small clock on the wall. It looked like most of the other thirty thousand Latter-day Saint chapels in the United States.

An unfamiliar man in a navy-blue suit and maroon tie walked quickly up the steps to the stand. He paused at the rostrum and began whispering in the ear of the bishop, who was the lay leader of the congregation.

The two engaged in a spirited discussion, which became so distracting that more than half of the churchgoers suddenly quit singing.

Dorcus, who was wearing a loud '70s-era flower-print dress, thick brown Coke-bottle glasses, and large costume jewelry earrings, couldn't see what was happening behind her and was growing increasingly agitated. She waved her baton vigorously, trying to coax back the energy.

"What's wrong with you people? I've never seen anything so lifeless. Come on, *sing*," she said—under her breath, she thought. Dorcus apparently didn't realize her voice was loud enough to carry through the chapel.

When someone caught Dorcus' attention and pointed to the stand, she turned and was instantly and fully enthralled trying to figure out the dramatic scene. Only a handful of people in the congregation sang the last few words of "How Firm a Foundation," which ended abruptly since the organist quit playing when her attention was also diverted.

After finishing the conversation with the stranger, the bishop stood up before the invocation could be offered. Wearing a conservative dark blue suit, white shirt, and yellow necktie, he walked to the pulpit and stood silently for a moment before addressing the congregation.

"I have just been informed that the river in City Creek Canyon is close to breaking its banks, and downtown Salt Lake is about to experience a catastrophic flood. We will partake of the sacrament, say a quick closing prayer, and then all able-bodied men and boys over the age of fourteen are to head home, put on your overalls, grab some gloves and shovels, and head downtown immediately."

The winter had been unseasonably wet and cold that year, with heavy snowfall, especially in January. Come spring, it was as if Mother Nature had slept through her alarm clock and didn't awake in time—evidenced by a crust of snow, which usually disappeared from our lawn in February, that was still on our grass in April. Cool temperatures pervaded until a few weeks into May, when Mother Nature suddenly awoke. She flipped the switch, and temperatures in the valley went from the forties and fifties to ninety-plus degrees in a matter of days. This heat wave melted the snowpack too quickly, overwhelming rivers and streams and creating flooding not just in downtown Salt Lake but throughout all of Utah. Overall, there would be more than $100 million in flood damage.

That Sunday afternoon, my father was in a hurry to get home following the prayer. I found myself stuck behind an old man with a walker and had to run to catch up. I anxiously met my father at the car.

"Please can I go, please? I know I'm only ten, but I'm almost as tall as some of the fourteen-year-olds. I promise I won't get in the way."

My father stopped and briefly contemplated the request. He had always been someone for whom the spirit of the law trumped the letter of the law, and likely realized this could be a memorable experience for me. As he opened the door, he smiled and voiced his approval, adding, "But you will need to follow my instructions, which might involve watching and waiting."

Dressed in jeans, old hiking boots, and a yellow "East Millcreek Love It" T-shirt complete with an illustration of Mount Olympus on it, I loaded shovels with my dad into the back of our old red Subaru wagon and headed toward State Street.

The city center looked different. It had been transformed into a war zone. Mountains of sand were piled twenty to thirty feet high in every open parking lot. Large trucks drove up and down State Street delivering pallets of gunny sacks. Armies of men and a few women worked with amazing precision in every direction as far as the eye could see.

The operational lines began with a volunteer opening and holding a gunny sack. Then another person would fill it with sand, someone else would tie the bag, and then the sandbag would be handed from person to person. Lines of hundreds of individuals snaked around for almost a mile. At the end of the line, men with big muscles, many wearing orange tank tops, would take the sandbags and tediously add each bag to the fast-growing makeshift dikes on each side of State Street.

Initially, my dad shoveled sand and I helped capture remnants that didn't make it into the bag, returning them to the pile. A news crew shot footage of my dad working. It not only made the ten o'clock news that night but was saved as file footage that would be used in stories about the flood for several years to come.

Later, my father helped move sandbags as one of the links on the massive human chains as I stood by and watched.

Nearly every congregation of various denominations canceled services and sent people to battle the flood on the front lines. Many who were agnostic or atheistic also joined the effort. According to media reports, more than 325,000 sandbags were filled that afternoon by tens of thousands of volunteers.

At around dusk, water broke the banks of the river, and a few minutes later the volunteers cheered as the first trickle of muddy water slowly meandered down State Street. I ran into the modest flow along with several teenagers, but we were quickly escorted back behind the sandbag dikes by firemen. The water level rose quickly. We watched as a wall of white water now rapidly made its way down State Street, running stoplights, racing through each intersection, and emptying out to the valley below.

There was an unusual air of excitement and a sense of pride among the people lining the shores of State Street that night. My father said it was similar to the feeling when the Salt Lake Stars won the American Basketball Association championship the summer before I was born.

In this case though, we had all worked together to save the city. As the water continued to empty into the valley, feelings of both elation and chills seemed to travel through the crowd.

This phenomenon of volunteerism wasn't new to Salt Lake City. In fact, it dates back to Utah's early history. In the 1850s, a few years after Mormon pioneers settled the area, European immigrants who converted to the religion began traveling in large groups to the Salt Lake Valley—a place they affectionately referred to as Zion. Because most couldn't afford to go by wagon, and the transcontinental railroad wasn't completed, they pushed and pulled small hand carts—large wheelbarrow-type contraptions that held all of their provisions and belongings—across the plains for nearly three thousand miles.

In 1856, two groups, the Willie and Martin handcart companies, got a late start and found themselves in a dire situation, caught in an unexpected October snowstorm on the high plains of what is now Wyoming. Nearly 1,500 pioneers were stuck with insufficient clothing and blankets and dwindling food rations.

When word reached Brigham Young, leader of the church and also the territory's governor, he immediately petitioned bishops, who called on their respective wards to help. Within forty-eight hours, the first rescue party departed Salt Lake City, driving sixteen wagon loads of donated food, blankets, warm clothing, and supplies. In the coming days and weeks, a diverse group of volunteer rescuers would make an estimated two hundred to three hundred wagon trips that would both aid and transport the handcart pioneers to Utah.

The rescuers ranged from grizzled veterans of the Mormon Battalion, who'd fought a decade earlier, to young men in their late teens and twenties, many of whom had very limited frontier experience. English-speaking Latter-day Saints, born in the United States and the United Kingdom, worked side by side with Scandinavian and other European immigrant church members, speaking in many different tongues. Multiple ethnic groups were also represented, including an African American who'd been enslaved. The rescuers put aside their differences and came together with a common purpose and focus: rescue the stranded immigrants.

While more than two hundred people perished in what was recorded as the worst nonmilitary disaster on emigrant trails, the rescuers were successful in saving more than 1,200 of the handcart pioneers.

The flood of 1983, the rescue of the Willie and Martin handcart companies, and scores of other events, big and small, were historical precursors to the search for Elizabeth Smart.

Her story captivated a state and a nation, opening hearts and minds, bringing an even stronger and more diverse contingent of people together. It is believed that the search for Elizabeth was the largest and most publicized since the search for Charles Lindbergh's baby in 1932. In the first week alone, approximately ten thousand volunteers from countless backgrounds came together and joined the effort, searching for the missing harp-playing teenager on foot, on horseback, and by helicopter, motorcycle, boat, airplane, and ATV. Tens of thousands of additional people joined the effort in the weeks and months that followed.

Selflessly serving and coming to the aid of others is part of the DNA of members of The Church of Jesus Christ of Latter-day Saints. This is the result of a combination of factors, including counsel in scriptural works. In the New Testament, James (James 2:14–26) teaches that "faith without works is dead." Additionally, in the Book of Mormon (2 Nephi 25:23), an ancient prophet states, "It is by grace we are saved after all we can do." As a result, the Latter-day Saint culture is sometimes perceived as focusing on works more than grace. This explains why church members will perform heavy labor for hours for little more than a chocolate donut and a glass of milk. That said, church doctrine does not in any way undervalue the grace and gift of Jesus Christ through His sacrifice and atonement for all mankind. It is understood, however, that grace alone isn't enough. We can and ought to do more.

In Utah, more hours are volunteered annually per capita, and more money is donated, than in any other state. Service is so prominent that sometimes too many people show up to volunteer at certain venues. For example, leading up to the 2002 Winter Olympic Games, nearly seventy thousand people—the vast majority who were Utahns—applied for twenty-seven thousand volunteer positions. This is believed to be an Olympic record for the largest number of rejected volunteer applications. The odds of getting tickets to some of the top Olympic events was better for many Utahns than the chances of having the opportunity to work for free directing cars in the freezing cold or helping clean up trash after one of the events.

Children begin learning to serve others at a young age. This is further fostered as they mature and participate in regular service projects and activities throughout middle and high school. As of this book's publication, more than sixty thousand young men (beginning at eighteen years old) and young women (beginning at nineteen years old) are currently serving on volunteer proselyting missions for The Church of Jesus Christ of Latter-day Saints on their own dime, for two years (males) or eighteen months (females) in locations around the world. Most return home and continue to serve in various capacities in the church and community. An additional twenty thousand retired individuals also work as service missionaries.

While service is an incredible antidote for breaking down cultural barriers and reminding us that we are more alike than different, its effect can sometimes be short-lived. When there isn't an urgent or obvious need, many of us revert back to our tribalistic human nature—being presumptuous and judgmental, and staying close to those who share our beliefs, opinions, and history. We can forget the experiences and lessons learned in working together in the trenches with, and often for, those who are different.

While helping save Salt Lake City in 1983 was profound in the long term for our city, it had a fleeting impact on my father and me. The very next day, we were working together in the carport when Baker appeared and began complaining about the noise. Within seconds, the battle of bickering and backbiting recommenced.

As I stare into the empty cultural hall on this early June morning in 2002, voices of volunteers echo through the darkness. I contemplate if this experience will be similar to previous ones. Will I forget what this feels like, to be united with so many in such an important, meaningful common effort? To see boundaries, biases, criticism, and a reticence to engage left at the door? Or will I take to heart and remember this feeling? Will I remember how much observing the volunteers at the search center, and being a part of this monumental effort, already has opened my mind and changed me?

CHAPTER 7

The Board

Looking around the long, rectangular table, I make a concerted effort not to show any trepidation. On the inside, however, it's as if I smell smoke, and a fire alarm is blaring.

The dozen or so men and women, some of whom I have become acquainted with during the week since Elizabeth's abduction, look directly at me as I take a seat. They seem to be sizing me up. I am decades younger and have significantly less professional and life experience than they do. Anxiously wondering if what I am about to share will be well received, I try to think positive, confident thoughts: *Fake it until you make it. Fake it until you make it.*

Looking around the room, I quickly realize I may be the only one without a graduate degree. Sitting at the table are a renowned cancer researcher, a lawyer, a pediatrician, the head of one of Utah's most prominent family foundations, an executive with a large energy conglomerate, a successful tech entrepreneur, the former mayor of Salt Lake City (who now heads the Hinckley Institute of Politics at the University of Utah), and a prominent artist.

The board consists of immediate and extended Smart family members, along with community and business leaders who live in Elizabeth's ward and neighborhood. They meet twice daily to oversee the search efforts, the investigation, and all other aspects in response to the kidnapping. Aside from starting and concluding with a prayer, the meetings are serious and orderly, often resembling those of a corporation or foundation.

Dr. Charles Smart, Elizabeth's grandfather and the seventy-five-year-old patriarch of the extended Smart family, presides over the group. He is balding, with white hair on the sides, rimless oval spectacles, and a voice and demeanor that remind me a little of the Dalai Lama's.

Dr. Smart pulls me aside a few minutes before the meeting to ask if I will brief the board, explain what's happening with the media, and share how we can be more strategic in our efforts.

Dr. Smart introduces me, saying: "I've asked Chris to join our group." Then he looks at me and adds, unexpectedly, "Did I ask you?" While at age seventy-five, a person's memory can be spotty, this isn't the case with Dr. Smart who seems to be solving multiple problems in his mind at any given time.

My heart skips a beat, and I feel faint. Already nervous at the prospect of addressing the board, I am now feeling an even more acute sense of flight mode.

Before I can answer, Dr. Smart, who is the quintessential multitasker, dives into the agenda. For several years, he doubled as the chief of surgery at LDS Hospital in Salt Lake while commuting and working full time as the director of the cancer division for the American College of Surgeons in Chicago. The man knows how to get things done.

"Wait, I'm getting ahead of myself," he says. "We need the Lord's help. Please kneel."

There's a brief commotion as the chairs are pushed aside and we all kneel down on the beige Berber carpet, fold our arms, bow our heads, and close our eyes.

"Chris, will you offer the prayer?" Dr. Smart asks.

Praying publicly is a common practice among church members. It is taught from a very young age and occurs at the beginning and end of three separate meetings each Sunday. We pray at youth events and other gatherings during the week, and as part of several leadership meetings. Latter-day Saints are encouraged to pray audibly together, both over meals and once or twice a day as a family (usually before school or work in the morning and before bed).

Praying publicly is nothing new for me. I have done this thousands of times growing up and numerous times each day while serving on a two-year church mission in South Korea. Yet this time it is different. I am tongue-tied, as if Dr. Smart has asked the favor of a lifelong atheist.

A long and awkward silence ensues. I don't know how or where to start. Worrying about how my prayer will be judged, I desperately want to utter the right words and phrases to pass the test. The pressure seems to increase exponentially with each passing second. Suddenly, Lois Smart looks up. I see the circles under her weathered, bloodshot eyes. Her face tells an unspeakable story of pain and anguish.

It causes me to quickly forget about my insecurities. I bow my head, and tears stream down my cheeks as I begin to speak. I no longer care how or what I say. Instead, I plead with God that He will bless Lois and Ed with peace and comfort. That He will protect Elizabeth and strengthen her and let Elizabeth feel the love of her family and community. That God will help guide this group in their efforts. That we may be inspired. I also ask for a blessing upon law enforcement and the volunteers, and then close with "in the name of Jesus Christ. Amen."

As I slowly stand up, I try to quickly conceal the tears, and then notice something unexpected. Everyone at the table is doing the same thing. And they're not necessarily crying from what I've said, but rather from a collective feeling. Often when an effort is being led and guided by God, and His hand is in it, a beautiful unification, love, and power are felt and shared by everyone involved.

As the meeting continues, I am completely at ease. The board and I communicate and collaborate openly. It's as if we have known and worked together for years.

In The Church of Jesus Christ of Latter-day Saints, members affectionately call one another "brother" and "sister," as in "Brother Hansen" or "Sister Smith." This practice dates to the early history of the church when members often banded together in groups of families to escape persecution, cross the plains, and build and establish new settlements. Because there was often a high mortality rate, the members of the group literally viewed themselves as members of one big family that worked and fought together. Over the years, the terms stuck. They also signify to church members that all people are children of a caring God, making the human family at large our collective brothers and sisters.

The Board

By the end of the meeting, I feel like I am part of a new family. Aside from the fences coming down in my neighborhood in 1983, I can't think of another time when I've experienced a group bonding so quickly and unexpectedly.

CHAPTER 8

Eccentric Personalities

A heavyset photographer with a wrinkled, untucked, mustard-colored shirt struggles, carrying a tripod in one hand and a large video camera in the other as he jogs swiftly down the large grassy incline in front of the Arlington Hills ward. It's become routine for members of the media to go back and forth from satellite trucks, trailers, and other mobile offices into the foyer of the church building, and to various points in between, but this photographer's urgency catches my attention.

Stepping outside through the front door of the church, I discover a growing contingency of reporters and photographers on the east side of the building, some yelling questions. Tom Smart stands in the middle, holding court. He speaks casually with the media, sharing erratic and emotional thoughts about the investigation, specific family members, and what he deems to be "truth in journalism."

Tom has been working maniacally and has not slept in more than a hundred hours since learning of Elizabeth's abduction, so his faculties are severely compromised. In the book *In Plain Sight*, which is a well-researched, in-depth examination of the police investigation and kidnapping that Tom wrote with Lee Benson, he confirms his commitment to finding Elizabeth and the weary pace he had kept: "During the nine months Elizabeth was missing I stayed true to my own monomania, a family trait of dogged—sometimes blind—pursuit that the kidnapping fully awakened."

Sharing his unfiltered stream-of-consciousness thinking with the media attracts more attention than if he were throwing out hundred-dollar bills. One of Ed and Lois' fellow ward members observing the circus pleads for me to intercede, saying, "You're the PR guy. You have to do something."

Quickly maneuvering through the melee, I whisper in Tom's ear, "The family is meeting, and they need you."

Tom puts his arm around my shoulder and pulls me close. Then he tells the media, "Chris is telling me I have to go."

The media scrum crowds even closer to us. Several journalists eye one another, giving each other cryptic cues that say, *Do whatever it takes to keep this going.* The questions continue:

"Why do you have to leave?"

"Is there something developing?"

"Can't you please answer a few more questions?"

Tom looks stoically at the crowd and pauses while he tries to process this last request.

"I guess the family can wait for a few more minutes. Ask away."

I glare at Tom, trying to communicate nonverbally before shielding my mouth with my hand in an attempt to conceal my words from the media.

"Tom, *we need to go.*" He doesn't budge. Instead, Tom turns to the crowd.

"Do you know Chris? He's a great guy, but we really don't need him since I am handling the media just fine. Am I not doing a great job?"

I take a few steps sideways. Tom follows suit, as I'm holding him in a death grip. We continue the awkward dance toward the building. The media follows. Questions continue in rapid succession. Tom struggles to walk and answer at the same time. His responses are largely incoherent.

I have heard a church described as a sanctuary, but I don't truly understand this notion until I get Tom inside the door and exhale.

Tom will later recall in his book that following this incident with the media, his brother, David, confronted him and told Tom he "was jumpy, rambling, can't stand still and the optics were bad."

It isn't one of Tom's best moments. I don't yet realize that this is simply the beginning of managing the crisis inside the crisis; if I did, I might run. Then again, I have a strange affinity for working with creative, eccentric people who are driven and won't take no for an answer.

* * *

The pitch and tone of my parents' voices carried through the wall that separated our bedrooms. At first, I couldn't quite make out what they were saying. I could only decipher my name being volleyed back and forth, so I moved closer to the wall. I was nine years old.

My mother said something about being embarrassed, and it had to do with "all of the neighbors."

My father interrupted: "You are so overreacting. You should be proud of Chris and instead you are going to kill his..."

The furnace kicked on, and a shushing sound muffled the conversation. The exchange continued, but I couldn't make out a word until the door to my parents' room opened unexpectedly.

"I don't care," my father said. "I'm not going to argue with you any longer. I'll take care of things, *alright?*" He hastily exited, slamming the door and walking down the hall en route to the garage.

"I can't wait to see what you come up with," my mom responded, but I was the only one who heard it through the closed door.

My father was a hustler, a huckster, an inventor, an artist, and the struggling owner of several fledgling small businesses. He had a degree in fine arts from the University of Utah and a passion for oil painting, but rarely had the time or focus to pursue this interest. He was a pipefitter and sheet metal worker for the Union Pacific Railroad by night and wore a plethora of hats during the day. Working the graveyard shift, he often skipped sleep for several days straight, pursuing an idea or chasing a buck.

Hustle and frugality are two common attributes in the culture of The Church of Jesus Christ of Latter-day Saints that my old man embraced. Because members of the church, especially in the Beehive State, tend to marry earlier and have larger families (Utah has both the youngest marriage age and youngest first-time parent age in the country), families often need to do more and get things for less to make ends meet. This may be part of the reason why Utah is considered the multilevel marketing capital of the world, a fact that some embrace and others find embarrassing.

Over the years, my father's pursuits included everything from purchasing junk at yard sales and welding the items into sculptures, to refurbishing antique furniture and reselling it through the *Thrifty Nickel* newspaper.

He was always inventing something. Among his illustrious innovations was a connector that allowed for the transfer of toothpaste from an extra-large tube into smaller ones, so someone could do refills for the entire family at a fraction of the price of purchasing new smaller-size tubes.

My father's most legendary venture began one day when he overheard someone talking at the grocery store about a particularly difficult golf hole at the Salt Lake Country Club. The person mentioned that he had hit dozens of balls into the water that day, and there had to be a treasure trove of them somewhere downstream.

My old man snuck onto the course late one night with a headlamp, found the hole, surveyed the stream, and spent the next week welding a contraption that would capture the errant water shots and guide the balls into a twenty-five-gallon drum that was submerged and hidden by fallen tree branches.

Within a few weeks, the drum was filled. My dad recovered the bounty, and we chipped literally hundreds of balls on the front lawn before he made the rounds selling them for a dime each to pro shops at all the local golf courses. The money-making scheme was working perfectly, and he was reaping hundreds of dollars from the side hustle. Then one night a security guard caught my dad rolling a bucket of golf balls under the fence to his car. My old man fessed up, and because he was forthright, the night watchman agreed not to call the police. However, my dad had to surrender the bucket and his contraption as well as agree to never trespass on the country club grounds again.

Despite acquiescing to the demands, my dad complained for years that the night watchman likely had never reported the incident to his higher-ups and instead was getting rich off my dad's ingenuity.

As a child, I emulated my father but on a much smaller scale. I sold chalk rocks door to door, collected cans and bottles for the deposit money, and begged several neighbors for odd jobs. I was hustling a few dollars a week, which wasn't enough. I knocked on every door in the neighborhood—well, almost every door. I never knocked at Baker's house. I still feared the old man and told myself I didn't want his money anyway.

While my father was proud of my ambition, my mother was becoming increasingly concerned. The neighbors were subtly voicing their annoyance with my persistence.

The argument I had overheard between my parents loomed over our house like the scent of burnt toast. That same evening before dinner, my father informed my mom that he was working on finding me a job. She couldn't contain herself.

"A job? Really? He's *nine years old*. I'm all for finding him something to occupy his time, but I don't want him hitting up the neighbors anymore."

My father promised to keep me busy and to teach me "a thing or two about the American Dream," all without bothering the neighbors.

I went to bed that night with grandiose visions of what lay ahead and the incredible wealth it would generate. Maybe I would be so successful that I could save up enough to buy a car. I could just see a story on the evening news: "Local kid buys Toyota—long before he's old enough to drive."

CHAPTER 9

Crawlers

Dr. Smart looks stern as he stares down at Tom and says, "Loose *lips* sink *ships*."

This is the first time I've heard the aphorism, and it won't be the last. In fact, several members of the board, including myself, will repeat the phrase countless times over the next nine months.

"From now on, no one goes in front of the media if they have not slept for at least four of the previous twenty-four hours," Dr. Smart proclaims. "Go home, Tom, turn off your phone, and stay away from watching or reading anything. *Get some sleep.*"

Dr. Smart's face and tone are more animated than normal, yet he still seems to be employing the bedside manner that served him well throughout his career.

"I was just trying to..." Tom is crimson. His blue eyes are dilated. His hands shake as he stammers, trying to plead his case like someone pulled over for a DUI.

"I love you. I love you all," he continues. "I really love you. I understand what...what you are try-trying to say, trying...to do but...but I'm okay. I'm just fine. Elizabeth...Elizabeth...needs me here."

Tom later will describe his mindset during this period by saying that a *New York Times* reporter likened him to Al Pacino's character in the movie *Insomnia*. Pacino plays a veteran cop who becomes maniacal when he can't sleep because he's obsessed with solving a murder.

Tom's two sisters, Angela and Cynthia, intercede and embrace him. They have been part of the impressive family effort from the start, helping at Ed and Lois' home and at the search center, doing interviews, and running errands, often with their young children in tow. They provide a soothing, friendly voice and presence, and on more than one occasion have put an arm around *my* shoulder to make sure I was okay.

After a few more minutes of trying to reason with Tom, they gently escort him out of the room and put him in the care of his colleagues and close friends, *Deseret News* columnist Lee Benson and outdoors editor Ray Grass.

Tom's impromptu press briefing and Dr. Smart's meeting to address the issue rob me of valuable time. My team and I are now behind in gathering statistics and details from the day's search, and in developing messaging, and we still need to prepare family members for the afternoon press briefing. On the fly, I pull together what I can before the press conference starts, but I fail to anticipate questions regarding Tom. The media want to know where he is and why he has been acting so erratically. During the briefing, Ed does his best to explain that Tom is sleep-deprived and headed home to rest, but it doesn't seem to mitigate the media's growing suspicion.

Following the press conference, members of the extended Smart family divide and conquer, participating in more than a dozen live interviews with various cable news channels and local news shows over the next several hours.

Caught up in the afternoon feeding frenzy, I realize *Larry King Live* hasn't booked its routine evening interview. The iconic journalist had transformed his show into what one Smart family member touts as "reality TV that trumps reality TV." The hour-long program would end up likely being the recipe for Andy Cohen's *Live After Show*, following episodes of the Real Housewives series, which would debut four years later.

Each night, King has been starting his broadcast with the latest news concerning the search for Elizabeth and the investigation, followed by interviews with one of the Smarts, local police detectives, journalists, and others who have developed close ties to the case. Then King, with his patent black-rimmed glasses, suspenders, and face for radio, brings in his panel, including Court TV's Nancy Grace, celebrity attorney Mark Geragos, and world-renowned forensic expert Dr. Henry Lee. They have been analyzing and speculating on every word, action, and expression of the immediate and extended Smart family, even taking occasional calls from viewers.

On this particular evening there are no cameras, microphones, or lights set up in the makeshift CNN studio on the lawn of the Arlington Hills ward. One of the monitors has been left on, so I stop to watch the show. Nancy Grace is sitting in for Larry. At the onset, she teases the lineup, including a person of interest named Bret Michael Edmunds, a drifter wanted on an outstanding warrant. He'd been seen in his parked car near the Smart home just before the abduction. This news is already a few days old, but you would think with the dramatic tone and words Grace employs, it is a breaking story. I roll my eyes.

Then Grace introduces the first guest, local milkman Charlie Miller, who saw Edmunds and reported the tip to police. I'm looking at my phone and not paying attention to the images on the screen until I hear "…and with him the uncle of the little girl, Tom Smart."

I do a double take. The screen pans to Tom, who appears as if he is in a trance, sitting next to Miller. The two are on the set of a satellite studio on the south side of the Salt Lake Valley. Tom had subverted the board and convinced King's producers to conduct the interview away from the church so no one could stop him.

I feverishly make several calls, trying unsuccessfully to reach Lee Benson, Ray Grass, and Tom during the commercial. I realize there is little that can be done, that pulling Tom from the show after he's already been introduced would likely create more attention and controversy. Still, I hope something I can say will help him avoid the inevitable.

Grace begins interviewing Miller, who describes an encounter in the Smarts' cul-de-sac a week or so prior. He had followed a suspicious green Saturn he feared was trying to steal a delivery from one of the Smarts' neighbors.

Miller is affable and folksy, and fits the persona of the quintessential neighborhood milkman, mentioning how he is friends with, and often provides refreshments to, neighbors as they're walking and jogging.

When asked if he knows Elizabeth, Miller explains that he usually stops in front of the Smart house to give her and her siblings free milk and juice before they get on the bus. This response triggers Tom.

In previous conversations, Lois has mentioned to Tom more than once how protective she is, and that the only time the kids aren't supervised is when they are at the bus stop. Putting two and two together, Tom is quickly convinced that Charlie is the perpetrator. He is now on a mission to get the milkman to confess to the crime, and to do so live on national television. In his book, Tom writes of his motivation: "I thought I just might be sitting next to the kidnapper. If that were true, I had to appeal to Charlie Miller to let Elizabeth go. I had to speak to Charlie through my interview with Nancy."

Tom initially plays it coy. The interview begins with him nonchalantly divulging details of polygraph tests, something that has not yet been in the news. He talks about Ed's going through "four hours of hell" and then mentions that he, too, has completed a polygraph test.

"Hey, hey, hold on," Grace says. "Why did you have to take a polygraph?"

Tom tries to downplay the slip, explaining that everyone is a suspect and that it's the police's job to question anyone with connections to the situation. When Grace asks Tom whether or not Ed and Lois have ever seen Edmunds, he shifts the focus.

"Nothing that they've said to me," he answers. "But I think—we're happy that Charlie's come forward with this—right, Charlie?"

Tom glares at the milkman, throwing visual daggers that catch Charlie off guard. Charlie offers a sheepish "yes."

Tom then begins spouting an odd series of words, and as involved as I am in the case, even I am not sure what he's saying.

"I believe that this person is not a bad person at all. And our family has felt strongly for a while. And there's been a comfort here for a while. This is just somebody who actually likes Elizabeth. We don't know—we have issues. We've been ripped apart by our polygraph. I don't know who has done what with my brothers. We all have issues. Anybody's taken— we've been ripped apart to the core. And we understand that everybody has issues."

Tom pauses, and there is an awkward silence as he glares at Charlie like a hypnotist before continuing his diatribe.

"And we pray hard that whoever this is will know that the family is full of compassion towards everybody because this is a wonderful story, in a lot of ways. Because it's about, foremost, a beautiful little angelic girl. But it's also about—everybody has issues, no matter what. It crosses the boundaries on everything. It's an amazing story."

I'm stunned. I feel like I'm trying to corral Bill Murray's neurotic character in the movie *What About Bob?*

During the next few days, I will try to explain, justify, and even apologize for Tom, over and over. Although it's frustrating, I'm not necessarily angry with him. His unusual behavior is something that became all too familiar while I was growing up.

* * *

Sitting cross-legged, wrapped in a red-and-blue striped blanket on the living room floor, I tried to muster the energy to shower and get ready for school. My fleeting thoughts of going back to bed and staying home sick were interrupted by the sound of aluminum and springs colliding, as my father struggled to free something caught in the screen door. He pushed and pulled, nearly tripping before emerging with a large wooden box adorned with a padlock. My father had spent the graveyard shift putting the finishing touches on his masterpiece, which, much to the chagrin of my mother, who was upstairs getting dressed, he now placed on the coffee table in the living room.

"Guess what's in here?"

Before I could answer, my father blurted out: "A ten-speed bike."

I was puzzled. *How can a ten-speed fit in a three-foot-by-three-foot box?* I didn't want to hurt his enthusiasm, so I nodded and said: "Oh, wow, a ten-speed."

"No, there isn't actually a bike in here. What's in here is the opportunity to earn the money to *buy* a ten-speed bike—and not just any bike, the best one on the market."

My dad continued by telling me about the KHS Junior Racer. It was a Japanese-made bicycle that was a little smaller than the standard ten-speed, perfect for a nine-year-old, and had all the bells and whistles of a Cadillac.

Handing me the keys to the padlock, my father beamed.

"Open it."

Inside the box I found a half dozen black-and-red flashlights he had "borrowed" from the train warehouse, all with the Union Pacific logo, along with a package of peat moss and a large stack of red-and-white plastic cups.

"You still don't know what this is, do you? Take a look at this."

My dad pulled out a beautifully stenciled sign he had welded and painted at work. I turned it around and read aloud: "Chris's Crawlers. Fifty cents per dozen."

At the bottom of the sign, my dad had welded a rectangular track and created a metal insert that on one side had our address, with a caricature of a night crawler in the shape of an arrow, and on the flip side had the words "Sold Out" in red block letters. A small padlock was affixed to a hole in the panel on the sign, allowing me to secure the insert so someone else couldn't change it.

I was blown away and, at the same time, could not begin to comprehend how fortunate I was to have a father who made me a small business owner at the ripe old age of nine.

While I was still trying to make sense of everything, my mom came down the stairs. She was wearing a lavender robe and exhibited the intensity of an air traffic controller trying to keep the runways on schedule.

"Hey, this doesn't belong in the house. Would you please put everything in the box and take it out to the garage? And you're running late; you'd better *hurry*, Christopher."

After school, my father and I jumped into the car and drove to Sid's Bike and Ski. It was love at first sight. The Junior Racer was sleek, sporty, and smooth, and fit me like a glove. I rode the bike effortlessly around the parking lot. It was nothing like my yellow Huffy. The difference felt like Baker's car with a thousand dents versus a Ferrari.

I was sold until I saw the price tag: $399.95.

"That's a lot of money," I said. "I've never had more than twenty bucks. It would take years to buy this."

I raised the kickstand and stepped back.

"Not if you work hard," my dad said. "I bet you can buy this bike before the end of the summer. I'll show you how."

Before going into the house for dinner, we moved the sprinkler to the middle of the yard and turned the water on full blast. Then, instead of going to bed at nine o'clock as usual, my dad and I headed out on our first hunt. It began with a lesson on catching crawlers. First, my dad demonstrated holding the flashlight at an angle so that it lit only the ground a few feet in front of us.

He crept slowly on his knees, holding the flashlight steady in his left hand, then set down a coffee can on his right as he gently pounced on a crawler, stopping its motion with his thumb and forefinger. Once the little creature was trapped, the tug of war began.

Extracting the crawler from its hole involved patience, finger dexterity, and perfect timing. If anything went amiss, the crawler would break in two and be worthless.

During my first attempts, I wasn't fast enough, and the crawler either disappeared before I was able to trap it or slipped between my fingers into the safety of the underworld.

I finally got the hang of trapping the crawlers but didn't have the right touch to pull the little creatures from their holes without breaking them. My lack of timing and coordination weren't doing me any favors. I kept coming up empty-handed. Despite the early frustration, I was determined to make it work.

Finally, after my dad's coffee can was a third of the way full, I successfully captured my first crawler. I then caught another and another. By the end of the night, I was getting the hang of things.

Around 11 p.m., we opened the bag of sphagnum peat moss and began counting and depositing our cache into the yellow and brown fibrous layers of organic plant material. We had nearly two hundred crawlers, and I was almost ready to open for business.

I discovered something else that night. Catching crawlers had given me such an adrenaline rush that I wasn't tired, so I grabbed a bowl of vanilla ice cream and turned on the TV.

A plump man with a funny round face appeared. He was riding a small BMX bike erratically, while trying to escape from several scantily dressed housemaids who were pursuing him on the grounds of an English manor. The chase ensued in fast-forward while a punchy saxophone soundtrack played and a voice announced, "The Benny Hill Show, sponsored by Dove." As the camera panned in closer on the portly man's face, he winked.

From that night on, Benny Hill became part of my routine: catching crawlers, taking a shower, serving up a bowl of vanilla ice cream, and enjoying the high jinks of Great Britain's favorite funny man before going to bed.

The late nights caught up with me though. I was regularly late for school. At parent-teacher conferences a few weeks later, my strict fourth-grade teacher, Mrs. Johnson, asked me why I was routinely tardy.

"I don't know," I answered. "I have a new job that keeps me up a little later."

I proudly smiled.

"What time do you go to bed?" she asked.

I was disappointed that she hadn't inquired about my job. *How many of your students have jobs?* I thought, almost saying it aloud.

"Around ten, ten thirty."

My smile was quickly dissolving into a wince.

"Are you sure?"

Mrs. Johnson proceeded to pull out a paper where I had listed all of my favorite things, including my favorite TV program, as part of a classroom assignment.

"*The Benny Hill Show, I never miss it*," I'd written.

"How do you 'never miss' *Benny Hill* if you are in bed by ten or ten thirty?" she asked. "It doesn't start until eleven o'clock."

I was trapped. I apologized and promised to be on time. My mom had other ideas.

"No more *Benny Hill*," she said. "I didn't even know you were watching it. That show is not appropriate anyway."

I agreed and then that night pretended to go to bed. After several minutes, I tiptoed back to the TV. My face was mere inches away from the screen so I could hear "Yakety Sax," the show's theme song, which is a fast-tempo saxophone-based instrumental, on very low volume. I wasn't late to school again that year. There was no way I was going to compromise my business or my affinity for *Benny Hill*.

We installed the beautifully stenciled sign on a telephone pole, on a busy street a block from my house, on a Friday night. The cars, trucks, and RVs started pulling up several hours later. The business would offer new opportunities as well as an unforeseen challenge: Baker.

While the confrontations between my father and Baker had become legendary in the neighborhood, I had taken the road of least resistance. For years, I had simply avoided the west side of the driveway and any type of interaction with the angry old man; I'd even avoided making eye contact.

This became impossible in the days, weeks, and months to come. The increased traffic, noise, and attention from Chris's Crawlers catapulted me into learning an unintended lesson in something much more difficult than running a small business.

CHAPTER 10

Hiccups

Overwhelmed with emotion, Sierra and Amanda Smart sob as they embrace outside the makeshift Fox News set on the lawn of the Arlington Hills ward. While tears are commonplace at the search center, their reaction to something is so demonstrative that I step away from shepherding someone in an interview with MSNBC.

"We were just attacked by Bill O'Reilly," Sierra says. "He is an…" She stops and rubs her eyes, trying to regain her composure, and then apologizes for not being professional.

I wasn't aware of anything being scheduled with O'Reilly, but the sheer volume of interviews—sometimes more than fifty a day—means that sometimes things slip through the cracks. This also often can be attributed to Tom's laissez-faire approach to the media. He has made it clear to me on several occasions that although my team and I manage interviews for the rest of the family, the structure is overkill and doesn't apply to him.

"Chris, I book and handle my own media, *got it?*"

The O'Reilly predicament is a result of this. The morning after the televised milkman incident, Tom's sisters took his phone and put him in the car of a family friend, who drove to a remote cabin where there is no cell service. Tom will write later that after 152 hours without sleep, he finally took an Ambien and succumbed. Because of the chaos and Tom's sleep deprivation, he failed to inform anyone about the interview. He also didn't tell me about something else that I won't start to understand until I watch the tape of the segment on O'Reilly's show, America's highest-rated cable program.

"Now for our top story tonight," O'Reilly says. "Salt Lake City police are *heavily hinting* that the person who kidnapped fourteen-year-old Elizabeth Smart was known to her. Joining us from Salt Lake are Elizabeth's two cousins, Amanda and Sierra Smart, and from San Francisco, Marc Klaas, who launched the KlaasKids Foundation after the kidnapping and murder of his twelve-year-old daughter, Polly."

O'Reilly delivers the opening lines to his show with his trademark indignant tone. What he fails to inform the viewers, however, is why Klaas is back in San Francisco and not still in Salt Lake City, where he was just a few days ago.

Klaas approached the Smart family under the guise of a father of a missing and murdered child who wanted to help. In 1993, Klaas' daughter, Polly, was abducted at knifepoint from a slumber party in Petaluma, California, spurring the largest modern-era search for a missing child until Elizabeth Smart. More than four thousand people, including the actress Winona Ryder, joined the effort before Polly's body was tragically found in a shallow grave off Highway 101 two months later.

At Klaas' request, Tom reluctantly facilitated a private meeting with Ed and Lois and agreed to allow Fox News to record the last few minutes of their discussion. During the meeting, Klaas was empathetic and provided some helpful advice to Ed and Lois. He also offered to make several connections, including arranging a meeting between famed forensic composite artist Jeanne Boylan and Elizabeth's sister, Mary Katherine, who had witnessed the abduction. After talking for about twenty minutes, Ed and Lois thanked Klaas and said they wanted to meet with Boylan and would get back to him.

After they departed, Tom and Klaas spoke. Tom knew that bringing in Boylan would be problematic, since it would go against the directions of the Salt Lake City Police Department.

Because it had been completely dark during the abduction, Mary Katherine didn't get a good look at the perpetrator. She gave a very limited description of his clothes and features; the one thing that was distinctive was his voice, and yet she couldn't quite place it.

The police determined there weren't enough visual details to create a sketch. At the same time, they didn't want this information to become public, because it could send the message to the abductor that they didn't have much evidence. It also could create additional pressure for Mary Katherine. Instead, investigators counseled the family not to publicly share what Mary Katherine had witnessed and to give her space—to avoid asking Mary Katherine questions about the morning Elizabeth was abducted. If Mary Katherine wanted to talk about it, the investigators advised, the parents could listen but shouldn't pry for details. If she were given space, over time Mary Katherine would likely remember something that could crack the case, law enforcement believed.

Without divulging specifics, Tom explained to Klaas that there were prudent reasons not to defy the police and bring in Boylan. Klaas wouldn't listen, and instead argued that working with Boylan was in the family's and Elizabeth's best interests, and that the Smarts should not be afraid to go against law enforcement.

Klaas dug in, and as he lobbied more aggressively, Tom became increasingly skeptical. After hearing him out, Tom pushed back and asked Klaas why he was being so adamant. Klaas hemmed and hawed. And then in a last-ditch effort to get Tom on board, he came clean and admitted he was working for Fox News and that the network was offering to pay for Boylan to come to Salt Lake City and meet with Mary Katherine in exchange for exclusive access to the family.

Tom not so kindly declined Klaas' offer and told him to stay away from the family. This occurred a few days before Tom's bizarre, sleep-deprived appearance on *Larry King Live*, which put an even bigger target on Tom.

After the dramatic introduction at the top of the show with Klaas, Amanda, and Sierra, O'Reilly wastes little time and attacks the elephant in the room: "Mr. Klaas, first up, how do you see this case? Are there problems here?"

"Well, there've been many problems from the inception—least of which is the fact that they seem to have absolutely nothing to go on," Klaas says. "And the one piece of solid evidence that might exist, which is burned inside the mind of the little nine-year-old sister, has not really been followed up on until today. I guess when they finally reinterviewed the young girl, they got some new information, which apparently is leading them directly to perhaps several individuals on the radar screen."

Klaas continues explaining about the prospect of having Boylan interview Mary Katherine, which leads to several follow-up questions from O'Reilly.

"I understand that the uncle, Tom Smart—Amanda and Sierra's father—is against that?"

"Well, it's been difficult. Tom has been a challenging individual, yes sir."

"And do you know why?"

"No sir."

O'Reilly switches to interrogate Sierra and Amanda, who are unaware of the incident between their father and Klaas. When Tom didn't show up for the O'Reilly interview, a Fox producer, who had seen Sierra and Amanda on *Good Morning America* earlier that day, frantically pressured them to fill in for their father.

"Now, Amanda and Sierra, you just heard Mr. Klaas, who's an expert on this, say that your father has kind of been not really on the same page as Mr. Klaas, at least. Do you have any reaction to that?"

"'On the same page'—what do you mean by that?" Sierra asks. She looks at her sister and then stares back into the camera.

"What I mean is that Mr. Klaas says he's trying to set up an artist coming up there, trying to do a rendition with the little girl. But your father doesn't want that to happen."

O'Reilly continues to badger Sierra and Amanda in his pugnacious manner, asking them questions about what their father had told them and why they aren't more familiar with the investigation.

"Look, I'm not pushing you ladies, and I know you're here because you want everybody in Utah and across the country to keep an eye out for your cousin, and we want Elizabeth to come home. But it is a little strange that in a close family like the Smarts, you wouldn't discuss this case with your dad in very specific terms."

The muscles on Sierra's and Amanda's faces are as tight and textured as the leather on Tom's cowboy boots. They repeatedly squint to contain their emotions, but their expressions can't hide their newfound disdain for O'Reilly and Klaas.

Following the O'Reilly fracas, the focus of media coverage throughout the day largely shifts from the search effort to Tom. The media wants answers as to where he is, why he wasn't available the prior afternoon but then appeared on *Larry King Live*, and why he took a polygraph test. They also ask repeatedly if the rest of the family, like Tom, believe the abductor isn't "a bad person" and if they "have compassion" for him or her.

Several hours later, the media's questions recirculate in my mind as I lie in bed trying to get some fleeting shut-eye. The flip phone on the nightstand next to me will start vibrating in less than three hours. My eyes sting each time I blink. My body aches like the morning after the first day of the ski season. The exhaustion is unlike anything I have ever experienced, yet I am unable to sleep.

What began as a feel-good opportunity to help the family of a missing child, by working with the titans of the media world, is quickly devolving into something very different. The situation feels like it is careening out of control. It is over my head.

It would be easy to shut off the phone, sleep in, take a day off, and then go back to working in the office. No one would blame me if I quit, but that's not an option I would even begin to entertain.

* * *

"Get your *damned* car off my grass, or I'm going to call the police."

Baker scowled, pointing in the face of a heavyset man holding a cigarette, standing at the end of my driveway.

It was the first day of Chris's Crawlers. There were cars, trucks and RVs—many with boats, lining the street waiting. I was running back and forth from the front yard to the backyard, grabbing handfuls of crawlers and loosely estimating the number I put in each order, because there wasn't time for a precise count. I kept returning with as many red cups as I could pinch between my fingers. After completing each transaction, I would put the money in my pocket and then go back for the next round.

"Go ahead," the customer said. "The police aren't gonna do anything. My tire is barely touching your lawn." He stood his ground and gave Baker an intimidating stare.

"Okay, if you're going to be belligerent, then I'm not calling the cops," Baker responded. "I'm going to take care of you instead." He pouted as he raised his inflamed hands to make a fist.

"I'd love to see it. *Bring it on.*"

My parents were nowhere to be found. I had no idea how to handle the situation, so I did the only thing that came to my nine-year-old mind. I pretended nothing was happening and ran into the backyard to continue filling orders. When I returned to the driveway five minutes later, Baker was mysteriously absent. I wondered if the customer had actually popped the old man.

"Here you go," I told him, handing him a cup of crawlers. "No charge. I'm sorry."

The man motioned for me to walk with him to his car.

"It's not your fault, son. I'm sorry you have to live next to that drunk. Never back down from him. He's all bark and no bite. Show him who's boss, and he'll go away scared…. Here's a five. Keep the change."

Shortly after the man left, Baker reemerged. Instead of taking the customer's advice, I still acted as though Baker wasn't there, as if he was invisible.

"This is a nuisance, an absolute nuisance," he railed at me. "I'm calling the county. You ain't got a business license, and they will shut you down. Do you hear me? They will shut you down…you bastard child."

I apologized to each customer during the course of that business day. Once the last RV pulled away, I went into the house. That didn't seem to deter Baker. He continued to yell and rant like a picketer, pacing up and down our driveway.

I had envisioned the first day of business being idyllic: hustling, working hard, making small talk with customers, and putting stacks of greenbacks and quarters into my new cashbox. Instead, the whole experience had been so disquieting, because of Baker's embarrassing and insulting display, that it was quickly souring my appetite for the Junior Racer.

Unfortunately, Baker's disdain and antics wouldn't change in the ensuing days and weeks, but I wouldn't give up. My drive and my dad wouldn't let me.

CHAPTER 11

Herb

"Sometime soon, this man could walk into your life and make you a millionaire." The camera panned to a couple of shiny black Florsheim shoes trotting down a sidewalk, then transitioned to a group of people in a fast-food restaurant, who stopped in their tracks and said in unison: "It's *him*."

"This man is Herb," the narrator continued.

The image shifted to a balding middle-aged man with large, round, black spectacles. He tightened his necktie as he walked into the building and was immediately mobbed by a horde of adoring fans.

"Now that Herb loves the Whopper, he is visiting a Burger King in every state. Study the Herb poster, because the first person to spot Herb in each restaurant wins five thousand dollars. And everybody there gets a chance at winning one million dollars and receives a free Whopper and a Pepsi. Spot Herb at any Burger King for five thousand dollars and a chance at a million."

The camera panned away from the restaurant full of Herb groupies and returned to the Florsheim shoes, which were now untied and walking in the opposite direction. The music faded, the commercial ended, and the intro to *Gilligan's Island* came on the TV just as the phone rang.

"Maynard, you have got to be freaking kidding me," my good friend Chad Ragland said. "Herb is going to make us millionaires. That's right: millllll-yawnn-airrrr-ssss. Do you have any idea how many baseball cards we could buy with a million bucks? Meet me at the corner; we have a date with destiny."

Chad was the first employee of Chris's Crawlers, and had become my fellow Herb bounty hunter.

Our nightly grass-and-flower-garden safaris included lots of goofing off, gossiping about the neighbors—Chad insisted that Baker had a basement full of weapons, including a bazooka and several hand grenades—and talking about the highlights of the previous night's episode of *Benny Hill*.

I had turned Chad on to the best show on television. As a result, it wasn't uncommon for one of us to be humming "Yakety Sax" as we trudged through the mud chasing crawlers and experiencing the late-night joy and freedom afforded to few other kids our age.

Chad not only became my first and best employee, but he also worked for hamburgers and baseball cards. After school, I would grab a handful of dollar bills and quarters from the cashbox and meet Chad at the corner, and we were off. Our first stop would be 7-Eleven. Once we had failed at saving the princess in Donkey Kong a dozen or so times, purchased several packs of baseball cards, and were amped up from downing twenty-two ounces of icy cherry-flavored corn syrup, it was off to get some real food.

Our introduction to Herb happened in the entrance of the neighborhood Burger King one afternoon. There was a strange life-size cutout of the nerdy man, who looked like an accountant. He was wearing a three-piece suit and holding a black briefcase. An accompanying sign read "Find Herb. Win $5,000."

At first, we thought Herb was a joke. When we learned it was real and that Herb was "the only person on earth who had never tried a Burger King hamburger," both Chad and I nearly swallowed our gum, we laughed so hard. It was the worst advertising campaign we had ever seen, which made us love Herb even more.

We set up shop at a table with a window overlooking the 7-Eleven, Willy Car Wash, and Utah State Liquor Store. Over the next several hours, we devoured Whoppers and fries while enjoying people-watching—of course, keeping our eyes out for Herb.

We opened and read, and then reread, the stats on every baseball card before finally chewing the rectangle of stale pink gum with chalk-like powder that accompanied each fresh stack of cardboard dreams.

"Rollie Fingers. This is the best baseball card ever," I said. "He has to be a great pitcher with a name like Rollie Fingers, and that curly mustache is unbelievable."

I gently held the new prize with my fingertips in order to keep it in mint condition. Chad eyed it with great envy.

"I'll trade you my entire stack—a Reggie Jackson and two new, unopened packs—for that card."

Before I could respond to the offer, we saw Baker driving. He slowly pulled into the liquor store parking lot next door. Chad chuckled.

"Heeeeere comes your best customer," he said. "Attention, ladies and gentlemen, you might want to hurry and head home before this car gets back on the road. There's a reason why it has a thousand dents...and, please, Baker, don't hit Herb. I need that five thousand dollars."

Chad caught the attention of other patrons in the restaurant, who stared as he dropped his hands, which had served as a makeshift megaphone. Their crimped faces had no effect on Chad.

Surprisingly, Baker's car was still parked at the liquor store when we left about an hour later. The next day while we sat eating Whoppers after school, the car with a thousand dents interrupted us yet again.

"Wow, he's already out of moonshine. Hurry and get your booze, folks—Baker is about to buy out the store again."

Chad cupped his hands, repeating the announcer schtick from the day prior. While we were joking about Baker's affinity for alcohol, it was a mystery as to why he was frequenting the liquor store so often.

Our afternoon routine of Slurpees, baseball cards, staking out Herb, and seeing the car with a thousand dents, continued for weeks. Chad and I were determined to both find the burger nerd and solve the mystery of why Baker was spending so much time at the liquor store.

We dared each other to venture into the store to see what the old man was doing there. The layout of the building made it impossible to see inside without stepping through the doors and around a barrier that likely served to deter people from running out with a bottle of booze. There was also another deterrent, a big sign that stated: "Absolutely No One Under 21 Allowed."

One night while walking on our hands and knees with coffee cans and flashlights in tow, Chad stopped suddenly. "Whoever catches the least crawlers tonight goes into the liquor store tomorrow. Go."

The competition was intense. We both moved as fast as we could while working to avoid breaking any of the miniature creatures.

"Okay, Herb, at 11 p.m., the flashlights go off and we count."

Chad, who had now started calling everyone Herb instead of Maynard, was so focused on the competition that ET's flying saucer could have landed in the backyard neighborhood and he wouldn't have noticed.

There was a flurry of activity during the last few minutes, then a ten-second countdown followed by the flashlights going dark. Chad and I headed to the big wooden box where we both dropped one crawler at a time, counting in unison, repeating each number in cadence.

"…One hundred forty-one, one hundred forty-two, one hundred forty-three, one hundred forty-four…"

We each hid our coffee can so the other person couldn't see inside. I was down to my last crawler.

"One hundred forty-five."

Chad dropped his can. He was out. I was victorious.

"Not so fast, Herb." Chad smirked, pulling out two crawlers from his back pocket.

The next afternoon my anxiety killed the routine. I didn't enjoy my Whopper, scarfed it down too quickly, and I picked the worst pack of Topps in the history of baseball cards, all commons.

Finally, it was time. I stood tall. Terrified but true to my word, I slipped around the barrier into the liquor store. The shelves of closely stacked bottles, coupled with the sun shining through the windows, created a kaleidoscope of stained glass. It was mesmerizing. I temporarily forgot my fear. Then from nowhere, Baker appeared. I jumped and my vision went blurry. The last thing I saw as I turned and darted out of the liquor store was Baker's name tag.

I sprinted until I was halfway home. Chad, who had been watching from the 7-Eleven parking lot, finally caught up with me as I was walking. I was so winded that I almost choked trying to catch my breath.

A few days later, after handing a customer a red cup with two dozen crawlers, I was scurrying up the driveway so fast with my head down, I didn't even see Baker at first. A mere second before what would have been a violent collision, he came into my view. I quickly zigzagged out of the way and tried to keep my balance but landed ungracefully on his lawn.

Baker was unfazed and surprisingly placid.

"Hey, I'm not mad," he said. "I just want to talk to you."

Baker's voice was markedly different. It was at least two octaves lower, with a hint of bonhomie. I was still apprehensive but at the same time curious.

"I seen you at my store the other day," he said. "I don't want you to ever go in that place again. And don't you ever, *ever*, try a drop of that stuff, you hear? Never. You're a good boy. Stay that way. Don't be like me."

Baker extended his hand. I looked awkwardly away, not sure how to respond.

"Now shake and promise.... *Shake*.... I ain't as bad as you think."

He held my hand for an elongated moment, and then apologized for having yelled at my customers and me. He promised to do better.

Baker's new attitude was short-lived. The next day when I approached him, he reeked of alcohol and brushed me away. Later that afternoon, his routine of harassing my customers and me continued. Breaking his promise though, was of little consequence to me. I was focused on more important things.

When Chad and I first saw the Herb commercial touting the new million-dollar prize, it was as if the pied piper had blown his flute and we were in lockstep. We should have applied for jobs at Burger King, because we were now spending almost as much time there as many of the employees. During our stakeouts, Chad watched one set of doors while I focused on the other side of the restaurant. We were certain we were going to win, and we had a deal in place to split the money: fifty-fifty for the five thousand dollars regardless of who spotted Herb first, and sixty-forty if we won the million bucks, with the lion's share going to the spotter.

Chad and I were both listening to the radio one afternoon in early August when it was announced that Herb would be visiting a Salt Lake–area Burger King the following day.

"Hey, Herb Junior. Your daddy's coming tomorrow. We're going to find him and walk away with a million bucks. Meet me at the corner at five thirty, and don't be late."

Before I could protest the early-morning meetup time, Chad hung up the phone.

The next morning, I grabbed two twenties from the cashbox and we waited outside Burger King until the manager opened the doors. Chad and I set up camp, and the vigil began. We ate nearly half the BK menu, waiting for the fame and fortune we knew would accompany being the first to identify the burger nerd.

The only time one of us left the table that day was to visit the restroom or go to 7-Eleven to purchase a fresh pack of Topps. The two large stacks of glossy cardboard, with low-res pictures and stats, grew higher on our table with each passing hour. When Chad was gone, I stood at attention scanning the two sets of doors in the restaurant. He did the same thing when it was my turn to leave. We worked Burger King that day like a couple of soldiers guarding the Tomb of the Unknown Soldier.

Around seven o'clock, my mother unexpectedly appeared.

"I have bad news, guys. Herb was spotted at a Burger King in Midvale—someone else won the money. I saw it on the news. They said Herb is headed to Boise. I'll give you guys a ride home."

Skunked. Our dream had been shattered, and even worse, there was no longer a reason to hang out at Burger King. In fact, we now despised the place.

"Thanks a lot, Herb ole buddy," Chad said, scowling. "We must have spent like five thousand hours and five hundred dollars trying to find you. What a huge disappointment. What a scam."

As we exited the restaurant, he hit the life-size cardboard cutout of Herb so hard that, like our dream, it toppled to the ground.

CHAPTER 12

The Hoop

I walked through the doors of Sid's Bike and Ski, clenching a large Ziploc bag full of mostly one-dollar bills. I felt an odd mix of emotions that ranged from proud to giddy. After wheeling the sleek metallic blue Junior Racer to the front of the store, I opened my bag and began counting. The twentysomething man behind the counter watched suspiciously as I laid the bills down.

"Where did this come from?" he asked. "Did you sell drugs?"

The salesman had a straggly beard, tousled dirty blonde hair, and wore a tie-dyed T-shirt. His stoic demeanor, glassy eyes, and expressionless face told me he was not kidding.

"No, I sold crawlers. Lots and lots of crawlers."

A short time later, I pedaled around the corner where my dad was waiting. He ran alongside of me with an eight-millimeter movie camera, capturing the moment.

"I want you to always remember this. You set your mind to something, you worked hard, and now you have the nicest bike in the neighborhood. You can do and be anything you want. You just *proved* it."

In less than three months of late nights laboring with a flashlight, and long days serving hundreds of customers, I had netted nearly five hundred dollars with Chris's Crawlers. Not only did I buy my dream bicycle with all the accessories, but I also had money to purchase just about anything

71

I wanted. Financial independence, I learned, was pretty easy to achieve at an early age.

I had always been tall for my age, which had earned me the nickname "Too Tall Thomas" on the playground. I also had an affinity for roundball, so when my father suggested I invest the next hundred dollars I would earn in a basketball hoop, it was an easy decision. Per his style, my dad wasn't going to allow me to settle for an off-the-shelf, mass-produced standard from Taiwan. No, he demanded the best. A basketball standard made from scratch.

My father drew up rudimentary blueprints on scratch paper, purchased wood at the local hardware store, and welded and painted the rim during the night shift at the railroad. Then we began installing the new standard together on the roof of our house—well, he worked, and I stood by holding a wrench, trying to look attentive. As my dad organized the wood and bolts we would use to connect the standard to the roof, I heard Baker's door open and then bang shut. Seconds later he appeared.

"What in the hell are you building?" he yelled up at us from the middle of the driveway, gesturing aggressively in our direction. A mist of perspiration coated his forehead. "I'm telling you right now, I ain't gonna tolerate this racket any longer."

I was puzzled. We hadn't even started hammering or doing any other noisy activity. My father tried to explain, but Baker cut him off.

"I'm calling the police, and then I am calling the county. You don't got a permit."

Baker's tone and his mention of the county building department, both all too familiar from our garage construction a few years earlier, triggered my dad.

"If you want some racket, I'll give you some..." he began, then took out a hammer and pounded loudly on a joint hanger.

Baker recoiled. He bent to one side and shuddered as if a shockwave were traveling through his body before he collected himself.

"I'm...I'm calling the...police, you...you son of a..."

He staggered across his lawn and back into his house.

Similar rancorous exchanges continued for the next few days before reaching a crescendo just as my father was putting the finishing touches on the project. We were standing in the cargo bed of our rusty gray 1970 Chevy pickup truck. I was holding a socket wrench. My dad was steadying the basketball hoop rim against the backboard, and suddenly we heard a heavy thump, followed by a bang.

My dad jumped, tripping back into me, nearly dropping the thin circular steel apparatus with a coating of rubber and bright orange paint. Baker had smacked the Chevy near the back fender with an open hand. Then he did it again. My dad lit into him in a tone I had rarely heard.

"Get off my property or I *will* call the police. You nearly caused a serious accident. I don't care what you think or what your problem is. Get out of here."

My father was incensed and, for a fleeting moment, almost sounded like Baker.

The angry old man took a few steps back onto his lawn but didn't back down with his words.

"You are a nuisance. No one should have to put up with you ingrates.... You people are the worst."

My father ignored Baker and went back to finishing his masterpiece. The springs from the socket wrench echoed in harmony as he affixed four bolts through the bottom lip of the rim. My dad stepped back, and then it happened.

We heard a creaking noise. It stopped momentarily, and then the backboard cracked across the bottom. Like a tree losing a battle with a lumberjack, the homemade rim crashed into the truck bed, nearly hitting me before landing on a heap of scrap lumber. The backboard was a complete loss.

Baker laughed, stepping closer and closer to the Chevy. "Serves you right. I told you it was dangerous. Now take that thing down and get rid of it."

In response, my father snatched up the rim and hesitated. I'm sure the idea of throwing it at Baker crossed his mind. He clenched the rim tightly in his fingers, then dropped it and walked into the garage, pushing the button to shut the door like a final and frustrated exclamation point.

The next day when I came home from school, I found a new backboard sitting on the porch. My father had spent the graveyard shift cutting and gluing two large sheets of particleboard together, nailing and caulking a tin border, painting the exterior white, and stenciling an orange square in the middle. This backboard was significantly nicer than our failed effort from the prior evening.

My dad had learned from his mistake as well, and this time purchased a lighter, mass-produced basketball rim from the local Fred Meyer superstore. We installed the bolts, and then my father propped me up by letting me step first on his knee and then on his chest to reach the rim. I dangled there for several seconds, my body twisting, my feet kicking the air. To our delight, it held. We were ready to play.

Despite Baker stepping out of his house to snarl and yell at us, my dad and I battled in a mean game of one-on-one. It was the first of many in the driveway together. He went easy on me and kept the score close that time, but in the end pulled away and beat me by a few points. It didn't matter to me though. I was euphoric. I now had my own home court.

In the months that followed, a constant mob of boys ran around the double driveway, jostling for position and fighting for the ball. The games of three-on-three, poison, twenty-one, dynamite, and others we made up would go on for hours. The competition was fierce, and it wasn't uncommon to have dirt and small jagged pebbles caked into our hands, along with scrapes and raspberries on our knees, from diving for the ball or getting fouled hard on a drive to the hoop.

Each time we started playing, it didn't take long for Baker to make an appearance. At first, my friends were taken aback and a little timid—most had never felt the wrath of an angry alcoholic. They acclimated quickly though and grew accustomed to his antics.

Baker's favorite tactic was positioning a sprinkler on the far edge of his lawn, right by our driveway, and turning it on full blast, showering water across the court. This caught us off guard at first, but we learned to adapt. We would either play on, with the water droplets providing some relief from the dry summer heat, move the sprinkler, or block the flow of water with a small sheet of plywood and a brick. Each time Baker discovered the fix, he would angrily cuss at us and kick over the makeshift shield. Regardless of how we responded, Baker returned every fifteen to twenty minutes to express his displeasure, always threatening to call the police.

Sometimes when we played, he would get into the car with a thousand dents and escape somewhere for a few hours. This was usually in the afternoon; he was likely working at the liquor store. I would try to organize basketball games so the biggest ones were when Baker was gone. The only problem was that he worked infrequently and never seemed to be away from his house for more than a couple of hours. When the car with a thousand dents wasn't parked out front, I was a lot looser and able to enjoy the competition. When Baker was around, it was onerous. It was as if he were a crazy uncle I had to deal with and try to explain to my friends.

While Baker generally had been an obstacle to any project, the basketball hoop was markedly different. He seemed more agitated, more anxious, more dug in. It was as if he were fighting some type of demon.

CHAPTER 13

Boom Mics

Early one Sunday morning in June 2002, David Hamblin, bishop of the Smart family's ward, asks to speak with me for a few minutes. It is the first Sabbath day the building is functioning as both a church and a search center. The search operation was initially located across the street, at the Shriners hospital; however, after several days of being deluged with volunteer searchers, it became necessary to distance the center from the hospital, to allow the medical facility to serve its patients.

The Arlington Hills ward has been functioning well as the search center during the second week following the abduction. It has welcomed volunteers while housing dozens of full- and part-time personnel who are organizing and managing the searches.

Search operations are minimal on Sundays. This is because members of The Church of Jesus Christ of Latter-day Saints generally observe the Sabbath day by attending services and refraining from activities, purchasing items, and participating in nonreligious events.

A skeleton crew works in the search center's situation room, and the handful of people who show up to volunteer are turned away. The most noticeable difference at the Arlington Hills ward from the prior Sunday is the large contingency of media, who have parked satellite trucks and trailers, as well as set up areas and makeshift sets, at the top of a large grassy area in front of the building.

Bishop Hamblin has dark circles under his eyes and tries not to yawn as he speaks.

"Will you take a few minutes at the start of sacrament meeting to explain about the media and how to avoid saying anything that could complicate things for the Smart family?" Sacrament meeting is the main congregational service on Sundays.

His primary concern is how ward members coming and going from services should interact if they're approached by the media. There's also a growing fear, planted by a technologically savvy church member, that the media might use boom mics to eavesdrop on churchgoers who are socializing outside the building. This is a relevant concern, since many ward members helping the Smarts are privy to sensitive and confidential information.

Bishop Hamblin asks me to also address this issue at this morning's ward council meeting. These meetings are unique in focus. Once a month, the entire leadership of the congregation meets to help plan and organize Sunday services and weeknight activities, and to discuss the spiritual and welfare needs of the families and individuals in the congregation.

The council is made up of representatives from several auxiliary branches of the ward. It includes the bishop, who is the head of the congregation; a female who is the leader of the Relief Society, a women's organization; two male priesthood leaders (one senior, for a group called high priests, and the other for younger adults called elder's quorum); two youth leaders (male and female); a woman who leads the children's group, called the Primary, and a handful of others who oversee and support various areas such as Sunday school and missionary work.

Each individual in a ward council is assigned through inspiration, by the bishop, and voluntarily leads in their respective capacity, without remuneration, for two to three years. All active members of the congregation are also given callings (volunteer assignments) and serve in various roles that support the auxiliary heads.

Each bishop and each ward are overseen by a stake president, which is the leader of a greater geographical area of multiple wards, known as a stake. Bishops, who serve for five years, and stake presidents, who serve for about a decade, are both lay leaders who continue to work their regular full-time jobs while devoting a vast amount of their free time to helping church members. But there is no pay and benefits aside from receiving blessings.

Because the bishop is responsible for the spiritual and temporal needs of all the members in his ward, he is often called upon at all hours of the day and night—to help when someone is ill or struggling with personal or marital problems, employment difficulties, financial issues, faith crises, loneliness, death, and other unexpected circumstances. If someone has significant needs that require additional help, the bishop will activate some, or all, of his ward council to provide it.

This organizational structure has played a crucial role in providing immediate help when Elizabeth was abducted and in organizing the search center.

After Ed called 911 on June 5, 2002, at 4:01 a.m., to report that Elizabeth was missing, his next call was to his home teacher.

In each congregation, every adult ward member is called to be a home (men) or visiting (women) teacher, and two pair of teachers are assigned to each family. Home and visiting teachers develop close friendships with their assigned families and make in-home visits monthly. They are the first line of assistance if a need or issue arises.

When the Smarts' home teacher received the call from Ed, he immediately informed Bishop Hamblin, who alerted the ward council, and in a matter of minutes, friends and neighbors were mobilized, ready to run to the aid of one of their own.

Bishop Hamblin also called the stake president, who began determining what resources and help he could make available from adjacent wards. The stake president then informed a regional authority over several stakes, who at some point may have informed the governing body of the church, known as the Quorum of the Twelve Apostles. They then informed the head of the overall church, who is a prophet, believed to be similar to the prophets in biblical times.

In the same fashion as a call to 911 initiates a police emergency, the call from a home teacher initiates a spiritual and grassroots response that, in some cases, could go all the way to the top of the church.

Before 5 a.m., the bishop and dozens of ward leaders and members were at the Smart home, assessing the situation. The Relief Society helped organize meals for the Smart family and determined how they could help with the younger children. Many members of the Relief Society joined with the priesthood group members to quickly activate a door-to-door search around the neighborhood.

Salt Lake deputy district attorney Kent Morgan would later tell the Deseret News that within a short time of police arriving, "We had neighbors running around, trying to find Elizabeth. It was the ward function of the year where everyone was trying to help."

This impromptu ward rescue team was later joined by members of Ed and Lois' extended families, additional friends, neighbors not of the faith, and others who simply came running to help. Many ward council and congregation members took the day off work to help. Approximately two dozen high priests and their spouses, who were retired, basically started new full-time jobs that day as volunteers for what would become the Elizabeth Smart Search Center.

On this first Sunday morning that the church is functioning as a search center, I step through a door adorned with a brown laminate plate and the words "Bishop's Office" in white letters. The room is small, with the bishop sitting at his desk and his two counselors, or assistants, on each side. The walls have images of Christ, a map of the ward with family names written in grease pen on each lot, and pictures of the Primary children. The other members of the ward council are crowded into chairs on the other side of the desk. They are dressed neatly in suits, skirts and blouses and dresses; most are holding pens and taking notes.

After Bishop Hamblin introduces me at the start of the meeting, I quietly observe while he discusses and checks off items on his agenda, working his way up to the topic of news media.

I can see from the faces of Bishop Hamblin and the other ward council members that the stress and rigors of the abduction have taken their toll. And yet, each one of them actively engages in the discussion and enthusiastically accepts assignments associated with the Smart family, along with other tasks involving their ward family. When we arrive at the topic of news media, Bishop Hamblin turns to me.

"We have lots of amazing talent and expertise in the ward," he explains. "However, a situation with media like this is outside anything anyone of us has ever experienced. We really need you to instruct the ward on what to do, Chris, including taking a few minutes from the pulpit."

While I don't really have experience managing a situation like this (likely only a handful of professionals in the country do), I don't let on to that fact. Instead, I focus on how we can steer things in the right direction.

"I'm not sure sacrament meeting is the best place for this. There will be media attending, many for the first time in a Latter-day Saint church, and they will report that the Smart family's publicist was telling people what to do and say."

I recommend having each leader speak to the group over which they have stewardship, and advise them that anything they say during Sunday services, or while walking in and out of the church, could find its way into media coverage. They should tell members they don't need to be afraid of the media or overly guarded, but they should avoid saying anything they wouldn't want to find printed in the newspaper.

Bishop Hamblin concurs, and each of the auxiliary leaders agrees to begin making phone calls. A prayer is offered, and the ward council concludes.

A few minutes before the beginning of sacrament meeting, Bishop Hamblin pulls me aside and says he may still have me say something from the pulpit—that I should be prepared.

I take my place in the pews, toward the back of the chapel. My heart pounds, and I can feel the anxiety cresting when, during the announcements at the beginning of the service, Bishop Hamblin speaks my name and asks me to share some advice. I walk slowly up to the rostrum, trying to formulate what to say.

I pause and look upon the congregation, which is a sea of colors, with dresses, suits, white shirts, and multicolored ties. The adults look attentively at me, while some of the children fidget with action figures, Matchbox cars, and dolls; many of the toddlers are eating Cheerios from small Tupperware containers.

"On behalf of the Arlington Hills ward, we would like to welcome the media who are sitting in the back rows," I begin. "We really appreciate everything you are doing to cover the story and bring awareness to the search for Elizabeth. Please let me know if I can explain anything to you, or serve as a guide, as you attend church today. For members of the ward, please be welcoming to our new friends in the media, and remember you are on the record—meaning anything you say or do can and will be used against you."

There is an audible laugh from the congregation. I breathe a sigh of relief, but the relief is only temporary.

CHAPTER 14

Annabelle

M r. Fowles, my fifth-grade teacher, looked up and down the aisles, surveying the room on an afternoon in April 1984.

"Who will serve as her defense attorney?" he asked the class.

As a former University of Southern California lineman, he was an imposing figure with the stature and glare of a bouncer. Mr. Fowles had unkept, wiry black hair with a few small patches of grey. His dark olive skin was outlined by an eternal five o'clock shadow, and when he passed by you in the hall or classroom, there was an unmistakable air of Aqua Velva.

"Alright, if someone doesn't volunteer, I will assign one of you. Anyone? Who will be the defense attorney?"

The face of the new girl, Annabelle, was both pale and crimson. She nervously twisted a strand of her strawberry blonde hair and sheepishly looked over her left shoulder, hoping someone or something would provide relief from the pressure that had been mounting since she left Alabama six months prior.

Although I would later learn that Annabelle had painted in her mind an idyllic picture of life in Salt Lake City, during the weeks following the move, her experience had been anything but what she had envisioned. Making friends and fitting in had been much more difficult than she had anticipated. Annabelle was an outsider, with a Southern twang, and she had a penchant for speaking her mind and going against the establishment.

Her cavalier attitude and approach were at the crux of a dilemma that had been brewing for several weeks, until things had finally boiled over earlier that afternoon.

It began when my peers and I arrived for school one Monday morning in the late fall. The bulletin boards had been stripped of all materials, the desks had been pushed against the walls, and two foreign plywood structures, which resembled Lucy's "Psychiatric Help" booth from the *Peanuts* comic strip, had been placed in the back of the classroom.

Trying to make sense of the situation, we noticed a pile of clipboards and No. 2 pencils with a note that stated, "Welcome to the real world. Please take one and sit on the floor." Mr. Fowles was transforming the classroom into a simulated city. All the students were required to get a job, after which we could purchase or lease our desks. Additionally, we would need to pay bills, balance a checkbook, and purchase and maintain a car.

The clipboard included a paper with a list of jobs and application forms. The hubbub in the room quickly surrounded the position of bank president, which was the highest-paying and most prestigious job.

While I was completely engrossed, writing about my experience running Chris's Crawlers, a fracas ensued between a group of boys and Annabelle. What started as sarcastic banter regarding which gender was superior quickly escalated when the ringleader of the group told Annabelle to shut up, go home, and make dinner. Annabelle didn't back down.

"Take that back right now. That is beyond offensive, y'all. A woman is as qualified, if not more so, than a man to run a bank. I know a girl who could do the job of bank president better than any boy in this class."

The ringleader could not believe Annabelle had the gall to stand up to him. The two argued for several minutes before Mr. Fowles finally interceded. Annabelle remained unapologetic.

The confrontation set the stage for the inevitable. Mr. Fowles interviewed candidates for each position. With my experience running a small business, I thought I was a shoo-in for bank president. In the end, Annabelle's grit and determination won out over my business acumen, and she got the job.

Before Annabelle could take her seat behind the pale blue bank structure, the ringleader and his henchman were already conspiring to get her ousted.

During the ensuing weeks, there would be several attempts to undermine Annabelle. With each seditious effort, she would grow more guarded. Annabelle was all business. The job was her identity, and in many ways, one of her only friends.

On a Friday afternoon in March, I saw the ringleader signal to one of his henchmen, just seconds after Mr. Fowles had stepped out of the room. Those boys, who ironically had landed jobs as classroom police officers, walked to the back of the bank. One began to write a ticket. The other attempted to grab the calculator Annabelle was using to reconcile accounts.

"Thief, thief, *thief*," he said, pointing at Annabelle's calculator. "Drop it and put your hands up."

Annabelle ignored the directive and instead walked toward her desk at the front of the room. The ringleader jumped in her path and ordered her to stop. He reached for the calculator. The two struggled for a few seconds until he successfully pried it out of her hands. That's when it happened.

All the insults, disrespect, and humiliation Annabelle had been harboring for weeks seemed to be channeled into the swing of her outstretched hand toward the boy's head. The impact was so significant that it not only knocked the ringleader to the ground but left a mark on his face that was still visible at the end of the school day.

Stunned and embarrassed, the ringleader dropped the calculator, trying not to tear up. Annabelle darted blindly toward the door, looking back just as Mr. Fowles barreled through. Her slender frame couldn't sustain a collision with the ex-college football player, and she crumpled helplessly to the ground.

The classroom erupted in a bevy of laughter and comments. Annabelle curled up in a ball and started sobbing. It took Mr. Fowles more than an hour to contain the situation, unpack the series of events, and determine a way to resolve the issue.

His solution was for Annabelle to be given a ticket for simple assault and larceny. She opted to contest the charges before a fourth-grade jury. Mr. Fowles then appointed a judge, and one of the henchmen immediately volunteered to be the prosecuting attorney, boasting how he would prevail since he would have the help of his uncle, who was a lawyer.

That's when Mr. Fowles asked for a volunteer to serve as Annabelle's defense attorney. After threatening to assign one of us, he asked yet again, likely hoping somebody would step forward so he could avoid further conflict.

My chest tightened. I rubbed my eyes. I looked up at the ceiling and then slowly stood.

"I will represent her."

The gravity of the decision was underscored by a flood of butterflies. I slowly took my seat again, maintaining tunnel vision on the blackboard to avoid the visual taunts and daggers.

I told myself that my motivation to serve as Annabelle's defense attorney was to right a wrong, to stand up for someone who was being mistreated. While there may have been a small degree of truth to the notion, I was actually more interested in an opportunity to go up against the ringleader and his henchmen, in a setting outside of the playground.

Like most kids, I wanted to feel accepted. At the same time, I was somewhat of an anomaly. Since I can first remember, my mom encouraged me to think and be different. So I did, in everything from the TV shows I watched, the mostly underdog teams I cheered for, and the way in which I wrote sentences with spelling words to the subjects I chose for class assignments.

When the customary report about a favorite animal was assigned in third grade, instead of writing about kangaroos, monkeys, or koala bears, I chose the squid. My mom purchased a large dead white-and-purple tentacled creature at the Asian market, and that served as a dynamic and smelly visual aid. After I finished the report, I got in trouble for using it to chase girls on the playground during recess.

In the church's cultural microcosm, which seems to value conformity over individuality, thinking and acting differently came with its share of challenges. One of the governing leaders of The Church of Jesus Christ of Latter-day Saints once said that from a national and worldwide perspective, Latter-day Saints were in a biblical sense "a peculiar people." The church encourages its members to embrace being different in their beliefs and standards, especially with friends, colleagues, and acquaintances outside of the faith, but that does little to change the culture's insularity. As a result, I was uniquely peculiar among the peculiar.

Thinking and acting differently put a target on my back, especially with the classroom ringleader and his henchmen. This had started in kindergarten and escalated each year, largely because I wasn't subtle or understated in my quest to be different. On the first day of fifth grade that year, I gloated to the group about a lingering issue, inciting further venom.

In fourth grade, while my friends were coming of age with music by Duran Duran, Def Leppard, Culture Club, and Michael Jackson, I was an unapologetic Billy Joel fan. I was the only person in my class who liked "the Piano Man." Aside from the faculty and staff, I was likely the only one in school who even knew he existed.

One day I brought my tan-colored Fisher-Price tape recorder to school, loaded with Billy's album *Glass Houses*. After I hit Play on the song "It's Still Rock and Roll to Me" during morning recess, the ringleader grabbed the recorder and ran off with it across the field. Before I could catch him, the playground monitor intervened, turning off the "new sound" and confiscating the player. My mother picked it up at the office later that day, and I had to promise to never bring it to school again. As a result, I endured relentless teasing for the rest of the year: "Hey, Billy, where's your tape recorder?"

The year 1983 was also my awakening to sports as I developed an affinity for the Los Angeles Raiders. I'm not sure if it was because of their silver-and-black uniforms, the pirate logo, or the hard-nosed play of Howie Long, Lyle Alzado, Marcus Allen, and Todd Christensen, but I loved this team.

For Christmas that year, I received one of my most prized possessions, a Raiders letterman-style jacket. Even though it wasn't warm enough to serve as a winter coat, I wore it everywhere, in every season. That spring, during one of the never-ending Nerf football games at recess, I became too hot, took the jacket off, and placed it in a pile with several other coats on the side of the field.

In the midst of battle, I eyed a large stray dog entering the playground. It bit my Raiders jacket and took off running into the neighborhood. The game stopped, as did most of the action on the playground, as the entire school watched the spectacle unfold. I loved my Raiders jacket and was not about to lose it, especially to a dog, so I sprinted after it. But I couldn't catch up with the canine, who finally stopped, dropped my prized possession, lifted its leg, and urinated on the jacket before running away. The field and playground erupted into laughter.

Embarrassed but not completely defeated, I pinched the end of the sleeve between my thumb and forefinger just hard enough to grip the saturated garment and headed back toward the building.

The ringleader sneered as one of the henchmen punched my shoulder, causing me to temporarily lose my grip on the jacket.

"That dog is smarter than you," he said. "He knows the Raiders suck. Oh, and I bet there is a pee-soaked Billy Joel tape in your pocket too. Everything you like sucks."

A few months later, during the summer of 1983, Billy Joel released *An Innocent Man*. The popularity of the album, which sold more than a million copies in its first two months, coupled with Billy's new girl-friend, supermodel Christie Brinkley, made him one of the hottest stars on the planet.

Wearing a Billy Joel T-shirt and my Raiders jacket on the first day of school that year, I felt vindicated. Billy was on top, and the Raiders were the favorites to win the Super Bowl. And I let everyone know about it, repeatedly.

This only increased the insults, attacks, and confrontations I had with the ringleader and his henchmen, but I didn't care. There were more than a few coarse words said, and a couple pushing matches that nearly went to blows, especially after I accepted the assignment to defend Annabelle.

Everything I knew about the law I had learned from the Honorable Joseph H. Wapner, the judge presiding over *The People's Court* on TV. The show was a staple at my house, and while many of my classmates relaxed after school by watching *He-Man and the Masters of the Universe*, I got my daily fix of Wapner, host Doug Llewelyn, and the venerable bailiff, Rusty.

I enjoyed watching and analyzing the often bizarre disputes, illogical arguments, and common sense (and lack thereof) from the eccentric people who weren't actors but were "actual litigants with a case pending in a California municipal court," according to the show.

The only problem with using *The People's Court* to help my classroom case was that it featured small claims disputes and everyday people acting as their own counsel. While getting a feel for what worked and didn't work in a television courtroom had some merit, it didn't give me much to work with in defending Annabelle.

There weren't a lot of places where an eleven-year-old could learn how to practice law in 1984. I didn't know any attorneys, and *Law for Dummies* wouldn't be written for another decade. Additionally, Annabelle was largely a stranger and still hadn't engaged with me to discuss the case, and it had been several days since I'd agreed to represent her. The clock was ticking; we had just over a week to prepare for the trial, and the stress and pressure were rising.

I couldn't sleep on Sunday night after waiting all weekend for Annabelle to call. Crawling out of bed, I turned on my family's off-brand beige computer, the Franklin Ace 2000, inserted a blue floppy disk, and created a new file.

Employing a poor man's rendition of hunt and peck, I typed and typed and typed. Despite the fact that the challenge was way over my head and the odds were significantly stacked against me, I feverishly continued to work as best I could.

I made a list of arguments in favor of Annabelle's case and then a list of arguments against her. I brainstormed possible questions. I also listed witnesses and captured what I thought each would say during the trial. My strategy was to make solid, convincing arguments and to have a playbook of strong responses, to help Annabelle navigate through the toughest questions the prosecution might throw at her.

When I didn't know what to do or where to go next, I just simply continued typing until something came to mind.

The cadence of the keystrokes was hypnotic. I got so lost in the work that when I finally looked up at the clock, it was 2:54 a.m. I was aghast. *How could that much time have transpired?* In a little more than three and a half hours, I had compiled nearly a dozen pages of single-spaced notes. I had never written so much in my life, let alone in one sitting.

I hit Save, pulled the floppy disk out of the drive, and hid it in the crack of the molding on the inside of my closet. I fell asleep quickly. It seemed like only fifteen minutes later when my radio alarm sounded with the sign-off from Paul Harvey's *News and Comment*: "This is Paul Harvey. Gooood day..."

Annabelle and I spoke briefly at recess. I learned she was acutely afraid of the repercussions from her father, who had recently retired from the Marines, if he were to become aware of the incident with the ringleader. As a result, she wanted me to do the impossible and prepare the case without her collaboration. I quickly concocted a plan based on something I had seen in a movie.

We synchronized our watches, and later that afternoon, at precisely ten seconds past 4:10 p.m., I dialed the last digit of Annabelle's phone number. She was perfectly in sync and picked up before the phone rang.

We were amazed it worked, and we planned another call at exactly ten seconds past 11:31 p.m., well after our parents would be in bed. Scheduling at this time also allowed me to keep my nightly routine of catching crawlers, showering, and then watching *Benny Hill* while devouring a large bowl of ice cream.

The first night, we barely talked about the case. Annabelle needed a friendly ear to bend. She told me about the challenges of being a "military brat" and how excited she had been to move to a permanent home in Utah, only to be met with challenges that made her yearn for their next transfer.

Despite being in that awkward stage when there is interest in, but often very little meaningful interaction with, members of the opposite sex—especially in the Latter-day Saint culture, where dating before the age of sixteen is discouraged—I felt guilty for not having been more welcoming. I hadn't previously engaged in a real conversation with Annabelle.

The last thing I remembered thinking, when my head hit the pillow and the late-night ether began robbing me of my consciousness, was that regardless of how the case turned out, having the opportunity to walk in Annabelle's shoes was illuminating. I was even more motivated now to do everything I could to defend her.

The calls at ten seconds past 11:31 p.m. became routine. We worked late into the night, thoroughly reviewing every detail of the trial, refining arguments, and practicing every possible question, scenario, attack, and curveball over and over again. After we hung up, I would typically work for another hour or two, fine-tuning the details before catching a few hours of sleep.

Several days into preparing for the case, I became so fatigued that my mother suggested I stay home from school. This would be the first and only time I would turn down a "get out of jail free" card. I felt I had no choice but to go to school.

In the rare instances when I was not working on the case after school, I would try to blow some steam shooting hoops. On the last day before the trial, I couldn't hit anything and was growing increasingly frustrated. Preoccupied, I didn't notice what was happening around me until I heard the guttural growl of the old man. He stood holding his sprinkler at the edge of the driveway and motioned toward me.

"Knock off this noi—"

"Don't say another word," I interrupted him, standing tall and ready to go to battle. The veins in my neck were bulging; I felt like I was Lou Ferrigno starting to turn into the Hulk. "*You* turn around. Go back in your house and *deal with it*. I'm not going to take any of your crap today. Go on, get out of here. *Now!*"

All the frustration, stress, and emotion had kindled a rage that for the first, and only, time seemed to affect Baker. He dropped the sprinkler and walked away without saying a word.

I shot hoops for another five minutes before finally making a basket. I never left the court on a miss, so now I had permission to get back to work.

As the midnight hour of the trial day approached, Annabelle and I, who had been working together for the past ten days, felt anxious yet excited at the prospect of presenting our case. I tried to reassure her, saying, "It will all be over today. If we aren't successful, it won't be for a lack of effort."

My rigid and disciplined demeanor seemed to be dissipating with each word. The extreme exhaustion was fading. I was functioning on adrenaline and becoming giddy. For the next hour, Annabelle and I talked and laughed on the phone about everything but the trial. When I was about to hang up, she said, "Wait. I need to thank you. I can't believe how much time you've put into this. I'm not sure anyone has ever done anything like this for me. You're a true friend."

I had no idea that this would be our last real conversation.

The trial during lunch recess attracted an audience of almost a hundred fourth, fifth, and sixth graders, who crammed into the back of the classroom, which had been transformed into a court. I ignored the onlookers and focused on my strategy of not denying or justifying Annabelle stealing the calculator or slapping the ringleader, instead working to demonstrate how the boys had conspired against her. This confused the prosecution, especially when Annabelle not only took responsibility for her actions but apologized. The prosecutor repeatedly struggled to respond, asking questions and trying to get Annabelle to admit her guilt, which she acknowledged each time and then explained how she had been the victim of a plot to get her fired. The ringleader and his henchmen hadn't prepared for cross-examination regarding their capricious behavior. As a result, they came across as arrogant, belligerent, and unremorseful.

After the jury was dismissed to deliberate, the room was a cacophony of conversations. So many people were speaking that it was difficult to make out any one exchange. I sat next to Annabelle. We both were quiet. I briefly contemplated how the experience was the hardest thing I had ever done. It had been more difficult than any assignment ever. But had we done enough?

When the bailiff opened the door five minutes later, few people noticed. He yelled to try to get attention, but to no avail. Mr. Fowles put two fingers in his mouth and emitted a screeching whistle. The room fell silent, the judge took his position, and the fourth graders walked slowly back to their makeshift box.

"Has the jury reached a decision?"

"Yes, we have," said a girl with pigtails. She pulled out and unfolded a page of thin lined paper. "We, the jury, *all* find the defendant, Annabelle, *not guilty.*"

It took a second for the news to sink in. At first, I wasn't sure if I had heard correctly. Then Annabelle grabbed and hugged me tightly, and I knew it was real. She held on for several minutes, burying her head in my chest to conceal her tears.

CHAPTER 15

Breaking News

For the first time in nearly a week of working twenty-plus-hour days, I arrive home before 11 p.m. I pace like a zombie between the kitchen and living room of our orange-and-tan brick 1920s Tudor. I stop and stare aimlessly out the stained glass windows, surveying our front yard and the tree-lined road, illuminated by an old-fashioned streetlamp. I am so frazzled that I don't see Laura until I feel her hand on my shoulder.

"Are you okay?" she asks. "You look terrible. When was the last time you ate more than a smoothie? Go lie down for a minute."

Despite having barely seen me in days and being constantly interrupted when she does, because my phone seems to never stop ringing, Laura provides a calming influence that seems heaven-sent.

I retreat to the den, lie down on the couch, and turn on the TV. I don't realize for quite some time that the satellite power box is off, and I've been watching white static.

I'm like the young girl in the movie *Poltergeist*. The only difference is that I'm not trying to connect with paranormal beings; rather, I'm so acutely sleep-deprived and emotionally exhausted that I feel like I'm about to join them.

I change channels, landing on a cable news program, and momentarily watch a story about the death of mob boss John Gotti. Because my capacity to focus is so compromised, the broadcast quickly devolves into background noise, and I check out even further.

Suddenly my phone vibrates, and I flinch. I answer reluctantly. It's a well-placed source with one of the television networks.

He gives me a heads-up regarding a development in the case. Pulitzer Prize-winning journalist Maggie Haberman and her colleague Jeane MacIntosh would later characterize the turn of events in their book *Held Captive* as something "that would ignite a media firestorm that threatened to rival the one surrounding the Jon Benet Ramsey case."

I feel a rush of adrenaline trying to digest the information when Laura appears with a chicken salad. I inform her of what is occurring and apologize, wanting to spend a little time together. She tries to hide her disappointment with an awkward smile.

"It's okay," she says. "I really miss you, but I know how much the Smarts need you."

Laura rubs my back and serves as a sounding board as I take a stab at formulating some initial messaging. Out of the corner of my eye, I catch a glimpse of a picture on the TV. It's a newspaper article with Elizabeth's headshot, and the headline reads: "Police Eye Extended Family: Kidnapping may have been staged."

I scramble to find the remote, and rewind TIVO a few seconds to the start of the story.

"And we have a breaking story," says veteran news anchor Randall Carlisle of the local ABC affiliate. "The *Salt Lake Tribune* is reporting that an extended member of the Smart family may be involved in Elizabeth's kidnapping."

He stares into the camera as the screen changes to the image of the newspaper story.

"The copyrighted article, slated to run in tomorrow morning's *Tribune*, says clues gathered from inside Elizabeth's bedroom are pointing to an inside job, including a revelation that the screen in the house, thought to have been the point of entry, may have been cut from the inside," Carlisle continues. "The *Trib* article goes on to say that investigators have been stumped, in part by the eyewitness account of Elizabeth's nine-year-old sister, which has not wavered since the alleged kidnapping took place. Once again, the *Salt Lake Tribune* is preparing to report that a member of the extended Smart family may have played a role in Elizabeth's disappearance..."

Before I can finish watching the story, my mobile phone, which I keep on vibrate, feels like an electric razor in my pocket. It buzzes incessantly as journalists aggressively try to reach me to get a response.

I ignore the impulse to answer and instead sit back down on my blue leather couch. I look up and fixate on a small crack in the plaster of the coved ceiling.

After a few deep breaths, I am ready. I answer the next call.

"The family can't respond to an article they haven't had an opportunity to read. We're trying to get a copy of the story. Do you have one? We'll respond once we have the story. Call me if you get it before I do."

I tell this to the first reporter, and several dozen that follow, who are also only aware of what the local ABC affiliate has reported. Aside from the station and the *Salt Lake Tribune*, no one has access yet to the actual story. Although the *Tribune* has an online site, articles aren't instantly accessible. In fact, it's not uncommon for news sites to post stories online early each morning, around the time when newspaper carriers are hucking their orange-bagged hard copies of heavily inked newsprint onto the porches of more than ninety thousand Utah subscribers.

I continue to take calls and repeat the routine as I drive to a meeting at the home of Angela and Zeke Dumke, Elizabeth's aunt and uncle, who are the tacit vice chairpersons of the Elizabeth Smart Search Center board.

When I arrive at the Dumke house, more than a dozen people are waiting anxiously in the living room. They are either debating amongst themselves how the family should respond or are on their phones—or, in some cases, doing both simultaneously.

They quickly update me on their conversations with the police chief, the mayor, and a half dozen other sources. The information they provide is helpful, but the task is still overwhelming.

While we're working to get a copy of the *Tribune* article, I reflect on the Jon Benet Ramsey case. I recall how when fingers started pointing at the family, they went into hiding and sent their attorney to respond to the media.

We need to do the opposite. But how?

I'm lost in thought, pretending to hear the people talking in front of me but not comprehending a word of what they're saying. I suddenly begin thinking aloud.

"We need to call and recruit as many members of the extended Smart family as possible to be out in front at the morning press conference."

One of the most important fundamentals in crisis communications is that you must demonstrate and communicate what you are doing, but not necessarily with words, in responding to the situation. The presence of family would boldly communicate that the Smarts are being transparent and up front in responding to the issue before any words are even uttered.

My non sequitur comment has caught the group off guard. There is some immediate resistance. Some people believe this tactic may be too risky.

I passionately argue its merits, explaining how we'd assign two members of the extended family to be spokespersons. Anyone who is approached by a journalist would strictly refrain from answering questions and refer them to me. I would then work to facilitate a response.

I am gaining traction. Several members of the board are now debating the advantages of the approach, with only a few dissenters. While we'll be interrupted before a final decision is made, not only will the presence of the family standing behind the spokespersons be an important aspect of the response the next day, but that visual of united support will become a hallmark at each press briefing that follows over the next eight months.

At around 1 a.m., Angela holds up a copy of the *Salt Lake Tribune* article, which the Associated Press has just faxed to her home office. She begins reading it aloud:

"Evidence from within Elizabeth Smart's Salt Lake City home has led investigators to theorize the girl may have been abducted by a member of her extended family, who staged it to look like the work of an outsider, the *Salt Lake Tribune* has learned.

"Since the fourteen-year-old girl's apparent kidnapping, police have scoured the family's Federal Heights home for physical evidence. Elizabeth's nine-year-old sister reported a man with a gun had taken the older girl from the bedroom they shared.

"Detectives have been unable to explain how the abductor—seen only by the younger girl—could have entered the house through the small window that appeared to be the entry point, according to sources in four law enforcement agencies. The window isn't in the girls' bedroom, but police have refused to specify where it is located.

"Investigators have surmised that someone who was already inside the home may have tried to make the window look as though a break-in occurred there. But the screen appears to have been cut from the inside.

"Still, detectives have been flummoxed by the fact that Elizabeth's little sister, who seems credible and whose story has remained consistent through three interviews, apparently did not recognize the kidnapper."

Before Angela can finish reading, she is drowned out by a chorus of comments, sighs, and quibbles.

Elizabeth's aunt, Cynthia, speaks up. "Chris, you may not know our family well, but I can assure you there is no truth to this. There is no way anyone in our family could have done this. *No way, no one, none at all.*"

Cynthia is calm and resolute as she looks at me with an expression that says, *You have to trust me.* She is difficult to dismiss. Cynthia, who followed in her father's footsteps—studying medicine and graduating from Yale University en route to becoming a pediatrician—not only has the credibility of a medical doctor but has impressed me as being genuinely thoughtful and trustworthy.

When I received the first call informing me about the *Tribune* article, it evoked some uneasy feelings, which are still lingering. While my focus is on the Smarts, in the back of my mind, I'm worrying a little about the repercussions to my reputation in the event that someone in the family was involved in Elizabeth's abduction. Cynthia's words are timely as the board continues to grimace over the article, but the feeling accompanying them is what gives me the confidence to move forward.

Obtaining a copy of the *Tribune* article wasn't easy. Crafting a response and getting everyone on board might be even more difficult. Many in the room want the family's response to blast the *Tribune* story as malicious and blatantly false.

There is a natural tendency in drafting statements like this to be long-winded and defensive, and to use lots of legal jargon. I recommend to everyone that the statement be succinct, employ common language expressing disappointment, explain what the Smarts are doing to address the allegations and why, and in the process, give the public the opportunity to come to their own conclusion versus telling them what to think or believe.

The strongest argument we can identify from the *Tribune* article is that the story incorrectly implies it is unusual to investigate the family.

Contradicting this and communicating the family's full cooperation with law enforcement will be key.

We go through a fair amount of debating and wordsmithing. Finally, at 2:33 a.m., the statement is finalized:

"The Smart family is disappointed by today's *Salt Lake Tribune* article, which is highly speculative and implies that it is unusual to investigate the family in this type of case. Investigating the family is common procedure. We continue to fully cooperate in every aspect of the investigation and urge the public and media to avoid distraction from what is most important, finding Elizabeth."

I blast fax the statement to approximately fifty media organizations and then place hard copies under the windshield wipers of a dozen network satellite trucks parked outside the church.

We are proud that the statement is delivered before the *Tribune* story is available online or on subscribers' driveways and porches.

Good Morning America leads with the family's statement, which is a victory. At the same time, the news is explosive and the coverage trends negative, as speculation runs rampant regarding the family's possible involvement. The number of people willing to volunteer in the coming hours will trickle down from two thousand to just a handful of faithful souls.

Later that morning, with more than forty members of the extended Smart family standing arm in arm in the background, two of Elizabeth's uncles address a large contingent of media. Reporters and photographers are pushing and shoving to get in position. Many are aggressively yelling questions before anyone can begin speaking.

The uncles make brief statements, both reiterating several times the key message of the family: that they have complied with all of law enforcement's requests, and that they are willing to do anything asked of them. They calmly answer questions, most of which they've already answered multiple times during a rehearsal for the press conference just hours earlier.

While the overall response is timely and thoughtful, it doesn't make the story positive, nor does it make it go away. Rather, the response is effective in providing some confidence and a level of public trust that the Smart family isn't hiding, and that they will meet any challenge or allegation head-on.

CHAPTER 16

Enquiring Minds

"All of the media are talking, and I'm hearing the story is credible," a local journalist tells me. "It could easily rival the *Tribune* article. You have your work cut out for yourself. I don't envy you at all."

This off-the-record conversation hits me hard. It feels like trying to maneuver around a screen set by a husky basketball player, only to get crushed and land on the ground with the wind knocked out of me. The prospect of enduring the public's wrath in another volatile situation, after several other challenging issues in succession, seems overwhelming.

Revelations surrounding rumors and innuendo are not uncommon. Each morning, between shepherding television interviews, I call a couple of trusted reporters and ask them what they're hearing through the grapevine: *What's the chatter? What's the scuttlebutt? What is the most outlandish question that the family might have to answer today?*

This intel is invaluable in preparing for the 11 a.m. press briefing and the ensuing interviews. I draft a question-and-answer document and then pepper Ed and the extended family members with the questions, posing them in several different ways. It's like an abbreviated version of debate prep that might be employed for a politician in a hotly contested race.

Unlike the family's prior controversies, this situation is different. It is both complex and highly personal. Information regarding materials found on Ed's computer, including some images of nude adult males, has been leaked. Complying with the requests of investigators, the Smarts surrendered all of their electronic devices in the hours following the kidnapping. Despite finding nothing of consequence on the machines, someone in the Salt Lake City Police Department leaked these private details, and now the *National Enquirer* is, according to several reputable journalists, about to break a big story.

The *Enquirer's* checkbook journalism practices, which often stretch the First Amendment, are infamous. At the same time, the tabloid has gone where others won't venture, breaking a handful of legitimate stories. This latter fact provides enough legitimacy that the media and public can't completely dismiss its coverage.

The traditional media is caught in limbo. Most organizations, especially local ones, don't want to play in the mud, but at the same time, the stakes are high. Such cutthroat competitiveness to break even the smallest detail surrounding the case has been constant since day one. This accounts for the media outlets' frequent calls and conversations. They're exploring every possible angle as they try to get family members and me to go down rabbit holes that are of little consequence, but that might provide a kernel that can be turned sensational, attract more eyeballs, and give them bragging rights over their competitors.

During the first few days of working with the Smart family, I warned them about American Media, Inc. Unbeknownst to many, this is the parent company of the *National Enquirer* and a camouflage reporters use when introducing themselves, so they can deceive and convince unsuspecting interviewees that they are mainstream journalists.

For several days, prior to learning about the pending *Enquirer* story, a man named Alan Butterfield had been frequenting the daily press briefings. Members of the extended Smart family had recognized his ruse when he first identified himself as a reporter with American Media. As a result, we've diplomatically avoided Butterfield by walking past him when he approaches and by ignoring most of his questions during press briefings. When Butterfield has been aggressive or complained, we've continued to be passive, while also working to be boring, so we can avoid the appearance of conflict or drama, which might attract undue attention by more legitimate media.

The day before the *Enquirer* story is released, Butterfield backs off, but a Salt Lake City police captain and public information officer mention the yet-to-be-released tabloid exposé to the *Salt Lake Tribune* and the

Associated Press, and now other legitimate media want the family to address the rumors surrounding it. It's a last-ditch effort by many reporters to come up with something even halfway relevant that can be spun into a story, so they won't look like they have been scooped.

After the 11 a.m. press briefing, I am cornered by a mob of media asking about Ed's sexuality, what was found on the computer, his relationship with Lois, and other salacious questions that seem more like something you would hear paparazzi shouting at a celebrity embroiled in a sex scandal as they exit a gas station on Sunset Boulevard.

While the pressure is intense, my answer is relatively simple and familiar to me, "Regarding your question about the rumored tabloid article, the family can't respond until they have seen it."

After repeating variations of this response several times, I retreat to the room where the board meets at least twice each day. Sitting alone, I am overcome with anger, but it's coupled with a new degree of melancholy.

How could this unifying effort of trying to find a young girl be devolving into such personal attacks on a family that, of course, is not perfect, but that is so vulnerable and sincere in doing everything they can to find Elizabeth? How can the media lose sight of the reality that the Smarts are real people enduring an unthinkable tragedy? Don't they have even a small dose of humanity? Don't they have children of their own? Sisters? Nieces?

My feelings for some members of the media border on hate. Deep in thought and agonizing over their attacks, deceptions, and misrepresentations, I stare aimlessly at the wall. My mindset unexpectedly shifts when a large framed print of Christ washing the feet of His apostles comes into focus. I realize that even in His darkest hours, Jesus loved and served others, including the sullied traitor who had sold his teacher and Savior for thirty pieces of silver. Even as he hung painfully on the cross, Jesus asked His Father to forgive those who mocked and crucified Him. His example of unrequited love and radical forgiveness helps provide some calm and perspective. A Latter-day Saint children's hymn, "I am a Child of God," comes to mind.

I think of the journalists who are disparaging the Smart family and remember they are imperfect children of God, just like I am.

While this thought makes me feel a little better, it doesn't make the situation or its gravity go away. I know the extended Smart family will continue to endure vicious attacks for at least several more hours.

Later that afternoon, as I'm walking between interviews in the grassy area in front of the Arlington Hills ward, the reporter who initially tipped me off regarding the *Enquirer* story hands me a copy of the article.

"You dodged a bullet," he says. "The *Enquirer* botched this one so badly, I'm not sure anyone is going to cover it."

The "world exclusive" *Enquirer* cover story begins with the headline "Utah Cops: Secret Diary Exposes Family Sex Ring." It cites anonymous police sources claiming that brothers Ed, David, and Tom are involved in a gay sex ring that led to Elizabeth's kidnapping. The article reports that police found a journal in one of the brothers' homes that details their escapades and how their wives even know about it.

When I brief the board about the story a short time later, there is a mixture of laughs and indignation. The women see the article for what it is—so preposterous, it's funny. They tease Chris Smart, who has been left out of the article, asking him if he feels bad that his brothers haven't included him in their exploits.

Tom is a little less amused, especially since he is the focus of the article and has been taking the brunt of the media criticism, which has insinuated for several weeks that he might be a possible suspect. We help Tom process the situation and convince him that the story is so ludicrous, any type of response would give it legitimacy and more attention. Only a couple of journalists casually ask about the *Enquirer* story, and they don't pursue any follow-up questions when we tell them the article speaks for itself and doesn't warrant discussion.

This *Enquirer* article would be far-fetched at this time in any American community, but in conservative Salt Lake City, it is so poorly received that most retailers pull the issue from their shelves and refuse to sell it. In a sense, the article is the best PR possible. It kills any further talk regarding the images on Ed's computer and seems to quell the media, which are more reluctant to pursue stories about the extended family being involved in Elizabeth's kidnapping.

CHAPTER 17

Cruel Summer

My mom burst into the living room with such vigor that it startled me. I jumped up from the couch, half asleep.

"Did you kiss Annabelle?"

It felt as if the room were spinning, as if I had been on the lam for several years and the police were making a surprise arrest. How could my mom possibly know about Annabelle?

After the trial had ended and the bell had rung the previous Friday, a large group of students, boys and girls alike, jeered at me as I walked out of school. I started running. The last thing I heard was a chorus of, "Chris and Annabelle sitting in court, K-I-S-S-I-N-G."

I'd hoped to sleep in on Saturday. Instead, the doorbell rang at a quarter to seven. The customers kept coming, at least every twenty minutes the entire day. I didn't think it was possible, but all of the crawlers in the large box were gone by 4 p.m. I pedaled the Junior Racer to the corner, unlocked the sign, and reversed the strip of metal to "Sold Out."

Chad and I hunted again until midnight that Saturday, and we brought in about 250 crawlers. Fortunately, Sunday offered a reprieve. As I've mentioned, a high percentage of Latter-day Saints and other people of faith in Utah kept the Sabbath day holy. For most, this means no shopping, fishing, skiing, movies, engaging in sports, or eating out. Some are more ardent and even abstain from watching TV, listening to popular music, or wearing anything except church clothes the entire day. For those who aren't as religious, observe a different day as the Sabbath, or are lax in adherence to the commandment, Utah Sundays are a godsend. The stores and malls are empty, it's easy to get a restaurant reservation, and the ski lift and boat dock lines are often nonexistent.

Initially, the Sabbath situation created challenges for Chris's Crawlers. I wasn't supposed to work on Sunday, yet every Sabbath morning, anglers would knock on my door, wanting to purchase worms. My mom worried that if we didn't answer the door, someone might break into our home while we were away attending our three-hour block of church services.

Thanks to my father's ingenuity in the early days of the business, we could take a break without losing any sales. On Saturday night, we would leave a Styrofoam cooler with crawlers, a stack of red cups, some envelopes, a laminated sheet with instructions, and a metal box with a slit on the top. The honor system worked. No one in the history of the business ever cheated us.

Finally getting a break on the Sunday after the trial made me realize how physically and emotionally exhausted I had become. After church I slept nearly the entire day, waking up only for dinner. I awoke again around 10 p.m., ate some ice cream, watched *Benny Hill*, and then tried to go back to sleep around midnight. I tossed and turned for what seemed like a couple of hours before finally succumbing.

As I lay in bed, I fixated on whether or not I liked Annabelle, and if the feeling was mutual. I thought incessantly about it as I was falling asleep. It would be a recurring thought for the next few days as I became increasingly tired and stayed home from school to recover.

This was precisely why my mom's question on Thursday afternoon sent shockwaves through my system. She had blindsided me. I was dumbfounded and not sure how to respond.

"What, huh? Why would I kiss Annabelle?" I mumbled.

I buried my head deep in the couch cushions. I had never felt, even to the smallest degree, the intensity of embarrassment I was experiencing at that moment. I wanted to take up residence with all the wrappers, pennies, and crumbs in the underbelly of the sofa and never come out.

"I spoke to Mr. Fowles. He told me about the trial. Why didn't you tell me about this? Mr. Fowles said you were amazing. He thought I had coached you."

I responded that it was nothing, trying to downplay things but still wondering why my mom had asked if I had kissed Annabelle. *Is she joking? Is she being mean?*

"Mr. Fowles called to see if you're okay. He told me that Annabelle has also been sick, so I called and spoke with her mom. Annabelle has mononucleosis."

I was silent. I had never heard of the disease but knew it couldn't be good.

"Don't you know? Come on, you know what mono is. It looks like both you and Annabelle have the kissing disease."

Despite seemingly not wanting to make me feel bad, my mom couldn't contain her laughter. The harder she giggled, the more I burrowed into the seams of the sofa.

I stayed on the couch with my face concealed in the cushions for the better part of an hour. I was about to get up and sneak down to my room when I heard my dad come in the back door.

"Oh, Fred, you have got to come here. I can't wait to tell you about the call I had this afternoon with Mr. Fowles. You will never believe what Chris has been up to."

No longer able to endure this punishment, I got up and stomped through the living room and down the stairs, slammed the door to my room, and turned on the radio so I could drown out their conversation.

I sneaked out that night. I needed a break; I was getting cabin fever. I was so humiliated that I couldn't face my parents. And just when I thought things couldn't get worse, they did.

"Hey, Herb. What is this about you and Annabelle having the kissing disease?" Chad snickered as he approached, pointing his flashlight directly in my face. I was stunned by the question and asked him where he had heard the news.

"It's all over school. Everyone is talking about it. I thought you didn't like her, huh? Sounds like the two of you have been swapping spit?"

The next day we got the test results, and to my great relief, they were negative for mono. The doctor told me to rest for a few more days. I did everything I possibly could to avoid going back to school. Each day I got all of my homework done, helped around the house, and avoided teasing my younger brother, Jeremy, who was six, and my sister Natalee, who was four years old. I even helped change the diapers of my newborn sister, Amy. My mom seemed to be buying it. Or maybe she was feeling guilty for having wrongly accused me of kissing Annabelle.

Then I stumbled. That Saturday was the busiest in the history of Chris's Crawlers, and the almighty dollar got me. Customers kept coming from sunup to sundown, and by end of day I had sales of nearly eighty dollars. I worked at a frenzied pace and then hunted late into the night, but bad news was just around the corner, and my mom would be the harbinger.

It was Sunday evening, and my mom and dad came into my bedroom to talk. I could tell my mom had something important to say.

"Chris, you're going back to school. I can't justify letting you stay home after how hard you worked yesterday." She gave me a sympathetic look as my dad nodded in agreement.

I dragged my feet on Monday morning. The anxiety was palpable. I put on a wrinkled blue T-shirt and a pair of Levi's 501 jeans. I could stomach only a few bites of Cheerios. I tried to talk my mom out of making me go, but to no avail. When I finally took my seat in the classroom, nearly half an hour late, Mr. Fowles welcomed me back and asked me in front of the class how I was feeling.

"I'm okay. I don't have mono. The test came back negative. I had a different virus, but I'm better now."

Despite my efforts at damage control, the peanut gallery ratcheted into full gear, asking where Annabelle and I had gone on our honeymoon. They surmised it must have been somewhere nice since I'd been gone for two weeks.

I withdrew, becoming reticent during the waning days before the summer break. I rarely said much in class; ignored the constant barrage of references to kissing, getting married to, and having a baby with Annabelle; and instead spent my recesses shooting hoops alone.

The school had one dilapidated basketball court. The asphalt was buckled in several places, creating trip hazards. The white wooden backboards were warped and cracked, and the rims had no nets, so it was hard to tell if a shot went in or if it was an air ball. It didn't matter. The time alone with just my thoughts on that miserable court provided a solace that kept me going.

Annabelle never returned to school, and was replaced as bank president. An election was held, and the ringleader won handily. In the end, the boys got what they wanted, even if it was only for a few weeks.

In years past, I had always grown sentimental as the final days of the school year wound down. I would ruminate about my fellow classmates and all the memories we had made. I knew these times wouldn't last forever. At the end of fifth grade, however, things were different. Aside from my tremendous appreciation for Mr. Fowles, who was one of the most gifted and greatest teachers ever, I couldn't wait for the final bell to ring.

I was counting down the days until I could finally escape for summer. Unfortunately, it would be, as the title of the Bananarama song touts, a "Cruel Summer." My two best friends during the summer of '84 would be Steve Stone and Harry Caray, the announcers for the Chicago Cubs on WGN-TV. That's because my real friends disappeared, and I was too afraid to even acknowledge Annabelle.

I had no one to hang out or play ball with on my homemade court. My next-door neighbors to the east, the Edwards, moved away after their parents separated. Chad's family's stature was on the rise, and as a result, he was living large in Park City and was rarely around. His father had worked his way up the ladder at one of the ski resorts, from laboring for near minimum wage as a lift operator to helping save the business and becoming its general manager. Throughout the process, Chad and his siblings had been working the resort like it was a family farm. This included organizing and executing a summer concert series.

In the rare instances when I saw Chad, all he could talk about was hanging out with Howard Jones, Kenny Loggins, and Jerry Garcia. I was beyond envious. For me, my TV friends—Steve, Harry, and Benny—would have to do.

Each summer morning, I would get up, play basketball for a couple of hours, and then take a break for an hour or so to watch a few innings of baseball televised from the "Friendly Confines," aka Wrigley Field. I would return to the basketball court during the middle innings and then race back to the TV in time to sing "Take Me Out to the Ball Game" with Harry during the seventh-inning stretch. After the game, I would spend most of the afternoon shooting hoops. My skin was like leather. I had built up an immunity to the sun that was on par with a construction worker's. The only time I wasn't outside in the late afternoon or evening was when the Cubs had a road game.

The increased basketball activity drew Baker's scorn. He became increasingly frustrated at the frequency at which I was bouncing the ball, and even more annoyed that I had become resistant to his tactics. I got used to playing on a water-soaked court. Even though it made the ball and pavement a little slippery, it also felt refreshing, akin to jumping in a swimming pool on a hot summer day. My enjoyment only made Baker more indignant.

"You need to knock it off now. You're irritating the whole neighborhood. No one can stand you. Do you hear me, boy? Why don't you go and find a hobby or, better yet, a friend? Ya big loner."

That hurt, but no way would I ever let Baker know. I stared off in the distance, ignoring his tirade, which he wrapped up yet again by threatening to call the police.

"Go ahead, you've been saying that for years. I'm waiting. I know they arrest a lot of kids for playing basketball. The prisons are full of them."

I smirked and dribbled the basketball as high, loudly, and obnoxiously as I could.

"You are the most damned smart-ass kid. Your parents didn't teach you no manners. You better watch out. I have lots of guns. If your ball comes onto my grass, I will shoot you. Do you hear me? I will *shoot* you."

I'd be lying if I didn't admit it made me stop and think. I wasn't sure how well Baker could aim and shoot a gun, but I continued more conscientiously and looked twice when the ball rolled into his yard. In the days that followed, I began to have nightmares. I could see myself wounded and bleeding on Baker's lawn as he laughed, took away my basketball, and walked inside his house with a braggadocious air.

The most difficult and poignant memory of the summer, however, wasn't the neighbors' moving. It wasn't Chad living like a rock star in Park City or my increased interactions with Baker. It was something that happened a few weeks after school got out.

One summer afternoon, several men began digging holes throughout the backyard neighborhood. The next day concrete was poured and the posts were installed. The two-by-fours and slats were delivered, and the closing of the backyard neighborhood was imminent. It was going out of business. The fences were returning. We were about to be separated again, sealed apart, quite possibly for another twenty or thirty years, maybe forever.

The neighbors scrambled to put together one last celebration. We dragged barbecue grills and lawn chairs into the center of the yards. There were tables with red plastic tablecloths replete with dishes for another bountiful potluck buffet.

The adults visited while the kids ran and played. I saw Annabelle from a distance. The situation was so awkward—with our parents' comments, the mono scare, and every kid our age gossiping about us—that we didn't dare talk to each other. Toward the end of the evening, one neighbor brought out a guitar, started strumming a few notes, and invited everyone to join in.

Neither Annabelle nor I acknowledged each other that evening, or in the years that followed, except for one brief moment when our eyes met as the group sang "Kumbaya." I never thought I had feelings for her, but my heart suddenly started pounding and I felt a fluttering that made me faint.

Unfortunately, it was too late. The situation was complicated, and I wasn't compelled to get out of my comfort zone and go after the girl. Or maybe I was simply too shy.

A few days later, the fences were back up. They were new, stained brown, and two feet taller than the original fences. They blended in better now with the trees and shrubs that framed Mount Olympus. With no easy access to the great backyard neighborhood, everyone returned to their cocoons. Sadly many, including Annabelle and myself, never interacted with one another in a meaningful way again.

CHAPTER 18

Turning the Other Cheek

A stranger follows Tom into the Monday-morning board meeting. He begins handing out papers as Tom stands at the front of the table and takes command of the meeting.

"I want to let you know I'm going to make an announcement at the eleven o'clock press briefing."

I grab and start reading a copy of the press release the stranger is distributing.

"My friend here is going to help us sue Marc Klaas and Bill O'Reilly," Tom continues. "What they did was unconscionable. We need to send a message."

Tom is back with a vengeance after a weekend break. While he is more rested, the attacks on him and his family, especially his daughters, are taking a toll. He appears high-strung and shaky, and his pupils still seem a little dilated.

In addition to the Bill O'Reilly-Marc Klaas ambush, Tom has been dragged into another controversy while he was getting rest and banished from the media and search center. Last Friday afternoon, Patty Henetz, a local Associated Press reporter covering the Smart story, asked to speak with me urgently. Patty was a no-nonsense veteran journalist who was aggressive and did not suffer fools gladly. (Sadly, she passed away in 2019.) While she could be irascible, Patty also had a softer side and a real sense of responsibility to do the right thing, whether or not it was popular or advantageous to her personally.

"I need to tell you something, and I need your word that you will never tell a soul I spoke with you."

Before I can answer, Patty proceeds to disclose that the *Salt Lake Tribune* already has a story for its Sunday edition about questions surrounding Tom's alibi on the night of Elizabeth's abduction. She says the article is damning and cites several unnamed sources and speculative evidence. It implies that Tom was responsible for the kidnapping and is at the top of the list of suspects created by many within law enforcement.

While I don't doubt Patty, I am taken aback, and ask her how she knows so much about a story that isn't from her news organization.

"Listen, I'm probably violating SPJ ethics," she says, referring to the Society for Professional Journalists. "Tom is a friend, but I wouldn't say anything if the story wasn't so scurrilous. Vern has read the article. He and I spoke and felt strongly that I should talk to you and then let you figure out how to handle things."

I don't ask who Vern is, but I quickly discover he is the deputy editor of the *Tribune* and is dating Patty.

After I learn about the pending *Tribune* story, I quickly find Angela and Cynthia. Tom has been ordered by Dr. Smart to continue his hiatus from speaking to the media and has been sent with a couple of friends to go horseback riding for the weekend. We fear they may all have shut off their phones to disconnect from the world and that it will be impossible to reach Tom.

Anxiously awaiting word, I retreat to the one activity that aside from prayer offers a small dose of peace and perspective, shooting hoops. Since the cultural hall is no longer being used for volunteer orientations after the broader effort has been transitioned to specific searches mostly on weekends, I have the court all to myself. The temporary reprieve and sound of the leather ball ripping through the nylon net is soothing when I can find a minute or two between meetings and assignments.

After grabbing a basketball and taking a couple of dribbles, I launch a three-pointer.

"Nothing but net. Nice shot, there."

I hear a distinctive voice with a Long Island accent behind me but can't quite place it. Then I do a double take when the man's familiar feathered brown hair comes into focus. It's Sean Hannity. He has slipped past the senior citizen security guards sitting on lawn chairs in front of the building.

"Hit me," Sean says, running toward the baseline. I hesitate and then throw him a pass. Sean catches the ball in stride and goes up making a fifteen-foot jump shot. I give him the customary change, which is when you pass the ball back after someone makes a shot in practice. Sean has some decent chops, hitting four out of five three-pointers. While basketball serves as the perfect icebreaker and I have nothing against Sean, I am still on edge from Bill O'Reilly. With the *Tribune* issue looming, the last thing I need is another quarrelsome journalist stirring things up.

We stop playing and converse for a few minutes. Before I can explain to Sean that there is no place for any type of politics in finding Elizabeth, he beats me to the punch. "I want you to know that I am here to sincerely help with absolutely no agenda. I know a lot of journalists say that, but I really don't care if I do a single interview. My main purpose is to lend my support."

While I am incredulous, Sean will surprise me. He won't pull any punches, and when he does talk about the kidnapping on his shows, it will always be sincere and about the family without drama.

After shooting hoops with Sean for a few more minutes, I'm interrupted by Angela holding her phone as she hurries into the gym. "Tom is in on the line."

I step away, explain the situation, and tell Tom we need to preempt the *Tribune* story by getting the *Deseret News* to publish an article on Saturday detailing Tom's alibi and his involvement with the search and investigation.

Tom is more than willing to defend himself, but the clock is ticking. It's after three o'clock, less than two hours before the publication's deadline. He wants to quickly call the newsroom at the *Deseret News*, to get everyone on board with our idea, and then circle back to prepare for the interview. Unfortunately, I don't hear from Tom for another hour. He tells me the reporter couldn't wait, adding that he really didn't need to prepare since he had lived through the series of events.

The next morning, the *Deseret News* publishes the story on the front page, with the headline "Elizabeth's Uncle Finds Speculation Ludicrous." The article states that "fueled by tight-lipped investigators, and a national media frenzy that's reached a fevered pitch not seen in Salt Lake City since the Olympics, the rumor mill has churned out Tom Smart's name as the extended family member authorities may be focusing on."

The article then denies the media conjecture that investigators have called Tom's alibi into question, and goes on to quote law enforcement saying that reports naming Tom as a suspect are "sensationalized speculations." It even quotes a police spokesperson as saying, "Tom Smart is no more a suspect than you or I."

The story has a significant impact on the Sunday *Tribune* article, which now criticizes the *Deseret News* for not being objective in its coverage of Tom, one of its own staff members. The *Tribune* also cites idiosyncrasies in Tom's quotes in the *Deseret News*, along with his erratic statements to several other media outlets, all of which paint a less-than-flattering picture. Fortunately, the *Tribune* story is largely ignored by other media and becomes a nonissue by the end of the weekend.

As we sit in the Monday board meeting listening to Tom rant about the legalities of suing Marc Klaas and Bill O'Reilly, it's obvious to me that the emotional fallout from the personal attacks on Tom and his family are impairing his thinking.

His proposal to take legal action is initially met with opposition from almost everyone on the board. However, an outspoken minority agrees with Tom and believes the family needs to quit being so diplomatic and take a stronger public stand.

I try to make a few arguments against pursuing legal action, but the discourse is pointed, and it's difficult to communicate more than a few words before I'm interrupted. After listening to the back-and-forth for several minutes, I finally stand up, walk to the chalkboard, write Elizabeth's name on the dark green slate, and circle it emphatically.

"Our mission is to find *Elizabeth*. Anything that distracts or takes us away from this should never be a consideration. Threatening to sue the media will only create more conflict and drama and take us down a path we don't want to go. We must keep the focus *solely* on finding Elizabeth."

The group is silent for a few long seconds, then Dr. Smart finally concurs. The board rumbles a unanimous echo, and we are once again united in a common purpose. Tom seems to understand the need for redirection and discontinues his crusade, but he stares me down with the frustration and defiance of an athlete who adamantly disagrees with a referee's call.

In the days that follow, Tom either avoids me or is aggressive in challenging how I'm doing things. I do my best to show respect. I understand that not only have I assumed much of Tom's original role of managing the media, but now he might feel like I'm trying to limit what he can say and do.

I know Tom's intentions are good. His passion and undying will are genuine—he wants to find Elizabeth more than almost anyone. I have come to love Tom, and over the next several days, when his words or body language seem less than hospitable toward me, I try to connect with him. I know it's in the best interest of finding Elizabeth to maintain a good relationship with him, but I also genuinely care about him.

Sometimes it feels like Tom is the big brother I never had. He has strong opinions and can be dominant and even abrasive, but at the end of the day, he still feels like family. Understanding his position, not backing down but being able to roll with the punches, and doing so while sometimes turning the other cheek, is not only key to working with Tom—it will prove to be necessary when navigating other strong personalities, especially those in the media.

CHAPTER 19

The Spokesperson

Former Salt Lake City mayor Ted Wilson and I file into a Sunday-school classroom overlooking the large grassy area in front of the Arlington Hills ward. It's a less eventful Friday afternoon than the previous one, in late June. Most journalists and photographers are sitting on camping chairs outside their trucks, trailers, and makeshift sets, biding their time. Ted and I know that at any minute the media will be whipped into a frenzy, and we want a front-row seat to witness the action.

A couple of hours earlier, I was with Ed as he was being interviewed by a *Deseret News* reporter. His cell phone rang and, as has been his habit, he pulled the phone out of his pocket and answered it midsentence.

"Ed, Bret Michael Edmunds has been arrested in West Virginia," the reporter and I overheard a Salt Lake City Police captain say. "He's in the hospital. We haven't had a chance to talk to him yet, but we don't think he is going to provide us with much…"

The reporter's eyes bulged as he quickly scribbled down the information. Although law enforcement had told the family more than a week earlier that it was unlikely that Edmunds was involved in the abduction, they wanted to speak with him. Shortly thereafter, the police made a big deal announcing Edmunds as a person of interest at a morning briefing, and the media were all too eager to play along, attracting international headlines.

As soon as Ed hung up the phone, the reporter asked him to confirm Edmund's arrest on the record. I quickly interceded and said it would be more appropriate to get the information from law enforcement. As a concession, Ed called the Salt Lake Police Department and asked an officer to help the reporter get official confirmation, and to allow him to be the first to break the story. The reporter hit a few roadblocks, and called me several times throughout the afternoon to provide updates. Finally, the reporter informed me he had confirmation and was about to go to press. Ted and I, who were the only members of the board at the church, quickly headed to our stakeout point to watch things unravel.

Almost on cue, a gray-haired female producer bolts out of the NBC trailer, looking frantically for a reporter and a photographer. The commotion catches the attention of a thirtysomething man wearing a blue baseball cap, sitting under an awning next door at ABC. Although he likely doesn't know what is happening, he can tell *something* is breaking, and he doesn't want to be left in the dust. As the man scrambles, the dominoes continue to fall, and we watch one media organization spark another media organization and another, until within minutes the area in front of the church is buzzing with reporters and photographers making phone calls and preparing for live shots.

While Ted and I are enjoying the spectacle, especially since the news is largely inconsequential, it occurs to me that we're missing an opportunity. The fact that Bret Michael Edmunds has been apprehended nearly two thousand miles away in West Virginia means that Elizabeth could be anywhere in the country. While this isn't necessarily a novel idea, it underscores the fact that this message could be a catalyst for getting people outside of Utah to be more involved, even vigilant, in looking for Elizabeth.

"Ted, you need to get out there and communicate this. We need to help change the narrative and make it about finding Elizabeth, instead of whether or not Edmunds might be the guy."

I motion eagerly at Ted, who is a longtime neighbor and friend of the Smarts and has periodically been quoted in the media as a family spokesperson. As the head of the Hinckley Institute of Politics at the University of Utah, Ted is the consummate teacher. He quickly assesses the situation, smiles, and looks me squarely in the eyes.

"I think *you* should get out there and communicate this. I don't understand why you've stayed behind the scenes, Chris. Are you afraid of being interviewed? Go."

Before I can explain that the best public relations professionals are the ones you never see or know about, he gently nudges me toward the door. Within thirty seconds, I'm live on CNN.

After I'm interviewed dozens of times that day in the glare of an unfamiliar spotlight, reviews from the family and several board members are positive. Ed even suggests that I become their full-time spokesperson, but then I remind him what happened when Jon Benet Ramsey's family employed a similar tactic—it backfired, creating significant speculation and suspicion surrounding her parents' possible involvement. We agree to compromise. I will handle weekend interviews, so the immediate and extended family can get a break and unplug from the craziness.

Although I'm happy with this new arrangement, I'll need to minimize the number of weekend interviews I agree to, so as to give my wife greater consideration. Since time with Laura has been rare, she has seldom had my undivided attention. Now that I'll have additional commitments as the family spokesperson, Laura and I agree to find a regular time each weekend for an uninterrupted date.

I also decide to inform the media that the Smarts won't be doing weekend interviews anymore unless there is a major development. I won't offer myself as the next option, but will instead suggest other people, like Mayor Anderson. In the event they ask me directly or the interview has a real purpose, I might sometimes oblige.

As I walk past the Fox News booth later that afternoon, a producer hands me his cell phone without explanation.

"This is Craig Rivera," the voice on the other end says. "I'm sure you know of my older brother, Geraldo. We're coming to Salt Lake in two days and want to sit down with the Smarts in their home for an exclusive interview. I just wanted to check and make sure this works with their schedule."

I kindly explain that the Smarts won't be doing any interviews over the weekend and that their house is off-limits.

Craig tries to make the case that the family somehow owes them something since Geraldo is personally coming to Salt Lake City, where he will be filming his show live on location. He tells me how much they care about the Smarts, and how much it would mean if they would make an exception and allow them into their home. I bite my lip to avoid laughing but tell him I'll get back to him.

After waiting twenty minutes, I call Craig back with the bad news. He proceeds to contact me several times over the next twenty-four hours, finally pleading with me late Saturday night to come on the show the next day. When I acquiesce, Craig tells me how grateful they are, and how awkward it would have been if they didn't have representation from someone close to the family who could speak on their behalf.

I arrive at the appointed time on Sunday afternoon and watch Geraldo interview Mayor Anderson and several other guests before it's finally my turn. As I wait for the preceding commercial to end, I realize I am about to be interviewed by the infamous mustachioed one—the legend who opened Al Capone's secret vaults and had his nose broken by a chair during a brawl on his daytime talk show. That brawl scene has been mocked and parodied multiple times in television shows and movies. While I'm a little skeptical of his show, being interviewed by Geraldo feels harmless and is just too much of a temptation.

Geraldo, wearing a gray suit with a white shirt and a black-and-gold tie, settles into his chair. A strange but fleeting appreciation wafts over me that I'm in the presence of a unique pop culture icon. I take my seat in the chair across from him. Geraldo and his mustache are larger than life.

Once the show returns from the break, Geraldo asks me about Ed, wondering why he talks directly to Elizabeth in his interviews, and if he thinks Elizabeth might have access to a television to hear him. I humor Geraldo with a response about Ed's sincerity, only to find out that this is his *only* question for me. He tells his viewers they are out of time but reiterates how much he wanted to have me on the show. It feels contrived and is as anticlimactic as watching Geraldo's play-by-play of the Capone vault excavation team finding debris and old bottles—instead of treasure, guns, and bodies—in Chicago's Lexington Hotel.

At first I'm a little annoyed, having sacrificed part of my Sunday afternoon to drive to the church and wait for the interview. A few minutes later, when I'm alone in the car and have had a chance to process the series of events, I high-five the roof. *That was off the charts and so apropos for Geraldo,* I think. *He really is larger than life.*

As I am about to pull away, my phone rings. It's Ed, and he sounds anxious.

"I need to fill you in on something. The police have told me some news that will likely break this afternoon. This one is complicated."

Ed's voice is an octave higher than usual as he informs me that his former handyman, Richard Ricci, has been arrested on a parole violation and has admitted to stealing several items from the Smarts. He also took valuables from another home near the Smart residence, where he worked for two of the other board members.

Ricci is affable and well-liked by the Smart children, who talked and played with him when he labored at their house. He drives an old white Jeep that Ed gave him as partial payment for his work. The vehicle likely contains Elizabeth's DNA, since she'd ridden in the car for several years before Ed gave it to Ricci.

The police make it clear that Ricci is being held on a parole violation. This is more of a technicality, because in actuality, he's being seriously investigated in conjunction with the abduction. Ed says he'll be surprised if Ricci has been involved but adds that he's also surprised that Ricci stole from him and lied about it.

The Ricci news creates a sticky situation that necessitates a strategic response, so we can avoid the narrative spiraling out of control. Working to formulate some messaging in my mind, I hang out near the church, figuring the media will converge on me once the news breaks. Within minutes, a producer approaches and asks if I would be willing to join his show for a live interview. I agree.

I sit on a bar stool waiting and listening to the live feed of the program. When the commercial break starts, the producer reappears.

"As a heads up, there may be something breaking, and we've had some issues with the IFB," he informs me. An IFB, or interruptible foldback, is a device that serves as an earpiece and a microphone. "If you hear a bunch of loud static, take off your headset and tell the talent you don't understand and can't answer."

I recognize that this is a setup and consider leaving before the interview starts, but realize that also could be used against me. The news team likely would report that once the Smart family spokesperson was made aware of the issue, he refused to be interviewed and walked off.

The sound from the headset is crystal clear during the softball questions at the beginning of the segment. Then one of the anchors places a finger on her earpiece.

"Sorry to interrupt," she says. "We have some major breaking news surrounding the Elizabeth Smart kidnapping. For more, let's go to the newsroom…"

When the show returns from coverage of a correspondent explaining the Ricci development, the anchor asks me if the Smarts are aware of the news. As I am about to answer, a producer in a New York studio control center pushes a button and a deafening blow of white noise penetrates my eardrum.

"Yes, they…they were surprised to learn Ricci had…had stolen from them and have been fully cooperating with law enforcement," I manage to say.

I focus on the top part of the camera lens, mustering every ounce of energy I have to hear the next question while not appearing flustered. I can't make out what is being said, nor can I read the anchor's lips, so I improvise once she stops talking.

"The Smarts are concerned and are doing everything they can to find Elizabeth. They support law enforcement investigating everyone and are cooperating in all ways."

I would later learn that the question she asked, which I couldn't hear, was about why I was acting so erratically. Was I uncomfortable with the question? Was there something I was trying to hide?

The white noise dissipates briefly, and I hear the producer's voice in the headset loud and clear: "Just tell them you can't talk any longer and need to go. Take off the headset."

I pause and take a quick breath.

"This is an incredible family. They are resilient and doing everything they can to find Elizabeth. The Smarts support law enforcement and have fully cooperated with everything that has been asked of them. What they want people to know is that they need them to be vigilant and keep an eye out for Elizabeth. Anything you can do to bring her home will mean more to the family than you can possibly know…"

When I finish speaking, I smile and look calmly into the camera. When I see the show has cut to the commercial break, I exhale and hand the producer the headset. I walk away before he can say anything to me.

While I constantly try to anticipate and plan for various questions and scenarios, something like this never crossed my mind. It's apparent that the producers were trying to create a situation in which I would appear visibly frustrated by the question so they could spin it into something it wasn't. The more drama surrounding the Smarts' response to Ricci's arrest, the more fodder for talking heads to discuss and speculate about, concerning Ed and Lois' relationship with the handyman and what could be perceived as embarrassing news.

Over the next few hours, I make the rounds, doing dozens of interviews and providing context regarding the family's relationship with Ricci, their concern regarding the stolen items, and their support of law enforcement in getting to the bottom of things.

Around 10:30 p.m., after live interviews with the local television stations, I speak with Ed. He tells me that while watching one of the breaking news stories about Ricci earlier that evening, he heard Mary Katherine's voice and noticed she had crept into the bedroom—and probably had been there for several minutes.

"Daddy, they don't think Richard took Elizabeth, do they? He wasn't the one in the room. It wasn't Richard."

Mary Katherine, who is typically shy and soft-spoken, was animated and adamant.

Ed informs law enforcement about Mary Katherine's reaction, but they discount her claim and keep the focus on Ricci for the next eight months. According to Tom's book, Mary Katherine also tells one of her cousins when they are playing one afternoon that "everyone thinks Richard took Elizabeth, but he didn't."

This misguided fixation on Ricci might have continued for years if Elizabeth hadn't been rescued from another man—the one who actually was in the room that night.

CHAPTER 20

Firecrackers

One of many peculiar aspects of living in the Beehive State is that Utahns celebrate the Fourth of July twice. That's right, twice.

After Latter-day Saints were violently exiled from settlements in New York, Ohio, Missouri, and eventually Illinois, Brigham Young led a group of pioneers to the Rocky Mountains. They entered the Salt Lake Valley on July 24, 1847. Young, who was ill during the final leg of the journey, stopped his wagon, sat up from the wooden wagon bed, surveyed the open desert valley, and said: "This is the right place."

The spot where this occurred is just one canyon to the south from the steep foothills where Brian David Mitchell tethered Elizabeth to a tree and held her in a rudimentary camp, dug into the edge of a rugged mountainside. He kept her there for the first few months of her captivity.

Each year the observance of July 24, or Pioneer Day, is a carbon copy of the Fourth of July festivities that occurred twenty days earlier. Salt Lake City celebrates with parades, barbecues, watermelon, and of course, fireworks. The only real difference between the two holidays in Utah is that Latter-Day Saint congregations stand and sing all four verses of *The Star-Spangled Banner* during the sacrament meeting before or on Independence Day.

And fireworks are a mainstay with both holidays. In fact, July should be deemed pyrotechnics month in Utah because of the incessant explosions and noise—especially at night—along with the smoke that permeates the air, and the white and yellow firework scars that stain our streets and driveways.

One of the ironies of Utah's obsession with fireworks is that the state prohibits most flying or exploding pyrotechnics. When I was growing up, the only permitted fireworks were smoke bombs, sparklers, snaps, and several variations of cones that emitted sparks resembling some sort of abstract flower.

The law must have been slightly loosened the summer I was eleven years old, because the firework shops began selling some new items—"tanks" and "paratroopers." The tanks consisted of a few small firecrackers and a lotus flower, glued to a camouflage box with wheels. The paratroopers were small bottle rockets with a green army guy affixed to a plastic parachute that usually melted when it was ejected, causing the little man to crash into the asphalt—all of which was part of the allure.

While I liked the paratroopers, I was obsessed with the tanks and would construct elaborate war scenes in my driveway with Lego buildings, green plastic army men, and perfectly plotted roads that I outlined with chalk rocks. Lighting the fuses of the tanks at separate ends of the city and igniting a smoke bomb, I would watch and revel in the ensuing mayhem.

During one particularly hostile battle, in which the two tanks were doing lots of damage to the town, the troops were suddenly blindsided. A stream of cold water came out of nowhere, stopping the tanks, dousing the smoke bomb, and ruining the other cardboard combat vehicles I had lined up, waiting for battle.

"What the…?" I said.

As I stood up, I could see the old man who had turned the hose on me.

"Serves you right," Baker said. "Those fireworks are illegal, and I will call the cops if you ever light one again."

I didn't try to explain to him that these fireworks were now legal. Instead, I ran inside the house and found my dad. He immediately stopped folding laundry, listened intently, then grabbed his keys.

"Get in the car, we're going to Wyoming," he announced.

My dad put on his shoes and grabbed his wallet, and we were off.

"Why Wyoming?" I asked, looking incredulously at him. "What does this have to do with Baker and my tanks?" I was sitting shotgun in our red Subaru wagon, clicking the button on the emergency parking brake between our seats like it was the trigger to a large artillery gun.

"Everything. You'll see."

We drove ninety minutes up Interstate 80, to Porter's Fireworks in Evanston, Wyoming—a large warehouse that sold a plethora of pyrotechnics. It was the candy store of fireworks, offering basically everything that was illegal in the Beehive State.

We entered to a thick aroma of gunpowder and sawdust. The large fabricated steel room was dimly lit. It had a backdrop of red, white, and blue streamers on the wall to break up the monotony. A Charlie Daniels song played overhead on a dilapidated speaker.

There were so many firework options, it was overwhelming. My dad started filling a box with bricks of M-80s and cherry bomb firecrackers, a case of whistling bottle rockets, and some long fuses. He then picked up several Roman candles. We spent enough money at Porter's that the salesman running the cash register, who was sporting a worn Stetson, threw in a couple of heavy red papier-mâché balls with large fuses on top.

"Now make sure you run as fast as you can when you light these suckers," he warned us. "They pack a powerful punch, buckaroo."

On our way home, my dad and I stopped at McDonald's for dinner. After we devoured our Big Macs, French fries, and root beers, he purchased two vanilla cones and a dozen helium balloons for the road. The Golden Arches had recently started selling yellow balloons with a red illustration of Ronald McDonald for twenty-five cents each.

Instead of returning home, we parked on Celeste Circle, which was directly behind our house. My father got out of the car, knotted a few balloons together, tied the end of the strings to a brick of M-80s, and tucked a long fuse into the package. I held the strings as he struck a match.

"Let go!"

We watched as the balloons ascended directly over the home behind Baker's toward Celeste Way. The M-80s exploded somewhere over the middle of the street.

"That was close but not a direct hit," my dad said. He proceeded to create a similar concoction, this time adding a brick of cherry bombs and a slightly shorter fuse. I held the string until he said, "Go!" The balloons sailed about ten feet past Baker's house before there was another series of explosions.

"Chris, we're getting closer but still not there." He was giddy, and at the same time uniquely focused on finding the precise combination. For the final attempt, he added three bricks of cherry bombs then ignited the fuse. I let the balloons go. They barely cleared the home in front of us and then seemed to skip in perfect rhythm onto Baker's roof, where hundreds of tightly packaged pods of gunpowder exploded in a spectacular fashion. The reverberating sound was deafening. Gray smoke filled the air. "Direct hit. Take that, you angry old man."

My dad raised his hand and gave me a high five. We waited a few minutes for the smoke to clear and then drove home. When I exited the car, my jovial mood was broadsided. Baker was yelling at the top of his lungs. His voice was so loud and shrill that his words carried through the red brick façade of his humble home. He was in a full rage. The worst part, however, was that he was berating Vaunna, his wife—a white-haired, angelic, grandmotherly type of woman who sat in front of us at church. I could hear her crying as she tried to pacify him.

"I'm sorry. Baker, please, please calm down, please…"

My stomach churned. My head ached. My emotions ran in circles. I felt intense guilt and remorse, the strongest I had yet experienced in my young life. I wondered if this was what it felt like to commit a serious sin.

I had never been more upset, sorry, or ashamed. I barely slept that night, and lay in bed reliving the events of that evening repeatedly. This caused a pit in my stomach, and every time I thought about lighting that last fuse, it evoked a deep, visceral reaction.

CHAPTER 21

Under Wraps

"There's a rumor that a suspicious break-in occurred at the home of one of Elizabeth's relatives in Taylorsville. What can you tell me about this?"

The reporter has pulled me aside so that none of his competitors can hear his question. Holding a pen in one hand and balancing a notebook and a tape recorder in the other, he looks up at me intensely. Trying to remain calm, I resort to an old trick.

"I'm sorry, I'm thinking about too many things at once and didn't catch that. Could you repeat it?"

His question is the one I have been dreading most. I've thought and worried about it for days, especially since there just isn't a good answer. Even worse, the reporter is KSL NewsRadio's Ben Winslow. He is one of the journalists I have come to trust and respect. Ben works hard, hustles, is tenacious, asks difficult questions, and, at the same time, is reasonable, considerate, and fair.

However, I wasn't necessarily fond of Ben at first. On the second day I was working with the Smarts, there were dozens of interview requests, but the family was exhausted. We decided that morning they would do only the twice-daily press briefings and not participate in one-on-one interviews, to provide them with a small breather.

Ben immediately went on the air and told radio listeners that a PR consultant was now working with the Smarts, and the family would no longer be doing interviews, that everything was being tightly managed and controlled. His reporting likely left some listeners wondering if there was something questionable surrounding the Smart family, the search, or the investigation. It also may have made many people wonder about the authenticity of what the family was doing and saying, since a professional crisis spinmeister was now on the scene and apparently calling the shots.

Ben had inflated the issue or was under the impression that this would be a standing protocol, when in reality, it was a coping mechanism just for that day. With his reporting, Ben had fired a shot over the bow, and it would have been easy to start a battle.

KSL, which is owned by The Church of Jesus Christ of Latter-day Saints, is the highest-rated radio station and one of the most (if not *the* most) influential media outlets in the Utah market. The news assignment desks at all the television stations and newspapers monitor it closely. So the issue couldn't be taken lightly. I knew immediately that we had to work to change the situation.

Introducing myself to Ben, I invited him to meet with me privately in the church, where I explained that the family was taking a one-day break since there had been an overwhelming number of requests. He understood, was appreciative, and then explained how the local journalists were getting pushed aside by the national media. Ben feared he and his local competitors would become an afterthought, as had happened on other stories that had garnered national interest. He helped me to better understand the local media's perspective, and how they had a vested interest in the community, because they were planning to cover the story for months and years, not days and weeks.

I looked at the interview requests and saw that only a handful were from local reporters. We compromised: I agreed to ensure that a member of the extended Smart family would be available for a short interview with Ben and the other local journalists, on the condition that they wouldn't brag or bring attention to this approach, as doing so would spark contention and jealousy among the members of the national media.

That meeting with Ben was the beginning of a professional friendship. Ben and I recognize we have many competing interests, but we respect each other. We also recognize that when it makes sense, working together can be mutually beneficial.

That's why I want to shrink when Ben asks me on this July morning about the attempted break-in.

The reason the answer is so difficult is because the Salt Lake City Police Department has pressured the family not to talk about or answer any questions surrounding it.

Law enforcement claims that they need adequate time to get evidence analyzed by the FBI in Quantico, Virginia, and to further investigate the incident. Some on the board are skeptical, wondering if the police really are just afraid of the increased pressure the news would generate. Regardless, everyone agrees to keep the details under wraps.

The incident happened on July 24 at the home of Elizabeth's fourteen-year-old cousin and close friend, Olivia Wright. In the early-morning hours, following Pioneer Day, a chair was propped up against the Wrights' house and someone cut the screen to the window in Olivia's former bedroom—she had changed rooms with her older sister a few weeks prior.

Once the screen had been cut from the outside, the intruder got his hand inside and began slicing the screen from the other side when he bumped a picture frame, which crashed to the floor. Olivia's eighteen-year-old sister, Jessica, awoke and screamed when she saw an arm poking through the window screen with what looked like a gun. The commotion caused the would-be intruder to flee. Within seconds, Olivia and Jessica's father, Steve, ran into the room and then released the family's Labrador into the yard. The police were summoned and, according to Steve, initially accused the family of staging the incident—since nearly every detail, including how the screen was cut, was a carbon copy of what had occurred at the Smart residence seven weeks earlier.

This was especially concerning since the detail of a chair being used to gain access to the Smart house wasn't publicly known and hadn't been reported by the media.

Elizabeth would later explain to investigators that one afternoon Brian David Mitchell, her kidnapper, was complaining about his mother and mentioned where she lived. Elizabeth blurted out that it was in the same neighborhood as her favorite cousin, Olivia. Without thinking, Elizabeth explained the features of Olivia's home, which Mitchell recognized.

The next day, Mitchell informed Elizabeth that God had commanded him to abduct Olivia. He would spend the next week planning the kidnapping for Pioneer Day, knowing that the distractions of the festivities and fireworks that evening would provide the perfect cover.

In *My Story*, Elizabeth recounts how on the afternoon of July 24 she was too sick to eat. Instead, she sat on a bucket and prayed: "I begged and cried and pleaded with God to protect my cousin."

Her prayers were answered when Mitchell was scared off and the scenario was averted.

On July 25, the board was briefed regarding the incident. We were told the break-in might be the most important lead in the investigation to date. That's precisely why it was vital that every possible precaution be taken to avoid this new information becoming public.

When Ben asks about rumors of an attempted break-in at the home of a Smart family relative in Taylorsville a few days later, it stops me in my tracks. But his question carries a detail that provides me with an easy out.

"I am not aware of a break-in at one of Elizabeth's relatives in Taylorsville," I reply.

Olivia and her family live in a suburb of Cottonwood Heights, so technically, my answer is truthful. I still feel guilty and disingenuous, but never show it. Ben nods and doesn't prod me for more information. In fact, he won't ask me again about the break-in.

A few weeks after my encounter with Ben, Scott McKane with the local Fox affiliate breaks the story. Following McKane's scoop, the other local media outlets barely cover the development, and it is largely ignored nationally. By this time, more than two months after the abduction, the media and public's interest in the Smart case is waning. So the information about the attempted break-in doesn't receive anywhere near the amount of attention it would have generated if it had broken at the end of July. This also can be attributed to the police, who tell the media they have thoroughly investigated the incident and believe it was a prank by a group of teenagers.

The break-in at Olivia's house is problematic for law enforcement, since it goes contrary to the theory that Richard Ricci was the perpetrator. Ricci had an ironclad alibi: He was incarcerated on July 24.

In the weeks leading up to the attempted break-in at the Wrights' house, the police had doubled down on Ricci publicly, communicating more suspicious information surrounding him that had all but convinced many among the rank and file in law enforcement, as well as the media and the public, that Ricci was indeed the one who had abducted Elizabeth.

The police announced they had spoken to the owner of an auto shop, who told them Ricci had dropped off his white Jeep for repairs but then unexpectedly picked it up just prior to Elizabeth's abduction and before the mechanics could fix the fuel pump. The owner claimed that Ricci took the white Jeep for a couple of days, and when he returned it, there were hundreds of additional miles on the odometer and the undercarriage was caked with dirt and mud. The shop owner said he witnessed Ricci remove a post hole digger, seat covers, and a couple of garbage bags, before leaving with the items when another man picked him up across the street (after he dropped the vehicle off the second time). Ricci repeatedly denied having ever taken the Jeep from the repair shop.

The attempted break-in on July 24, like several other developments in the coming months, contradicts Ricci being the perpetrator, and yet law enforcement always seems to quickly dismiss contradictions like this.

For years I will wonder how things might have been different if I had allowed the news to break that day when Ben asked me the dreaded question.

Would the story have been taken more seriously because of its timeliness and the fact that law enforcement didn't have any concrete reasons to dismiss it? Would the media have dug deeper and discovered just how similar the attempted break-in at Olivia Wright's house was to what occurred the morning of Elizabeth's abduction? Would these details have made Ricci less of a slam dunk and opened the media's, the public's, and law enforcement's minds to alternate theories and options—maybe even regarding how it could have been another man in the room the night Elizabeth was abducted?

Instead, by providing my creative answer, I have unknowingly helped perpetuate the premise that Ricci abducted Elizabeth. This will bother me for years, yet at the same time, I take some solace in knowing I stayed true to the direction and wishes of my client.

CHAPTER 22

The Potted Plant

On a warm summer afternoon in 2002, an anchorwoman with short, perfectly styled golden blonde hair sets a decorative potted plant from a hip nearby nursery on the doorstep of the Smarts' home. Media organizations are notorious for trying a myriad of tactics to gain exclusive access and interviews from individuals who are prominent in the news. This includes everything from sending flowers and small gifts to having the who's who of the journalism world make personal phone calls. However, with the Smarts, these types of efforts generally do little more than generate a modicum of goodwill.

That is largely because of a media response structure we implemented with the family during the first day my team and I worked at the search center. It resulted in the Smarts, including Tom (although it took him a while to acquiesce) diligently following a specific media protocol, which involved referring all interview and information requests to one of my colleagues or me.

This structure seems bulletproof, but we'll soon discover its Achilles' heel. This vulnerability, coupled with events that no one will see coming, will create a myriad of challenges over the ensuing months, including a very complicated situation that will have the potential to compromise Elizabeth's rescue.

The potted plant on the doorstep is accompanied by a handwritten note addressed to Lois. Weeks later, this gift giver will end up wielding significant influence over the family's response to elements of the abduction. The journalist's motive will be the result of a combination of extreme pressure and a will to win, along with her leveraging of religious ties.

Competitiveness is an all-too-common aspect of the culture of The Church of Jesus Christ of Latter-day Saints. Beginning at an early age, church members are instilled with a drive to excel, not always overtly but sometimes even by an osmosis of sorts, as they absorb the communal compulsion toward perfection and achievement that is all around them.

Children in the culture are generally taught to work hard, delay gratification, and find a way to succeed even when the odds are against them. This is often encouraged and even pushed by parents, many of whom are high-achieving and skilled professionals in their work spheres, individuals who have been rewarded for academic prowess or excellence in sports, music, and other dedicated activities. Additionally, many parents have served as full-time volunteer church missionaries for eighteen or twenty-four months, and have overcome frequent and intense adversity or rejection, often while speaking a foreign language as they try to find those interested in their gospel message.

I believe that the many ways in which parents verbally or nonverbally value and encourage their children to excel has likely contributed to the competitive nature of our culture. For many, this competitiveness fosters motivation, productivity, and achievement, but for others, the effects can be much less desirable.

A few statistics reinforce this assessment of the Latter-day Saint culture: Utah has more pianos per capita than any other state in the country, and one of the highest percentages of high school students who pass advanced placement college tests. Utah's Junior Jazz youth basketball program is among the most successful in the NBA, with more than sixty thousand participants annually and fourteen thousand volunteer coaches and organizers. According to the Annie E. Casey Foundation, Utah ranks among the top states in the nation for children's well-being based on health, education, and family stability—despite the state being near the bottom nationwide for per-pupil funding for K–12 public education.

On the flip side, Utah has among the highest percentage of children with mental health disorders, has one of the higher suicide rates in the country and, despite being at or near the bottom nationwide when it comes to alcohol and drug use, has one of the highest rates of overdose. As an interesting aside, the Utah State Correctional Facility is believed to be the only prison system in the world with a full orchestra, which regularly performs and rehearses weekly.

It is important to note that the above statistics are inclusive of all Utahns, not just those affiliated with The Church of Jesus Christ of Latter-day Saints, who comprise approximately 70 percent of the population. But they do help to illustrate both the positive and adverse effects of a state dominated by a certain faith and culture.

As illustrated, there is more motivation and pressure in many Utah communities for kids to participate and prosper in a variety of activities, from academics and music to dance, debate, and athletics, including my personal favorite, basketball.

* * *

The score was tied at forty-one. With less than a minute left in the game, two groups of parents on opposite sides of the cultural hall jawed at one another, while a teenager wearing an old referee's jersey two sizes too large tried to ignore them.

"Call it both ways." A middle-aged man with a receding hairline jumped to his feet, hollering with disgust at the volunteer official.

Another guy, in a red plaid shirt, stared down the man from the other side of the court and threw his own remark into the ring: "I don't know what you're complaining about. They've been calling it your way the entire night."

The first man couldn't contain himself and got animated, shouting: "Zip it, and sit down!"

Before things could escalate further, a volunteer at the scorer's table held down the electronic buzzer, which drowned out the contemptuous bickering. The stake athletic director, a volunteer who was responsible for organizing sporting events among the congregations, walked past me down to the center of the court.

"We are in a church," he told both fan bases. "This is a sanctioned activity. These are twelve-year-old boys. Please act appropriately, or we will call the game."

After the crowd settled down, one of my teammates stole an inbounds pass and made a layup. At the other end of the court, I got a defensive rebound, was fouled, and hit both free throws to put us up by four.

On the next possession, with time ticking down, I anticipated a cross-court pass and intercepted the ball, but was violently clotheslined. Reeling from the collision, I was enraged. As I got up, the boy who'd fouled me sneered and stepped aggressively in my direction. I stood tall and got in his face. He continued to talk trash, so I shoved him away and attempted to throw a punch. But before it could land, one of the coaches from the opposing team grabbed me in a bear hug from behind. This infuriated my coach, who was an older, inactive member of our church. He pushed the other coach, and before long, a handful of parents came storming onto the court. The volunteer at the scorer's table again held down the buzzer, creating even more commotion.

While at first it looked like the parents were going to break into fisticuffs, instead they grabbed both coaches and worked to rectify the situation. After a few minutes, I was instructed to apologize. The other boy stepped out. We shook hands, not making eye contact, and both of us muttered an obligatory "sorry."

Ward ball, which starts with a prayer and rarely ends without a fight, is supposed to unify neighbors and bring people closer to Christ, but here it had turned into something more like a Roman gladiator fight than a friendly ball game. This scene didn't just play out in our ward building that day. Similar scenarios were repeated in Latter-day Saint churches throughout the country, but for some reason, the intensity seemed more pronounced in Salt Lake City.

* * *

Ed finds me and pulls me aside before the afternoon press briefing. His serious expression makes me fear he is about to share another Richard Ricci-type development.

"Chris, I need to give you a heads up…I don't quite know how to tell you this…. Uh, Lois had lunch with Jane Clayson. Yes, the same Lois who wants nothing to do with the media. All of a sudden, she's becoming best friends with a member of the group she used to consider the enemy. Jane has been talking about flying the family to New York…"

I struggle to hide my disdain. I feel betrayed. This revelation is almost as surprising as seeing Tom sitting next to the milkman when I watched *Larry King Live* a few weeks ago.

Lois has always been appreciative of and cordial toward me, but early on, she made it very clear she would be involved with the media only when it was "absolutely necessary." Sometimes, that was a challenge. On several occasions, she even tried to make a case for not participating in any interviews at all.

"Ed is in charge of the media and investigation," she'd say. "I take care of the kids and the house. Can't Ed just handle this? Do you really need me to be there?"

Our established media protocol, by which all requests for information and interviews go through one of my colleagues or me, helps to maintain order and creates a quick, effective, and consistent response to media requests. But it has one main purpose: to protect the family. It allows me to serve as a buffer. That way I can be the "bad guy" who diplomatically says no or, on the flip side, negotiates any details if it makes sense for the family to participate in an interview, a segment, or a special prime-time network program.

Media protocols work, however, only if family members (or employees, in the case of a company) are diligent in referring all requests to the media point person, without offering any type of comment or consideration. If a journalist penetrates this firewall by getting the subject to cooperate directly with them, the ability of the public relations professional to effectively manage the media and advocate on behalf of the client is compromised.

Journalists frankly don't want to deal with an extra layer of defense like this. They know they are much more likely to get what they want through their own pathways and volition. This includes buddying up to the subject and showing extreme concern and interest for the individual or family. Sometimes the journalist will provide advice and counsel, including an insider's view on how to manage the media, often discrediting the public relations professional in the process. For many people, receiving this kind of attention—being pursued by a person on TV who suddenly wants to be your best friend and help you during your darkest hour—can be alluring.

At this time in 2002, Jane Clayson is perhaps the most prominent journalist who is also a member of The Church of Jesus Christ of Latter-day Saints. Jane graduated from church-run Brigham Young University in 1990, but instead of following the path of most broadcast journalists, who work their way up the ladder at stations in small towns like Redding, California (the 134th largest market in the United States), or Butte, Montana (189th largest), Jane skipped a couple of rungs and secured a job right out of college with church-owned KSL-TV in Salt Lake City (30th largest).

She rose quickly through the KSL ranks, going from entry-level reporter to on-air anchor, winning the coveted Edward R. Murrow Award in the process. After six years, she took a job with ABC News and moved to Los Angeles, where she worked as a correspondent for *Good Morning America* and *ABC News Tonight*, covering big stories like the O. J. Simpson trial. Her strong work ethic, likable demeanor, and good fortune continued, culminating in her very own Cinderella moment.

In 1999, CBS News launched its heavily publicized Operation Glass Slipper. The network was looking to find a cohost for Bryant Gumbel, in an effort to rename and revamp its morning show, which ranked dead last in ratings out of the three TV networks. Jane was the lucky girl who was a perfect fit, and soon CBS and the national entertainment media were swooning. They covered details of her life, like when she was moving into her New York City apartment, getting up in the morning and choosing which outfit to wear, riding in a limo to *The Early Show*'s studios, and even explaining how she operated without drinking coffee, since it was against her religious beliefs.

Jane anchored *The Early Show* from 1999 to 2001. She is probably most remembered for her live coverage of 9/11 and her interview with Martha Stewart during a cooking segment. Stewart—famed businesswoman, writer, and television personality—refused to answer Jane's questions about felony insider trading charges, and instead took out her frustration on the salad she was preparing.

A few months after Gumbel left the show in 2001, Jane was reassigned as a reporter and an occasional anchor for the *CBS Evening News*, and worked on the network's true crime show, *48 Hours*.

One year later, in the summer of 2002, Jane left that potted plant on the Smarts' doorstep, and her relationship with Lois blossomed. As a result, Lois agreed to give *48 Hours* an exclusive interview. She would collaborate on a prime-time hour-long television special that would be filmed over several months, and then air during one of the annual rating periods known as "February sweeps."

After breaking the news about Lois and Jane Clayson, Ed looks at me as though he's seeking counsel on how to navigate the situation. Frustrated by the news, I silently ruminate. Why does Lois give Jane the time of day? Why isn't she going to lunch with Ashleigh Banfield, Connie Chung, or Barbara Walters (all three of whom have aggressively been pursuing an exclusive interview with the family)?

Despite feeling somewhat defeated and at a disadvantage, I recognize that I can either continue to complain about the situation, or look for ways to influence the process and be a voice for the family's best interest.

I forge a relationship with Nancy Kramer, who is the head producer of the *48 Hours* special. Nancy is a caring yet relentless journalist, with an infectious smile and a laugh reminiscent of Ernie's from *Sesame Street*. She doesn't have any children of her own but possesses a loving, maternal quality that is magnetic. Elizabeth and her siblings (and fifteen years later my own children) will come to know Nancy as their "New York auntie."

While Nancy and I will have many spirited discussions, we respect each other. She knows what the network is working to accomplish, and at the same time is trying to listen and be considerate of my position, with a desire to also do what is best for the Smart family. The conflicts, however, that will arise during the coming months of filming, coupled with developments in the investigation, alchemize into something neither of us could have anticipated. It will test our resolve like nothing we have yet experienced in our careers.

CHAPTER 23

The Ask

Growing up, I believed there were four great commandments: Love the Lord thy God, love thy neighbor, honor thy mother and father, and cheer for the Utah Jazz with all thy heart, might, mind, and strength.

While I struggled mightily with loving my neighbor, I tried to make up for it with my passion for and devotion to the Jazz, the NBA's professional team in Salt Lake City. This, to me, was the highest form of basketball worship.

My grandfather took me to my first game when I was seven years old, shortly after the Jazz moved to Salt Lake City from New Orleans, and I was hooked. By 1983, I didn't miss a single game. I watched, listened, or scraped together enough money to see the team in person. On more than one occasion, to the chagrin of the box office, I paid for a ticket entirely with coins.

In my free time, I listened around the clock to a talk radio station that periodically gave away tickets, and I won a handful each season. During the summers, I religiously attended a basketball camp organized by my idol, Adrian Dantley, an NBA All-Star and the public face of the Jazz. I was such a big fan of A. D. that decades later, I would lead an effort to get his number retired by the team to improve his chances of getting inducted into the Naismith Memorial Basketball Hall of Fame.

In 1984, for the first time in the franchise's history, and after being picked by the media to finish near the bottom of the Western Conference, the Jazz qualified for the NBA playoffs. Experiencing the team's unlikely rise became a part of me and I found my mood often mirroring the ups and downs of the season. By the time the Jazz won the Midwest Conference and the playoffs started, I was so elated that I had trouble focusing during school.

The Jazz took on the persona of the community as a group of underdogs who worked harder, scrapped, and outhustled the competition, striving to find respect and legitimacy on a national stage.

The playoffs that spring were fruitful. The Jazz surprised the Denver Nuggets by winning an emotional first-round series that cemented Utah's affinity for the team. Despite the success and drafting future of Hall of Fame point guard John Stockton, the team was experiencing hard times a few months later. Rumors began to swirl that the franchise was in serious financial trouble. At the start of the next season that fall, the Jazz subtly dropped Utah from its jerseys and promotional materials, and the team played a quarter of its games in Las Vegas. News would soon leak that the franchise was for sale.

Despite an effort by a consortium of prominent Utahns to pool their money to buy the team, there just wasn't enough support, and the team's ownership began negotiating with groups in Miami and Minnesota that were bidding to buy the franchise and move it out of state.

Each day as the news grew grimmer, my parents tried to prepare me for what seemed inevitable. I wasn't receptive. I wouldn't give up the faith. I prayed for a miracle.

Upon returning home from school one afternoon, I heard breaking news come on the radio. The announcer said local car dealer, Larry H. Miller, was making a last-minute attempt to buy the Jazz and keep the franchise in Utah. He was seeking financing and had a five o'clock deadline that very evening. Encouraged by the news, I immediately called my grandfather and begged him to take me to the game that night. My mom's father, Thomas Reese, lived with my grandmother, Mary, in a modest home two blocks away from my house. He was a regular fixture in my life and had taken me to several college and professional games. We also regularly watched sports together on TV.

While driving to the arena, my grandfather made an offer I couldn't refuse. He would buy the tickets if I would write a story about the game for my elementary school newspaper.

Sitting in the second row from the top of the arena, I took detailed notes, capturing the mood and atmosphere. A few minutes before tipoff, the stadium announcer, Dan Roberts, informed the sellout crowd that Miller had secured the financing and would be purchasing the team. Fans leapt to their feet as Miller walked onto the court and was presented with the game ball. The crowd's response was deafening. Jumping up and pumping my fist in the air, I dropped my blue, ballpoint pen.

When we returned home, my grandfather told my mom about the article I had been writing. "Why don't you call Larry Miller tomorrow and request an interview for your story?" she suggested.

I protested, because I thought Larry had more important things to do than talk to a sixth-grade journalist, but the next morning, my mom dialed the number to Miller's office and handed me the phone. I stuttered and stammered, repeating myself twice before Miller's secretary understood my request. She took my name and number and told me she would pass the message along.

Refusing to go to school, I waited anxiously by the phone. After a couple of hours, my mom was nagging me to get ready and head out the door when the phone rang.

"Hello. This is Larry Miller. Is Chris available?"

It took me several seconds to respond. I swallowed so hard, I could feel my Adam's apple popping out of my neck.

"Ah, yes, this is he."

"I understand you're writing an article about the Jazz. How can I help?"

"Well, I have just a few, quick questions…"

Fumbling through my notebook, I finally found the page with the list of questions I had prepared earlier that morning just in case Larry called back.

"Take your time. I'm happy to take as long as you need. The press can wait," Larry said. He sounded calm and relaxed, and as though I was his only focus.

I struggled to read the first few questions. Then I got in a rhythm. Larry and I spoke for the next fifteen minutes. He was warm, engaging, and thoughtful in his answers.

After I asked my last question, Larry explained that he had given me a scoop. This had been his first interview since signing the papers to buy the Jazz. In fact, his staff and the media were waiting for him to finish our interview so he could make the official announcement.

"Chris, if you only remember one thing about today, I hope it will be the power of asking. I granted you the first interview because you asked. Always be willing to ask. You never know where it will take you."

Miller, who had sought the counsel of the hierarchy of The Church of Jesus Christ of Latter-day Saints before risking his fortune to purchase the Jazz, was told that saving the team not only would be beneficial for Utah's image but would serve as a catalyst for him to *do* good.

My interview was the first of his countless acts of kindness as the owner of the Utah Jazz. Larry went on to build a multibillion-dollar business empire, elevate our community, and make a difference, enriching numerous lives, especially mine.

CHAPTER 24

The White House

" **I** honestly think we should go to Washington, DC, and protest," Ed tells me. "I will stand outside of the White House holding a sign that says, 'Don't politicize child abduction,' and then the Bush administration will *have* to explain to the media why we aren't inside that building."

Ed's frustration is boiling over. It's not yet to the tipping point of unrestrained laughter, but it's close. On several occasions, something—be it law enforcement, extended family dynamics, the media, the reality of Elizabeth being missing—would trigger Ed, and a laughing cycle would begin. He would start to unpack the situation. His voice would get faster and higher-pitched as he recounted each detail, all of which further reinforced his frustration. Then, just when it seemed like steam might blast out of his nose, mouth, and ears, Ed would pause and then burst into uncontrollable laughter, like a child being tickled. It was so infectious, I couldn't help but follow suit, and when we finally stopped and sighed, Ed would say, "Laughing sure beats the other alternatives."

Ed's laughter would often reset the situation for both of us. It was something I didn't always know I needed, but on a crisp morning in late September 2002, I desperately want a good Ed Smart laugh. During the three months following the abduction, managing most of the incidents meant intense days of problem solving on steroids. Issues like the attack on Tom's daughters by Marc Klaas and Bill O'Reilly, the *Salt Lake Tribune* article about the kidnapping being an inside job, and the *National Enquirer* cover story on the "family sex ring" each dominated a day or two of my time, and then we moved on. Now, as I enter my third week of trying to crack a new and stubborn dilemma, I am experiencing acute mental fatigue.

It began in early September, when Ed and Lois and I were leaving a taping of *The John Walsh Show*, a new daytime talk program on NBC. John shook my hand, gave Ed a hug, kissed Lois on the cheek, and then said, "I'll see you at the White House in a few weeks."

This was the first time we had heard about the White House Conference on Missing, Exploited, and Runaway Children. Ed and Lois were curious and began asking questions. It was then that John realized the Smarts had not been invited. He did his best to try and tap dance around the issue, but it was as awkward as a childhood playground exchange, when one friend discovers his pal has been left off someone else's birthday party list.

"I'm sure they'll send you an invitation," John said. "You deserve to be there."

The news of this exclusion, or what we initially thought may have been an omission, was surprising, since Elizabeth's kidnapping was the first, and highest-profile, of the abduction cases during what would become known as the "Summer of Missing Children." Previously the main strategy was printing images of missing children on milk cartons, but the attention surrounding the Smarts had pierced the national consciousness and spurred the media, who were now broadly covering each new kidnapping. These stories weren't just trending in the news; the public was talking about the issue of missing children more than ever before. A new energy had taken hold of people regarding this issue, despite the fact that there were approximately the same number of stranger abductions in 2002 as there had been during the previous several years.

Not receiving an invitation was confusing, because during the few months since Elizabeth's kidnapping, we had become familiar with how to work "inside the Beltway"—that is, with politicians and federal agencies in Washington, DC.

In early August, when the satellite trucks left the Arlington Hills ward one by one and the twice-daily press conferences were reduced to a weekly briefing, Ed went stir crazy. Very few searches were taking place, the investigation had slowed, and the interview requests were sporadic. I approached a handful of staff members from Utah's congressional delegation, whom we had worked with in various capacities since the early days of the case, and asked if they had any ideas on causes or legislation that Ed might help champion.

Senator Orrin Hatch's office recommended the perfect opportunity to channel Ed's energy: lobbying for the national Amber Alert. Ed and I dove into meeting with key sponsors of the legislation by phone, then took the story to the media. Our mission to educate politicians and Americans about the national Amber Alert provided an opportunity to talk about something of substance, while keeping Elizabeth's story alive. In Washington, DC, Ed and I walked from office to office on Capitol Hill, talking with staffers and the handful of senators and representatives who made time to meet with us.

As a result of these efforts and passion, Ed's discontent surrounding the White House conference stemmed not just from being excluded, but more from the prospect of not having an opportunity to help further the national Amber Alert legislation.

For weeks I assertively work every contact and angle possible to get an invitation for Ed and Lois to attend the conference. Our greatest chance, I believe, is with Orrin Hatch, who is Utah's senior Republican senator, chair of the Senate Judiciary Committee, and has a strong relationship with President Bush.

Hatch's state director, Melanie Bowen, had been a tremendous ally in helping us make connections surrounding the Amber Alert and was always willing to collaborate with the Smart family. When I first approached Melanie about the predicament, she said Senator Hatch would personally request an invitation from the White House and she was optimistic it wouldn't be a problem. As time dragged on, however, the tenor changed, and all she could tell me was that Senator Hatch had made multiple requests but was still waiting to hear. Despite talking to Melanie almost daily, and making calls to other members of Congress and John Walsh, I wasn't getting any traction.

Five days before the conference, Melanie informed me she had spoken with the White House. They'd told her there was a problem with inviting the Smarts because the conference had been moved to a smaller venue with very limited space. It was possible they would even have to uninvite some policymakers who were planning to attend, but they said they would see what they could do for the Smarts.

For Ed, this explanation was on par with a poorly concocted excuse a teenager might offer when they don't want to go on a date with someone.

Each time I call Ed, he gets more and more animated about the situation. He still hasn't burst into laughter, but his voice remains elevated, and he talks quickly. Ed is becoming even more adamant about his idea of protesting. I propose that we instead go to Washington and lobby for the national Amber Alert on Capitol Hill, so when the news breaks about how the Smarts weren't invited to the White House, Ed will be seen doing something constructive.

Ed's patience continues to wane. On the Thursday morning before the Wednesday conference, Ed decides that he and Lois will not be attending. I ask him to give me twenty-four hours. There isn't much else I can try, but I call a source, who informs me there is concern among the White House staff that the Smarts could upstage the president and distract from the focus of the conference. Equipped with this intel, I call Melanie.

"I need you to pass along a message to the White House," I tell her. "The Smarts are willing to refrain from doing any and all media at the conference. They are happy to be discreet in how they enter and exit. Ed and Lois simply want to be there to meet the other parents of missing children and learn as much as possible."

Melanie seems reluctant to make the call and tries to reassure me that Senator Hatch and his staff are doing everything possible to help the Smarts get an invitation, so I double down on the pitch.

"For reasons I can't explain, it is imperative this message be communicated to the White House. Will you please make sure this info is passed along?"

When we speak the next morning, Melanie informs me that the White House doesn't have an issue with the Smarts doing media interviews surrounding the conference. The problem is that there are limits regarding how many people the fire marshal will allow in the room. I then throw a Hail Mary pass.

"*Good Morning America* is aggressively trying to confirm a live interview from Washington, DC, with Ed and Lois the morning of the conference. Will you ask the White House how they want me to handle the request?"

After hanging up, I continue to ignore Ed's calls that morning, hoping someone will miraculously catch that pass, as time is quickly expiring. A few hours later, I can't hold Ed off any longer. I finally answer, and he is despondent.

"Will you please call Hatch's office, and everyone else you've been speaking with, and let them know that Lois and I absolutely will not be coming? We shouldn't have to beg. If the White House doesn't want us, then we don't want to be there."

I reluctantly follow Ed's directive and relay his sentiment in a message on Melanie's voicemail.

Melanie hasn't listened to her voicemail when she calls me at the end of the day. She explains how her staff and the senator worked most of the afternoon to finally get Ed and Lois an invitation to the conference. I am at a loss regarding how to respond, so I simply thank her and say I will let the Smarts know.

News moves fast. When I reach Ed, he has already accepted the invitation. John Walsh has called to inform him and has booked airline tickets for the Smarts, so there's no way they can say no.

A member of the White House communications office calls me over the weekend to coordinate media. The person wants to know what interviews I have scheduled for the Smarts. I say that outside of tentatively confirming *Good Morning America* after receiving the invitation, I haven't made any other commitments. Since I don't know the details regarding the conference location or schedule, and other media haven't contacted me since Friday morning, I have been standing pat.

The White House instructs me to send all interview requests to them, and they will handle everything. I agree but ask that I be there during media availability at the conference to shepherd interviews with Ed and Lois. This way I can ensure there is someone representing them who can run interference as needed and provide the media with equal access. I am told this is very unlikely, but they will see what they can do.

I catch a red-eye flight to New York late Monday night with Angela, Cynthia, David, and Tom's wife, Heidi. Once we land, we drive to Washington, DC, and while we're in transit, I receive a call from *Good Morning America* canceling the Wednesday interview. I'll learn later from a trusted producer that the White House offered ABC an exclusive interview with Attorney General John Ashcroft to get the network to agree to bump the Smarts from the broadcast.

That afternoon we tour the National Center for Missing and Exploited Children, where we meet Elizabeth's case worker and later join up with a group of parents of abducted children for dinner. The parents include Patty Wetterling, whose eleven-year-old son, Jacob, was taken at gunpoint in Minnesota in 1989 and hasn't been seen since (his remains will later be found in 2019), and Colleen Nick, whose six-year-old daughter, Morgan, disappeared at a Little League baseball game in Arkansas in 1995 (and is still missing). This is Ed and Lois' induction into a club that no parent ever wants to belong to.

Patty and the other parents are warm and gracious, providing insights, understanding, and a unique kinship that is exactly what the Smarts need. This makes the frustration and struggle of the previous three weeks feel worth it to me. At the end of the evening, Patty hugs Ed and Lois and gives them a reassuring smile as though everything is going to be okay.

"We'll see you tomorrow morning at the White House," she says.

This is the first time the Smarts are hearing about a special breakfast for the parents of missing children. It is to be hosted by the president and First Lady. As soon as Patty informs us of the event, I try to downplay things, but she isn't about to let it go.

"Of course you're invited. If it wasn't for you, this conference wouldn't be happening."

I briefly explain the challenges we've faced. Patty is aghast and says if the Smarts aren't invited to the breakfast, then she and the other parents shouldn't be going. She says she'll make some calls to make sure the Smarts are included. We convince her that it isn't a big deal and to please let it go if she isn't able to make any progress.

An invitation to the breakfast never comes. The White House calls me early Wednesday morning to let me know they have received more than thirty interview requests for the Smarts, and they need my help during media availability. They instruct me to be at the Ronald Reagan convention center a few minutes before noon.

Arriving an hour early, I proceed through a metal detector but can't find anyone in the appointed room. I wander for several minutes until I find the back entrance to a large area with scores of people sitting around dozens of round tables. There is a stage at the far end of the room with a podium and a half dozen officials sitting on each side, facing the crowd. The background has royal blue draping, an American flag, and a banner with black-and-white pictures of children along with the signage, "Missingkids.com 1-800-The-Lost."

I notice there are at least ten empty tables at the back of the large room. *I guess they uninvited several policymakers*, I think. I see Ed and Lois sitting next to Marc Klaas. Ed uses my entrance as an excuse to move to one of the empty tables, telling me that Klaas wouldn't stop interrogating about the investigation and pestering him about several uncomfortable details.

Fifteen minutes later, President George W. Bush and his wife, Laura, enter the ballroom. The audience stands and applauds. The president speaks to the group and announces several new federal measures, including funding for local Amber Alerts and post-abduction care for families and survivors.

After his remarks, as the president and First Lady are walking out of the event, I grab Ed and Lois and push through the crowd toward the couple.

"Hey, Mr. President, Elizabeth Smart's parents would like to meet you."

They stop. One of the president's aides whispers something in his ear, and then President Bush comes over to us and shakes hands with Ed and Lois. While they speak, reporters and photographers push and shove trying to capture the candid moment. They get there just in time to hear President Bush tell Ed and Lois, "God bless you both," before he departs.

Later that evening, I remind Ed how just a few days prior I was trying to talk him out of protesting and he starts laughing uncontrollably. While it catches me off guard, I smile and giggle. Anytime I see a smile on his face and the mood is elevated, I'm grateful.

CHAPTER 25

The Riccis

The Smart family is making a concerted effort to maintain an open mind when working with a diversity of media organizations (except the tabloids), and is employing a similar approach with the local and broader community. They happily welcome and work with a variety of individuals and groups, ranging from other families who have missing children to advocacy organizations such as Bikers Against Child Abuse. While we've been screening people after the Mark Klaas incident, at this point, a few months after Elizabeth's abduction, we've vetted and then partnered with just about everyone in that realm. When we get requests for meetings, phone calls, or supporting events and initiatives, we usually don't think twice; we simply say yes. That is, until Nancy Pomeroy calls.

Nancy, who is the publicist for the Ricci family, calls a few days before Richard Ricci is to be arraigned in August 2002. Ricci was indicted by a grand jury two weeks earlier for brandishing a firearm and robbing a Far West Bank in Sandy, Utah, for a total of $1,700 in November 2001. The charges are completely unrelated to the Smarts.

Nancy asks if Ricci's wife, Angela, can meet privately with Ed. My initial thought is that while the meeting likely would be harmless, it also could be fraught with potential landmines. What if the conversation were to go south, and Angela twists things and maligns the Smart family in the media? Could the meeting itself with Angela be perceived negatively? There has been significant criticism of Ed's practices of hiring and bringing in questionable characters like Ricci, not only to work at his home but to labor in the presence of his children. From a public relations perspective, the prudent thing might be to kindly decline the invitation, but my gut tells me otherwise.

Instead of immediately presenting the request to the board, which is customary, I speak with Nancy a few times. I want to flesh things out as much as possible to improve the chance of the meeting happening the right way. We agree that it should be completely private, that nothing would be said about it publicly, prior to or after the meeting, and that it would be 100 percent confidential. We should also wait until well after the court hearing, when the media will have left, and meet in a private room, with zero media access. If something leaks and becomes public, there will be agreed-upon response messaging.

The board has a mixed response when I present the request. Many members have the same concerns I initially did. Others make the argument that by allowing the two to meet, Ed might be able to get Angela's help in asking Ricci to explain to investigators why he had picked up the white Jeep, and where he had gone.

Ed is fully on board and confident that he can be empathetic, while standing firm on the facts of the case. Regardless, we believe that if something surrounding the meeting were to become a public issue, we could position the meeting as another example of how the Smarts are trying to do everything possible to find Elizabeth.

A few days later, Ed and I sit on wooden benches on one side of the courtroom while Nancy and Angela sit on the opposite side. When Ricci enters, Angela gasps and then sheds a few tears, smiling lovingly at him. Wearing an orange prison jumpsuit and chains around his wrists and ankles, Ricci looks adoringly at his wife and mouths "I love you" before walking past her and returning to his stoic disposition.

The judge reads the bank robbery charges against Ricci. Through his attorney, he pleads not guilty. He's then escorted back to the secured holding area. The door closes. The hearing concludes in mere minutes.

Angela and Nancy leave the courtroom while Ed and I sit and wait for the court's public information officer to direct us to the meeting room. After twenty minutes, she leads us to an elevator, where we're surprised to find Nancy, Angela, and Angela's father, David Morse. When the elevator opens on the second floor, reporters and cameras are waiting. Someone at the court has tipped off the media. As Ed tries to work his way through the crowd, he awkwardly explains that he is meeting with Angela in the hope of getting more information about the abduction.

Once we navigate through the media and are inside the room with the doors shut, Angela thanks Ed for being willing to meet with her. She tearfully speaks about how much she has worried and prayed for Elizabeth and hopes she will be found soon. Before Ed can say little more than "thank you," Angela continues in a fast-paced tone.

"Ed, you need to know that Richard had nothing to do with Elizabeth's abduction, nothing. He was with me the night she was taken. He has told the truth about everything they have asked him. You have to believe me…"

Angela sobs, looking as though she is pleading for us to release Ricci from prison. Ed thanks Angela for her prayers and acknowledges how difficult the circumstances have been for her, then bravely addresses the elephant in the room.

"I feel really sorry for you. But respectfully, I'm not sure that Richard has told the truth about everything. He lied to me about the items he stole from my home and he's not being forthright about what happened with the Jeep."

Wearing a navy-blue polo shirt, Ed is composed, his tone conciliatory. He looks at Angela with the compassion of a clergyman.

"Ed, Richard has told me how he has answered the questions about the Jeep several times, but the investigators won't listen, and they don't believe him. He never picked up the Jeep or drove it far away. I would have known if he had been gone for a long period of time."

Ed asks Angela if she will talk to Ricci and plead with him to tell investigators what he knows about the Jeep, as well as the identity of the person he was seen with when he returned the vehicle.

The tenor of the conversation suddenly shifts. Angela wants to know how Lois and the children are holding up. Ed then asks Angela how she is coping. They speak about resilience and trusting God. The two connect. My eyes shift downward as I blink away emotion. These two individuals, who come from very different places and have diametrically opposed interests, are finding common ground and coming together in such a meaningful and unexpected way.

As we leave the courthouse, Ed tells me that while he doesn't trust Ricci, he has a lot of compassion and sympathy for Angela. This feeling is even more pronounced a month later (almost three months after Elizabeth was abducted), when Ed receives some difficult news and calls me in a haste.

"We have a really challenging situation. I need your immediate help. Will you please meet me at the church?"

I continue talking to Ed as I get into my car and begin to drive. He informs me that Ricci was having trouble breathing in his jail cell and called for help. When the guards arrived, they witnessed him collapse onto his bunk. He was rushed to the hospital, where he is on life support and isn't expected to live more than a day or two.

"Chris, I am heartbroken for Angela, especially after all she has been through the past few months. She is a genuinely good person who doesn't deserve this."

Whenever there is a death or serious injury, the rule of thumb in communications is for any statement or commentary to begin with a sincere expression of sympathy. It is generally advisable to keep details to a minimum and to focus on the impacted individual and their family. If more information is required, this is usually included in a communication sent out the next day or even several days later.

Ricci's impending death creates a complicated situation. The Smart family needs to balance expressing condolences to his family with doing everything possible to keep the investigation and search for Elizabeth active. Otherwise, many will believe the hope of finding Elizabeth will pass with Ricci.

The board deliberates and examines the situation from several different angles. Once Ricci passes away, it might be possible to get accomplices, or others in the know about the white Jeep, to come forward with information. At that point, they might be more inclined to cooperate. We determine that keeping the investigation alive comes down to answering two questions: Who picked up Ricci when he left his white Jeep at the repair shop on June 8? And who was responsible for the attempted break-in at Olivia Wright's home in Cottonwood Heights on July 24?

These questions simply communicate that there is more to the story and investigation than Ricci as the sole suspect, and that both law enforcement and the public need to continue working if we're going to get answers that help us find Elizabeth.

One of the board members offers a three-thousand-dollar reward for answers to each question. We hope this will add some gravitas and increase attention while providing a vehicle to better define the narrative. The family believes Ricci's death might be an opportunity for others to come forward. We need to be proactive rather than allowing the story to take its course and then trying to respond to two presumptions: that Ricci's death negatively impacts the investigation, and that the mystery of Elizabeth's abduction might have died with Ricci. The only way to accomplish this is to communicate the news about the reward aggressively but diplomatically when the story breaks.

I volunteer to be the front man. If the plea for answers and the accompanying reward come off as contrived or insincere, Ed and Lois will be protected. I'm willing to take a hit to my reputation, if necessary.

Once the story of Ricci's condition breaks, I am deluged with calls and interview requests. In an effort to mitigate the risk, I begin and end each response for taped and print interviews with a message of sympathy or condolence for Ricci's family. Although this sounds awkward to the journalist conducting the interview, it helps to ensure that any sound bite used will include a statement of empathy to help counterbalance our ask.

When the media pose questions implying the reward is insensitive, I go back to the sympathy-and-condolence message while stressing that the family is doing everything possible to find Elizabeth—and that they can't stay silent.

The lead sentences in the stories about Ricci being in a coma, and later the ones about his death, all cite the Smarts' positioning and messaging, and make the case that the mystery of Elizabeth's abduction is larger than the former handyman.

Fortunately, none of the media criticizes the family or me for being proactive in communicating the questions and reward. There is enough public sentiment for finding Elizabeth that we're able to sidestep the communication rules surrounding a death or serious injury.

In the end though, no one comes forward with any answers. The confluence of Ricci's death with the lack of new information creates a sense of moroseness among all of us working on the case. Without a new development, finding Elizabeth seems hopeless. Little do we know that the next few months will not be uneventful, nor without significant setbacks and challenges.

CHAPTER 26

Not of the World

Adorned in a blue wool blazer, white shirt, red silk necktie, and fake gold Rolex, I sat down in my first-class airline seat, contentedly owning the look of a teenage anomaly.

"Are you coming or going?"

A middle-aged Black man with a salt-and-pepper beard initiated the conversation with me as he took a drag on a cigarette and eyed me curiously from the adjacent seat.

Before I could answer, a flight attendant handed my seatmate a Heineken. Sitting next to a stranger who was smoking cigarettes and drinking alcohol had become passé for me by this point.

"Heading home. Just saw my first night game at Wrigley. And…we nearly got mugged on the South Side."

I smile confidently, at ease as I talk with the man, who must have thought I was either the son of a Fortune 500 CEO or knew I was an airline brat flying standby.

In 1986, it became necessary for my mom to go back to work full time. Our family could no longer make ends meet on my father's modest Union Pacific Railroad income. Before I was born, my mom had taught second grade. Then when I was three years old, she began working periodically at a preschool part time. Although teaching was her passion, she wanted to expand her four children's horizons, so she took a job at a reservation call center for Eastern Airlines (and later Delta Airlines), complete with travel benefits.

My mom grew up in an agnostic household but attended the neighborhood ward of The Church of Jesus Christ of Latter-day Saints with her best friend. She wanted my family to understand and appreciate the outside world and its mores, while holding true to our church culture and religion. The essence of her desire was captured in a popular Latter-day Saint saying, loosely adapted from the Book of John (John 17:14–16) in the Bible: "Strive to be *in* the world, but not *of* the world."

Because of my family's limited discretionary income, we could rarely afford to stay at a hotel. Instead, we took red-eye flights through Atlanta to cities in the Midwest or on the East Coast, and returned home on the last flight of the day the following evening. My mom put her teaching skills to work and helped me use atlases and encyclopedias to plan each trip. I learned about the demographics, geography, and history of each location. Once on the ground, we traveled by mass transit, which meant quickly learning the bus and subway systems. Little did my mom know that she was not only teaching me but preparing herself for a future career. Decades later, she would accept a clandestine position as a CIA officer, working at headquarters in Langley, Virginia, to deploy and evacuate secret agents to and from dangerous locations around the globe.

My family's form of travel required us to adapt quickly, think on our feet, function well with little sleep, accept less-than-favorable circumstances, and do so with a smile. Flying standby required my dad and me to wear a jacket and tie, and the whole family had to take whatever seats were available. Sometimes we slept in airports or had to figure out alternative routes home, when flights were canceled or there just wasn't capacity for freeloading airline employees.

Because Utah has the lowest number of people per capita nationwide who smoke cigarettes, largely because of the church's Word of Wisdom, most of the open airline seats going to and from the Beehive State in the 1980s were in the smoking section.

As the oldest and most independent of my siblings, I ended up sitting alone in the smoking area most of the time. At first, I struggled to endure even the shortest flights inhaling that foreign smell of burning tobacco. Not to mention that in my mind, smoking was a big transgression. I had never known anyone who smoked, and I couldn't help but think that those who did were vile sinners. At thirty thousand feet, however, I quickly learned that whether someone adhered to my religious standards or not did not determine their goodness or character. I often found myself connecting and having interesting discussions with many smokers, even about Mormonism. To my initial surprise and later delight, I made friends while en route to cities all over the country.

Life on the equivalent of a high-class hobo railroad was romantic, and I quickly developed an insatiable case of wanderlust. I was constantly researching, planning, saving, and dreaming about our next trip. When I was traveling, I generally cherished all the exploration and experiences that pushed me outside of my comfort zone, and I genuinely took joy in meeting people who were vastly different from myself.

This experiential learning had a steep learning curve, however, with a few bumps and interesting growing experiences along the way.

On a trip to St. Louis when I was fifteen years old, I was making small talk with the cashier at a gift shop when he asked me where I was from. After I responded, he asked if I was Mormon. When I answered in the affirmative, the man asked me how many wives my father had. He wasn't being flippant or facetious. His was a question of genuine curiosity.

I tried to conceal my slightly hurt feelings when I responded, but I was offended by his ignorance. In my fifteen years of living in Salt Lake City, I had never met or even seen a polygamist. My church disavowed the practice of polygamy in 1890. While there are small groups of extremists who refer to themselves as fundamentalist Mormons and continue the practice of plural marriage in Utah, these small splinter groups live in the shadows and have not been part of The Church of Jesus Christ of Latter-day Saints for nearly a century. Today, approximately 1 percent of Utahns practice polygamy, and the vast majority of those people live in rural southern Utah.

Standing in the gift shop, I recognized that the cashier's ignorance provided a very small glimpse into the many misunderstood, misinterpreted, and marginalized groups within our national and global community.

Another growth moment for me occurred as a result of my love for the Chicago Cubs. I had been religiously watching "the Lovable Losers," as the Cubs were known, on WGN since 1983, when we had cable TV installed in our house. As a result, the Windy City was at the top of my travel list, and I quickly figured out how to navigate it. My dad and I would catch Cubs games in person at least a couple of times each summer. Our routine consisted of taking a red-eye, changing out of our dress clothes and ditching them in an airport locker, and then venturing out to find different locations from the film *Ferris Bueller's Day Off* before riding the L to the north side and worshiping at the Friendly Confines of Wrigley Field. The Cubs were the only Major League Baseball team that played their home games exclusively during the day, which fit perfectly with our travel schedule.

When lights were erected at Wrigley Field in 1988, I saved enough money for my dad, my brother, and I to stay in a reasonable hotel on the outskirts of downtown. Our first game under the lights was exhilarating, despite the Cubs losing to the Dodgers that night. Afterward, I discovered it was necessary to take the L to a stop on the predominantly African American South Side and then transfer to Metra, a heavy-rail line, in order to get back to the hotel.

Before switching trains, we grabbed dinner at McDonald's near the train station. I knew we weren't in Utah anymore when we were approached several times while we were eating by people trying to sell us food stamps. Once we left the restaurant and headed back onto the street, a group of rough-looking young men began to congregate about twenty feet ahead of us, right in our path.

My dad discreetly told my brother and me to stand our ground, look confident, and not make eye contact. As we got closer, a speeding car skidded around the corner, its tires screeching. Blue-and-red strobe lights suddenly bounced off the brick walls of the ramshackle buildings behind us, and the group quickly dispersed.

The police car stopped next to us as we increased our pace down the sidewalk, and I looked over to see the passenger window slowly rolling down.

"Who do you think you are, and what in the hell are you doing here?" asked a heavyset Caucasian female police officer, with two blackened eyes, shining a large flashlight at us. She scolded us for several minutes and then drove alongside us as we walked to the Metra station a couple of blocks away. The officer told us to go into the station, wait near the tracks, and not talk to anyone. Her parting order was one that we would take to heart.

"And never come back to this area *ever, ever* again."

We huddled in the station, quietly trying to unpack the experience. Fifteen minutes later, two men who looked like they were from the neighborhood approached me. They were each holding an oversized aluminum can of alcohol, with a brand I had never seen before.

"Ya got some quarters?"

As I heard the man's voice, I cowered and looked for an escape. The only option was to jump onto the tracks.

"If ya got dollars, we's can make change."

I was petrified and temporarily at a loss for words.

"Ah, sorry, I only have a twenty..." As soon as the words left my lips, I wanted desperately to take them back, but it was too late.

"No problem, we's got lots of quarters. Gib me da twenty."

I sheepishly dug into my pocket, pulled out the bill, and held it between my fingers. The man snatched it and, to my surprise, started counting out quarters in my hand. He and his friend proceeded to teach us to "toss." This game involved picking a crack in the sidewalk and tossing quarters. Whoever threw closest to the crack without going over picked up the bounty.

An hour later when the train finally arrived, I was as disappointed as a young child leaving Chuck E. Cheese. We had bonded with the men and a handful of other people who had joined the game. They were surprisingly kind, thoughtful, self-deprecating—and also poked fun at us. We laughed so hard that at times it was difficult to throw with any type of accuracy. While I left with only a small handful of quarters, this would rank as one of my all-time-favorite travel experiences.

CHAPTER 27

The Mayflower Hotel

t is nearing 1 A.M. Just as I turn out the light and try to get settled between
the sheets in my creaky hotel bed, the phone rings.

"We've got a *problem*. Lois has packed up and taken the kids to the
lobby. She refuses to stay here." Ed's voice is hoarse and replete with
exhaustion.

* * *

Since the moment I began working with the family, producers from major
television and cable shows have aggressively pursued the Smarts, trying to
convince me to get Ed and Lois to fly to New York for interviews. They
remind me of relentless timeshare salespersons.

In the early days, the answer was easy—the Smarts didn't want to be
away from Salt Lake City in the event that Elizabeth was found. As the
story got bigger and took on a life of its own, Elizabeth's parents became,
as they say in the industry, an even bigger "get." Landing the first exclusive
interview in New York would not only give a successful media organization bragging rights but also draw a big audience and increase revenue.

Pressure continued to build in the months following Elizabeth's
abduction, and my response changed as things loosened a little with the
Smarts. Lois said she wasn't willing to leave the children behind and would
consider going to New York only if the network was willing to cover travel
expenses for the entire family. Several producers said that wouldn't be a

problem if the kids would speak on camera, but interviewing the Smart children had always been a non-negotiable item and an absolute *no*.

Requiring travel to be paid for the entire Smart clan was enough of an ask that I thought it had solved the New York interview problem, since it was unlikely that anyone would be willing to make such a big commitment. Every time a producer called, I proposed flying the whole family out and they would ultimately decline. That was until the producers of *The John Walsh Show* called. The famed *America's Most Wanted* host was taking a stab at a daytime talk show on NBC that would debut in September.

His producers, Jamie Kotkin-Hammer and Alexandra Jewett, were kind, considerate, and at the same time tenacious in their pursuit of the Smarts. They knew an interview would bring strong national attention to the new show and would help to put them on the map with viewers. When we first spoke, Jamie and Alexandra didn't balk at covering the entire Smart family's travel expenses. Instead, they saw it as an opportunity to give the family, especially the kids, a chance to escape Salt Lake City and the stress and drama of the search and investigation. When I told Ed and Lois the producers had accepted the offer, they were surprised and a little overwhelmed at the prospect of traveling.

They initially dragged their feet in deciding, which frustrated the producers, who were calling me several times a day, wanting an answer.

"We'll do the New York trip on one condition…" Ed finally said.

I interrupted him and explained that the show and producers had already agreed to several of our conditions. Ed kept pressing, however.

"Okay, but Lois won't agree to go unless they also pay the travel expenses for a nanny. The thought of wrangling five children in New York City in our state of mind is more than we feel like we can handle."

When I informed Jamie and Alexandra, they were disappointed and told me the network executive who'd approved covering the entire family's travel expenses had been hedging from the beginning, and it was unlikely he would agree to spend another cent. The Smarts weren't willing to cave, and things remained in limbo for a couple of days before Jamie called and informed me that John Walsh had agreed to personally cover the travel expenses for the nanny.

I didn't know it at the time, but in addition to working with the producers, preparing Ed and Lois for the interview, and coordinating travel on the ground, my responsibilities would entail shepherding and helping to entertain all five of Elizabeth's siblings. This came as a surprise and, while the experience would have its share of challenges, I would grow fond of the Smart children.

Riding in a large van on the way to 30 Rockefeller Plaza, I sit in the middle row between Ed and Lois and the kids.

Elizabeth's siblings are sizing me up. They ask me several questions regarding where I live, what I do, and if I have seen the latest Spiderman movie. As I've interacted with them periodically while working at their home, or when they've come to the church, we've established some rapport, but the tone has always been much more formal.

Once we arrive in the green room, Ed and Lois are whisked away to get their makeup done, and the fun begins.

"If you place a Big Red wrapper on your skin, it will burn. Wanna try it?" Edward Junior smirks as he raises his hand and jumps up and down, trying to get me to take the gum wrapper. The eight-year-old is gregarious, has an endless supply of energy, and seems to view me as a novelty.

Edward Junior's older brother, Andrew (age twelve); his sister Mary Katherine (ten); and their baby brother, William (three), soon join in the gum wrapper dare while Charles, the oldest (sixteen), rolls his eyes and fidgets with a wristband of frayed blue ribbons and heart-shaped beads he wears on his left wrist in homage to Elizabeth. Andrew tries to tackle me, William grabs my left leg, and Mary Katherine pushes me from behind. While I am trying to respond and maintain a modicum of decorum, Edward Junior takes the Big Red wrapper and presses it hard against my forehead. I feel a shooting pain, akin to someone pouring bleach on my skin. I gently but hurriedly push the children aside, remove the wrapper, rub my head vigorously, and grab a bottle of water.

When Ed and Lois return to the green room, they are layered with more makeup than a mortician applies to a corpse, and I have a large crimson welt on my forehead. Charles tells his parents what has transpired, and they are both apologetic and a little angry. Their nerves in light of the impending interview seem to be coming to the surface as they rebuke Edward Junior. I walk over to Ed and Lois and redirect them back to the moment.

"It's okay. I'm fine. Don't worry about it. Just take a few deep breaths. They'll be coming to get you any minute. Let's focus on the interview." I smile, lower my voice, and speak slowly. It's a technique I observed

MSNBC's Ashleigh Banfield employ several months ago when Ed and Lois expressed frustration with some of her interview questions when the four of us spoke after an interview. This approach seems to work now and helps to temper some of the anxiety in the final moments before they walk onto the set.

Sharing a bond with John Walsh as fellow parents of abducted children helps the interview to be genuine and emotional. This feeling spills over to the studio audience, who are all wearing blue ribbons in Elizabeth's honor. More than a few people cry. The show's segments are well produced, and when it airs a couple of weeks later, the Smarts will be happy with the result.

After taping *The John Walsh Show*, we return to the hotel. That evening Lois and the nanny, who is also her best friend, Cheryl, leave to go shopping. It catches me off guard, but in the end, Ed and I are okay with them going, and try to reframe the situation as a unique opportunity.

Thankfully, I'm familiar with the subway system from visiting New York several times during my teenage years, as well as with my wife on business trips, so Ed and I take the kids to see the city—from Central Park to the Statue of Liberty. We trade off carrying William on our shoulders. He grabs and twists the tops of my ears, and by the end of the night, my ears are raw and red, matching the wrapper welt on my forehead.

The next day, during our adventures, the kids discover Canal Street, and it quickly becomes their favorite place in New York City. They shop for trinkets, try to find bootleg DVDs of movies they want to see, and purchase additional packs of Big Red. We spend hours walking through the shops and stopping for dim sum.

At one point, I find myself deep in conversation with Charles. He is ambitious and wise beyond his years. Charles wants to know how I got into public relations and what advice I have for him as far as careers and classes go. I tell him to focus on writing, and to take debate. Andrew and Edward Junior, who are eavesdropping, want to know why. I explain that communications skills are applicable to any career and will make them better at whatever profession they choose. Mary Katherine tugs on my pant leg to get my attention and then tells me about her teacher, how she is learning cursive, and how much she loves art.

On that trip, I develop a real love for the Smart children. They are curious, thoughtful, funny, and occasionally rambunctious.

I also gain a new understanding of and appreciation for Lois. A little change of scenery has allowed both Ed and I to see what a heavy toll losing her oldest daughter has taken on her. They say a mother's love is endless. I'm witnessing that this also can be true of her grief. Not only has Lois lost Elizabeth, but Mary Katherine experienced her own trauma the night of the abduction, causing a level of bereavement most young mothers will never comprehend. It's incredibly gratifying to watch her escape with Cheryl and find a small amount of the solace and rejuvenation she has been so desperately craving.

A couple of months later, on another trip to New York, the first question the kids ask when the plane touches down at JFK is, "When can we take the subway to Canal Street?" It's after 11 p.m. and a car is scheduled to pick up Ed, Lois, and me at 4:45 a.m. for an interview on *The Early Show*.

"Tomorrow," I tell them. "We'll go tomorrow. I promise."

I smile and giggle. There is something magical about reconnecting with Elizabeth's siblings in the Big Apple.

As we pull up to the hotel in a red cargo van, I notice a couple of homeless people lying in blankets on the sidewalk. The Mayflower Hotel at Central Park West, between 61st and 62nd Streets, is drab and pedestrian on the outside. There is sloppy patchwork across its eighteen-story façade, attempting to cover areas where neoclassical ornamentation has been removed. Inside the lobby, the carpet and furniture are coarse and heavily worn. As we approach the front desk, I notice a few motley characters who don't quite look like they belong, walking toward the exit.

The check-in process is long and laborious. It's as if the hotel hasn't updated anything, decor or technology, since the late 1970s. The hotel manager finally hands me a pair of metal keys affixed to a tacky plastic ornament.

The room is even worse than the lobby. It reeks of tobacco, and the antiquated tan polyester bedspread has more than a dozen holes from cigarette burns. I quickly brush my teeth, climb into the bed, turn off the lights, and try to reassure myself that I can endure this for just one night. After all, I slept in worse rooms while backpacking through Europe. That's when Ed calls to inform me that Lois, Cheryl, and the kids are waiting in the lobby.

"Chris, she refuses to stay here. You have to do something."

I get on the line with the ABC network's travel department. The hosts of *The View*, the popular ABC talk show started by Barbara Walters, will be interviewing the Smarts after *The Early Show*. The producers of *The View* are the ones who booked and paid for the rooms. I explain the issue with the hotel, and the travel agent informs me that the Rockefeller tree lighting ceremony was that evening, and every hotel in the city is booked solid. He examines several options before explaining that the best he can do is secure something the following night.

I plead. I ask if anyone can pull some strings. He apologizes and tells me that no one is going to be able to find a room. I call and wake up the producer I've been working with from *The View*. While he's making some calls, I open my computer and try several travel sites. Neither of us can find anything in the city. The producer is initially apologetic but then, with some East Coast edge, essentially tells me that the Smarts need to "suck it up." I tell him this outcome is not going to be well received, and it's possible the Smarts might not do the interview with *The View* as a result of the ordeal. He becomes angry and starts yelling at me.

I explain the predicament with the rooms to Ed over the phone and can hear him repeating my words to Lois. Then Ed seems to cover the receiver, because I can't make out their conversation. After about thirty seconds, Ed asks if I can come to the lobby.

I walk down the hall and he pulls me aside.

"Chris, I tried. Lois won't go back in the room. She is staying in the lobby until you find something. I'm really sorry. If it was up to me, I would just sleep in that icky room for one night."

Before he can finish, Lois arrives and tells me she doesn't feel comfortable staying here, especially with the children. The hotel manager overhears the conversation and intercedes. He and Lois proceed to bicker. I step away. I'm running out of options.

I call the producer of *The Early Show*, Audrey Wood, a fellow member of The Church of Jesus Christ of Latter-day Saints, whom I have worked with several times since Elizabeth's abduction. Audrey is incredibly kind and hospitable despite being awakened a couple of hours before she has to get up for work. She jokes that if she can't find a solution, everyone is welcome to crash at her apartment.

While I've been talking with Audrey, the hotel manager, who is offended by Lois' complaints, has been invading my personal space, inching closer and closer as I step backward. When I hang up, he launches into a tirade. I periodically nod, but my eyes glaze over and I don't hear anything he is saying. After I endure his lecture for several minutes, Audrey finally calls back.

"You're not going to believe this. I pinged one of the higher-ups at CBS, who called in a favor. Not only did he get you rooms, but *suites* at the Parker Meridien, and *you can stay for a few days.* The car service will pick you up in ten minutes."

Despite our obvious change of plans, the hotel manager continues to spew his wrath, yelling at me and even walking alongside the minivan as we depart. By the time the family and I check into the Parker Meridien, it's almost 2:30 a.m. I sleep for what feels like five minutes when my alarm blares and the phone rings with a wake-up call.

A short time later, we walk into CBS' Plaza Studio on Fifth Avenue and 59th Street. I hug Audrey as she greets us in the green room. The interview goes off without a hitch. It's unlikely anyone knows that Ed and Lois haven't slept more than two hours. The dark circles under their eyes are covered by makeup, but I know those circles have been there since Elizabeth went missing.

When we return to the Parker Meridien, Ed and I are exhausted, but there's no time for naps. The kids are waiting, eager to catch the next subway to Canal Street.

CHAPTER 28

The Roadshow

Before Broadway welcomed *The Book of Mormon* musical, there were *actual* Mormon musicals, called roadshows. These were competitions among local congregations, held every few years, in which church members would create and perform somewhat original productions. The roadshows would travel from church to church, performing multiple times over a two-night community event, before independent judges would crown a winner.

The primary difference—and there were many—between the real Mormon musicals and the Broadway sensation is that the former couldn't incorporate any religious material. This was so they would appeal to a broad audience of both church members and those not of the faith.

Although the objective of the roadshows was for people to come together as a community and have fun, the competition and pressure were fierce. This was partially because winning the contest was akin to capturing a Tony, at least for some members of the East Millcreek North Stake, especially the young wannabe thespians.

The productions, which were highly anticipated by some and equally despised by others, were basically dramatic works in which campy musical theater met "Weird Al" Yankovic. It was not uncommon for one of the actors, or even the entire production, to be so bad that the show was good. Think of it like "Springtime for Hitler in Germany" from *The Producers*, only more politically correct.

My ward had never won a roadshow crown. We'd even been ridiculed by the other congregations more than once over the years. This underdog status might have fueled the creative energy and enthusiasm that began building one evening when my mom and a few neighbors were hanging out, drinking Tab, and eating chocolate chip cookies. Something sparked an impromptu brainstorming session, even though it was several months before the local roadshow committee would announce the competition's theme, dates, and details.

These creative collaborations, which often went late into the night, continued for weeks. My mom, who became one of the lead directors, and several of the other ward members were obsessed with bringing to life new ideas, characters, and even songs. They filled the pages of multiple notebooks with these creations.

Their roadshow concept revolved around a teenager whose mother was constantly nagging him to avoid junk food and eat healthier. In the first scene, the boy falls asleep and escapes to a magical world, where he is met by a larger-than-life vending machine. Each time he pulls the lever, a different giant candy bar comes out, along with a host of singing and dancing versions of each sweet treat.

The committee created songs such as "Hershey Bar" (adapted from "Wunderbar," from the musical *Kiss Me, Kate*), "Old Soft Chew" (adapted from Dinah Shore and Tony Martin's "The Old Soft Shoe"), "Snicker Place" (adapted from "Everybody's Got a Laughing Place" in Disney's *Song of the South*), and "Baby Ruth" (adapted from Harry Akst and Benny Davis' "Baby Face").

During the musical numbers, the teenager ate the candy while a giant balloon underneath his nightshirt inflated, getting bigger and bigger until it popped just as the finale began. At that moment, the ensemble appeared, dressed as fruits and vegetables, singing about being healthy. The lyrics included "If you carrot all, if you are big or small..." adapted from "I Ain't Down Yet" from *The Unsinkable Molly Brown*.

On a cold Tuesday night several months after the first brainstorming session, the ward cultural hall was a beehive of activity. Echoing through the church building was an odd symphony of hammering, scissors clanking, kids singing off-key, and my mom and her committee of directors barking out orders.

UNEXPECTED

A group of silver-haired women, led by Vaunna Paxton, cut fabric and sewed and assembled costumes on a long table at the back of the gym. My father stepped away from the chaos to take a few measurements. He then walked down onto the gym floor, dodged some boys playing basketball, eyed the stage, and connected his thumb and forefinger on one hand to the thumb and forefinger of the other to form a square. He held up the makeshift viewfinder, squinted, and proceeded to make a few rudimentary sketches of the giant vending machine.

My dad led the scenery committee, which was made up of a handful of men who were gathered at the other corner of the room. The men would step outside periodically to cut two-by-fours and sheets of particleboard using a power saw, then return to organize, assemble, and paint the background scenery and props with primer.

The "lucky" few who had been cast as leads worked on the stage. The remaining adults and kids were organized into lines, according to their roles, on one side of the gym.

Chad and I were goofing off, ignoring Tresa, the director who was responsible for the ten- and eleven-year-old boys. Despite being distracted, we heard the familiar crinkling sound of a wrapper and turned to see Tresa pulling an Oh Henry! candy bar out of her purse. She had our attention.

"In order to embody the role, you need to know everything about an Oh Henry!—including how good it tastes." Tresa smiled, looking at our group of boys, who instantly became attentive. She handed each of us an Oh Henry! bar. As I tore the wrapper off, I noticed that the corresponding candy bars for each of the other groups were also being passed out.

Tresa introduced us to the Oh Henry! bar lyrics, an adapted version of Fred Murray and R. P. Weston's "I'm Henry VIII, I Am" made popular by Herman's Hermits. Her voice projected a mix of enthusiasm with a dose of sarcasm, which resonated well with my friends and me.

We're Oh Henry the eight we are
Oh Henry the eight great candy bars
We are peanuts, caramel, and fudge galore
We've been rolled in chocolate, seven times before
And everyone wants an Oh Henry
You wouldn't want a Snickers or a Mars
No way!

166

We're the eight great bars Oh Henry
Oh Henry's the greatest candy bar

Despite her best effort to make the song sound cool, we still rolled our eyes as Tresa finished singing. Then she demonstrated the choreography that would accompany our number.

While many kids our age might have been paralyzed by the prospect of performing on stage in front of hundreds of adults dressed as a candy bar, my peers and I, while slightly nervous, were largely unconcerned. In The Church of Jesus Christ of Latter-day Saints, most kids are brought up performing in various capacities. Many families start their children on an instrument. Not all kids continue to play through childhood (sorry Mom), but they usually have the opportunity to learn. Even those who aren't musically inclined or have parents who can't endure haranguing kids to practice, aren't left out.

Beginning at the age of three, children attend Primary, which is held after sacrament meeting, the main congregational worship service, and features classes for each age group, as well as an hour of singing time and group lessons about Christ, the Bible, and the Book of Mormon. This often involves learning from a teacher as well as from other children.

Each child is assigned to speak, usually a couple of times a year, presenting a two-minute talk to the larger group, which is divided by age into junior and senior Primaries. The entire Primary also presents a yearly program for the adult congregation during sacrament meeting. This hour-long program features each child speaking, usually in a small part, and everyone singing, with many kids also playing music.

By the time I graduated from Primary, at twelve years old, I had spoken dozens of times in front of my peers, as well as to large groups of adults, so getting up in front of an audience didn't seem too intimidating. For some kids, performing was second nature. Others who were more introverted didn't relish it but found it doable.

As the weeks of rehearsals began to wind down, the directors scheduled late-night sessions to put the finishing touches on their masterpiece. We felt at times during this period as if nothing else mattered beyond the success of our roadshow.

On the first night of performances, my mom and I were backstage just minutes before the curtain opened. She was pacing nervously, then peeked into the crowd and grabbed my shoulder.

"Christopher, do you see who is in the fourth row, third seat?"

I parted the curtains and looked into the audience. I noticed a balding man in a crimson sweater who looked vaguely familiar. But before I could respond, one of the other directors interrupted and we were ushered offstage.

My mom said something, but I couldn't make it out.

"Mr. Goodbar, bring me a dream. Make it the sweetest that I've ever seen..."

A group of thirtysomething women dressed in the signature yellow, brown, and red wrapper of the iconic chocolate peanut treat had taken the stage and were singing in harmony an adaptation of Pat Ballard's "Mr. Sandman," which was made famous by the Chordettes.

Once the production started, I couldn't get my mom's attention, so I went back to the makeshift green room and waited for the Oh Henrys to be called.

The judges, who were from outside our stake, reviewed each production only once. Roadshows were always a traveling act that moved from church to church—talent, scenery, props, and all. Every ward performed its musical at each building, and the judges would be at only one church, the location of which was supposed to be a tightly held secret; however, it always seemed to get leaked.

Right on cue as the show was beginning, one of the directors learned that the judges were at the S-curve church, which was a few miles to the south of us, situated between a set of windy roads that crossed Mill Creek Stream. The first performance of our roadshow would be at our church building, to an audience made up largely of our own ward members. It was a warm-up. The next one would be for all the marbles.

When the Oh Henrys were called, I wasn't necessarily nervous about performing in front of several hundred people, as I've mentioned, but I was worried about my complete inability to do any of the dance steps in the last section of choreography.

My rhythm at the end of the song was so bad, it elicited a friendly laugh from the audience. I felt a twinge of embarrassment that quickly disappeared—what lingered was my knowledge that musical theater was not my thing.

Fortunately, the finale didn't have any dance moves. All I had to do was stand on stage and sing a few lines dressed as a giant celery stick.

At the end of our debut performance, the audience stood and cheered loudly. There was little time for celebration. My father and his stagehands already had begun disassembling the scenery during the ovation. They quickly loaded it into four pickup trucks that were waiting in the parking lot. Teenagers grabbed costumes and props and carried them to a large van. The directors helped the cast get into designated cars that were numbered and parked in formation, with assigned drivers. There was a forty-five-minute limit between performances; getting to the next performance in time required the focus and precision akin to an Indy 500 pitstop.

When we arrived at the S-curve church, the doors opened and I glimpsed the keys of an upright piano shining unevenly in the light of the dimly lit cultural hall. The accompanist from our roadshow walked through the doors, unpacked her white canvas tote bag, and began to organize her sheet music.

Once settled, she started her warm-up routine, playing the first number by dancing her fingers across the keys without pressing them down, never making a sound.

Suddenly, a piercing shriek interrupted a man who was doing a ventriloquist routine to entertain the crowd between roadshows. The accompanist, who had screamed, stormed out of the gym as the audience strained to see what had happened.

"The piano keys have been frosted with several layers of Vaseline."

The accompanist was livid as she found one of the directors and informed them of the prank. We had about five minutes until showtime. If the roadshow started late, we might lose points. At a minimum, a delay would make a bad impression on the judges.

A couple of stagehands grabbed rags and feverishly worked to remove the sticky petroleum jelly from the piano keys. When they had removed most of it, a high-pitched bell rang, marking a two-minute warning. The accompanist tried to resume her intro but to no avail; several of the keys wouldn't stop sticking.

With literally seconds to spare, a couple of teenagers came bolting into the cultural hall, pushing another piano they had found in the primary room on the opposite side of the church.

The accompanist quickly reset and struck the first key. The candy bars lined up, and our roadshow went off without another hitch.

At the curtain call, we received an ovation that surpassed the energy of the one at our home ward. Before packing into cars, the directors high-fived everyone.

We were quite the circus as we packed up and then pulled into town (two more churches) that night. Since the judging was over, the cast and crew were much more relaxed and able to have fun. The production hit its stride.

By the end of the evening, several of the younger children fell asleep after returning to the green room following their numbers. While most of the cast members were experiencing a similar fatigue, our directors were on top of the world. They were euphoric and could smell victory, like a politician late on election night cautiously celebrating when the returns look good.

This confidence carried over to the second night of roadshows. On this night, the performances took place at one ward house, so the cast and crew from each congregation could see the productions of their fellow competitors. After the final performance, the judges would announce the winner.

A ward that had won the crown two out of the previous three times went first. They were the self-proclaimed favorites.

Right before they started, a man in a white button-down shirt tapped my mom's shoulder. She got up and was escorted along with another woman to an empty classroom. The door shut, and we were left wondering what was transpiring. While we didn't know exactly what was going on, we had a good idea within minutes of the first roadshow's opening number.

Their production was about…a teenage boy with a nagging mom. He had a dream about…candy bars. It was uncanny. Not a carbon copy of our roadshow but close. The biggest differences were the costumes, the songs, the set, and some of the candy bars they used. About halfway through the show, Tresa yelled, "Bring out the Oh Henrys! Or is it time for the Snickers?"

While several people in the audience looked back, Tresa stood resolutely unapologetic for her outburst.

Toward the end of the show, the door to the classroom opened and my mom appeared. I followed her and the other directors as they rushed into the hall.

Once the involved parties were behind closed doors with the judges, my mom and the other ward's director had been asked about the similarities between their two shows. The other director spoke first and implied that our ward had cheated.

In the hall, a growing group of my ward's directors and cast moved closer to my mom as she tried to maintain a whisper.

"I couldn't believe what I was hearing. The judges asked us a series of questions. I was able to explain the inspiration for every single number. The other woman fumbled through one or two answers, then finally apologized, explaining that they never meant for the productions to be so similar. They were disqualified."

My mom's body language was almost more animated than her face. The group hung on her every word.

"Although the judges didn't say it, I'm relatively sure we won."

Hot on the heels of this development was our call to take the stage.

In the weeks to come, our cast would piece together what had occurred. Right before the theme was announced, one of our directors' teenage daughters had bragged to her friend in the rival ward about our roadshow. Word traveled fast through the rumor mill, and some of the teenagers who'd seen parts of our initial rehearsals relayed some ideas and intel to their ward.

Minutes before our final performance, my mom went backstage and gave the cast and crew a pep talk.

"They copied parts of our roadshow and then accused us of cheating. The best way to settle the score is to show them who's king. Let's put on the best show ever."

There were shouts and loud applause from the cast and crew. A few minutes later, when the curtain rose, the energy was infectious. My ward, in our humble opinion, put on what had to be one of the best performances in roadshow history.

By the end, most of the members of the rival ward had left. The audience, made up of the rest of our competitors, stood and applauded.

Backstage we hugged, gave high fives, and even did a chest bump or two. Although none of us would ever come close to performing on any type of reputable stage, we got a small taste of the adrenaline that must fuel professional thespians.

A few hours later, after all the other roadshows had performed, suspense hung in the air. We could hear the chatter. The entire audience already knew the result. The judges came to the mic and made their announcement:

"First place goes to...the East Millcreek Third Ward for their roadshow *Sweet Dreams.*"

We returned to the stage, victorious. It was a scene reminiscent of the Raiders winning the Super Bowl, but with more hugging and jumping up and down in a circle. A few minutes into our celebration, I heard a familiar voice behind me, and someone patted me on the back.

"Nice job, Chris. Congratulations."

I turned around.

"You haven't been playing basketball much, so I thought I better come and check on you, to make sure you are okay."

It took a minute for things to set in. The man my mom had pointed to before the first performance was Baker. He was barely recognizable—freshly shaven and neatly dressed.

I shook his hand and muttered, "Thanks so much for coming." It was the only thing I could think to say.

That production was the first of three straight roadshow titles for the East Millcreek Third Ward. Our streak was snapped only by the roadshow program itself. The drama surrounding these competitions only escalated over the years and throughout the church. Eventually, the leaders at the headquarters of The Church of Jesus Christ of Latter-day Saints found the un-Christian-like behavior surrounding roadshows to be off-putting and incongruous with church principles. They canceled the tradition, and more than twenty years later, it still hasn't been revived.

CHAPTER 29

The Epiphany

Sitting next to Laura in sacrament meeting on a Sunday in early October 2002, I am about to doze off when my phone begins vibrating. Ed's name appears on the screen. I step outside the pew, sidestep a few people in the chapel, and walk into the foyer.

"Are you at church?" Ed asks. "I need to update you on a development, but it can wait until after the three-hour block of meetings."

From Ed's voice, it doesn't sound like it's anything of significant consequence. At the same time, the ward member who is speaking from the pulpit (because there are no professional clergy, ward members take turns preparing and delivering talks each week) isn't keeping my attention, so this is a good excuse to get a hall pass. I tell Ed it's fine and to go ahead.

"Chris, Mary Katherine knows who kidnapped Elizabeth."

Caught off guard by this earth-shattering information, I begin pacing anxiously past the foyer and into the hallway, listening to Ed explain the events from the prior evening.

"She was awake when we came home from the temple last night and told us it was this homeless man Lois met downtown, who worked on the roof one afternoon. I'm surprised Mary Katherine could remember him at all."

That Saturday evening, Mary Katherine had been in her room, reading the *Guinness Book of World Records*. For months she had been trying to match in her mind the voice of the abductor with someone she had previously met. As she was reading a passage about the world's strongest woman, for some inexplicable reason, the name "Immanuel" suddenly popped into her head.

During the four months since Elizabeth's disappearance, the Smarts have been following law enforcement's recommendations, which dictate not putting any pressure on Mary Katherine, or even asking her questions about the abductor. Investigators told Ed and Lois that if they followed their advice, it was likely that Mary Katherine would eventually remember the man who'd been in the room that night.

Surprisingly, the police don't seem interested in Mary Katherine's revelation.

Ed had called the Salt Lake City Police Department just before me and was told they would get back to him.

Later that Sunday afternoon, Ed follows up with the police multiple times. First, they tell him that someone will call him on Monday. When Ed insists they do something immediately, they tell him to bring Mary Katherine to the station the next morning.

Each time Ed calls to update me on the progress with the police department, his confidence level regarding Mary Katherine's recollection seems to diminish. In only a few hours, what had first been "Mary Katherine knows" devolves into "Mary Katherine thinks she might know." And later, Ed explains that "Lois isn't sure about what Mary Katherine is saying, but we should still look into this."

Over the next several days, the Salt Lake City Police Department seems incurious about Mary Katherine's epiphany. They do work with Elizabeth's brothers, Charles and Andrew, to try to create sketches of Immanuel, but the boys didn't spend much time with him. Ed complains that the two renditions look nothing like the man he had spent more time with than anyone in the family. When he insists they try again, working with him to create a sketch, the police don't even use their own staff artist. Ironically, a woman shows up unsolicited at the station that day, wanting to audition to be a sketch artist, and despite her having no police or forensics experience, they bring her in to work with Ed.

While Ed and I envision holding a joint press conference that week to release the sketch and ask the public to help find Immanuel, the police department has other plans. According to Tom's book, when Ed approached Cory Lyman, commander of the police unit investigating

Elizabeth's abduction, about when they would be going public with the Immanuel info, Ed was told, "Probably never." Cory explained that this was because investigators didn't have much to go on and the name was an alias. This marked the commencement of a long tug of war between Ed and Lois and the police.

The situation is complicated, because Ed and Lois have differing perspectives on the situation and what course of action we should pursue. Much like her family, Lois leans toward trusting authority, a common notion in Latter-day Saint culture. Like his siblings, who believe in questioning everything, Ed feels they should either push the police to release the information or do it themselves. This dichotomy creates paralysis within the Smarts' inner circle, and with each passing day, everyone's frustration mounts.

Initially, the police drag their feet, saying they need more time to investigate and follow up on leads surrounding Immanuel. As the weeks languish, law enforcement's response becomes more passive-aggressive. To our surprise, they reiterate their belief that Richard Ricci is still the perpetrator and inform the Smarts that they haven't found anything of significance surrounding Immanuel. Yet they ask the family to refrain from saying anything public because they are "still working on it."

This impasse creates a predicament when Jane Clayson and the *48 Hours* team come to Salt Lake City to begin shooting their prime-time special. It is generally my protocol to avoid giving new information or breaking news exclusively to one media source. While the benefactor would usually do the story justice, their competitors would be more likely to dismiss the development or be critical of the news in *their* coverage. Giving one organization an exclusive is never perceived favorably by the other media because it often appears that the family or its representatives are playing favorites.

As a result, in the first few days of working with the family, I established an order with the morning shows: The Smarts would go live with whichever media source was next in line—no varying regardless of any new developments. The family also pre-taped interviews with the two networks that didn't get to go live, and all three shows usually ran their interviews with the Smarts at the same time. Although many people watching at home don't register the importance of the chyron on the screen saying "live" during an interview, the distinction is a huge deal for news executives and network bosses.

I explain my concerns to Ed about the layers of issues that could arise if we give *48 Hours* the Immanuel information exclusively. It could mean relinquishing control of the story and the timing for announcing the new development.

Lois is unsure about releasing the information in the first place, so we decide to stay the course as though Mary Katherine *hasn't* remembered the possible identity of the abductor, and at the same time prepare for questions so that our answers broaden the possibilities beyond Richard Ricci.

The *48 Hours* issue represents a crossroads of two non-negotiable rules the family established in the early days of working with the media (no interviews at the Smart residence and no interviews with Elizabeth's siblings), which I'd been telling journalists from the start would never happen.

When Ed informs me that Lois has given Jane the okay to bring a camera crew to the house, I ask him how we will explain this to the other media. He brings this to Lois' attention, and they come to a compromise: Jane can film and conduct interviews with Ed and law enforcement in the backyard but not inside.

When I arrive at the Smart home later that day, Jane is talking casually with Cory Lyman. I am glad it is Cory and not Detective Don Bell, who seems to have an agenda and goes out of his way to try to discredit anyone or anything that doesn't align with his views.

I like Cory. He is affable, down to earth, and the older stepbrother of a girl I knew in elementary school. Instead of six degrees of separation, it's more like two degrees for Latter-day Saints in Salt Lake City. The church makes for a small world in which everyone seems to know everyone, via some connection or another.

Even before Cory goes on camera, the conversation about the case revolves around Ricci. Cory's comments are even more pointed than what law enforcement has said in the past, and it seems like the police department has tightened its messaging about the case.

Jane interviews Ed next. Her initial questions for him are highly focused on the Ricci theory. At one point, I interrupt and pull her aside.

"Jane, you need to know that there are many people in the family and law enforcement who don't believe Ricci was involved at all. The police seem to be zeroing in on him more than ever now that he is dead. Look at all the options, including those outside of Ricci."

Jane is annoyed and gives me a disbelieving look. I am the dreaded flack (a derogatory term journalists sometimes use to describe public relations professionals) who is making her job more difficult. She tells me that she trusts what the police are telling her but will try to keep an open mind.

After Ed's interview, Jane does a few standups. This is where a reporter appears in front of the camera on scene to introduce a story or segment. In one of the standups, Jane points over her shoulder and explains how Ricci stole property from a neighbor who was just "a stone's throw away."

I interrupt and ask Jane if she knows that the neighbor's house is actually down a large hill and three streets over, nearly a mile away. Jane tells me she has been by the neighbor's house and it's indeed a stone's throw away. I argue that by pointing to the house next door and saying "a stone's throw," she is implying that the house Ricci stole from is adjacent to the Smarts'. I know this detail isn't the most significant, and yet I'm highly sensitive to anything that points undue attention to Ricci.

The next day I receive a surprise as I'm driving to a downtown hotel, where crews have created a makeshift living room set for Ed and Lois to do a formal interview with Jane. My phone buzzes and it's Ed.

"Chris, I'm going to apologize before I even tell you this—you're not going to like it…Lois has agreed to let Jane interview the children. I know this goes against the rules we established, but I don't know what else to do."

Ed explains that to maintain the children's privacy, *48 Hours* is going to blur out their faces and possibly disguise their voices. They also have agreed not to ask Mary Katherine anything about what she witnessed when Elizabeth was abducted.

Sitting in my car outside the hotel, I am disgusted. I feel powerless and momentarily contemplate going back home and skipping the interview, because I wonder if what I do is respected and appreciated by Ed and Lois. The reason for having a publicist is so that you don't get pressured into doing things.

Walking in late, I enter the room as Jane runs frantically in the other direction. Ed and Lois are busy attending to one of the children. The culprit? Projectile vomit. While crews were getting the children settled next to each other in chairs, Jane was making small talk with three-year-old William when he became violently ill and promptly threw up all over her.

"Karma's a..." Ed quips under his breath, raising his eyebrows and looking in my direction, mere seconds before Jane reemerges in fresh clothing. I can't help but laugh.

Once Jane is back in the saddle and William has consumed a Sprite, the interviews begin. The children are articulate and charming. Edward Junior is in his element, answering questions like a child movie star at a press junket for a new film.

Charles drives the other children home after an hour of questions from Jane. Then Ed and Lois begin their interview. This taping takes several hours, and I am relieved when it's over. Being constantly reminded of the genesis of the special and how it has devolved takes a toll. I try to be gracious and bite my tongue, thanking Jane and the *48 Hours* crew as we leave.

The roller coaster of the debate regarding whether or not to release the sketch of Immanuel continues long after the interview, hitting a fever pitch in early December. Tom has been visiting Lois almost every day for two weeks, making the case for why it is essential to go public with the Immanuel news. Lois is incredibly strong-willed and isn't going to let Tom's pressure influence her decision. And yet when Tom proposes a reasonable compromise, Lois bites.

Tom's idea is for Ed and Lois to talk with John Walsh regarding the sketch and agree in advance to follow whatever counsel he provides. During our recent time in New York, interviewing with *The Early Show* and *The View* a week prior, John Walsh's producers contacted me. They wanted the Smarts to fly back ten days later to tape a year-end episode of his daytime talk show. Despite the rigors of the travel, we agree.

I call John and, without disclosing anything regarding Mary Katherine's epiphany, explain that the Smarts want to have a private conversation with him after taping the show. I ask if he would be willing to remove his journalist hat and talk to them as a father of a missing child, with full confidentiality. He agrees.

A few days later, we travel to New York for *The John Walsh Show* taping, which is a reunion of his top guests and stories from the first year of the program. John and his guest cohost, Paula Zahn, spend a disproportionate amount of time interviewing Ed and Lois and talking about

Elizabeth's abduction. Once the taping is complete, John welcomes us into his dressing room and shuts the door.

I reiterate what I said on the phone about confidentiality and how the Smarts might never go public with what they are about to share, but that they need his objective counsel. John, who is wearing a black mock turtleneck, a dark textured blazer, light gray wool slacks, and black loafers, reassures us that we can trust him.

When Ed tells John about Mary Katherine's epiphany, he nearly jumps out of his chair.

"This is *more* than significant; it's the most important lead *yet*. Ed and Lois, you owe it to your other children to find this man and bring him to justice. I am sorry to say that not even a religious cult would keep Elizabeth alive this long, but for the sake of your other kids, you need to go public to get answers."

John tells us that his track record of catching "bad guys" rivals that of any law enforcement agency, and he cites at least a dozen cases that *America's Most Wanted* helped solve, in which local police departments had made mistakes. He stresses that the police are doing their best but are not well paid, have limited resources, and deal with extreme stress and trauma.

Because it is the middle of December, six months after Elizabeth disappeared, I recommend waiting until the first week of January to stage a press conference, so the news doesn't get lost in the middle of holiday celebrations. John says he will try to fly to Salt Lake City for the announcement, but if he can't, *America's Most Wanted* will still give the new development lots of airtime.

After the meeting, Ed and Lois feel a sense of relief, having come to a decision that they both feel good about. Their bigger concern now is Christmas. The prospect of not having Elizabeth home looms large and feels like a heavy burden. I tell Ed I won't bother him for the next two weeks unless something significant arises, and I will handle the miscellaneous media requests. He agrees, and we plan to get together on January 2 to finalize details and prepare for the press conference.

CHAPTER 30

Happy Holidays

"Happy Thanksgiving, neighbor."

My father was speaking to someone, but I couldn't figure out whom. Craning my head around the back of our red Subaru hatchback, I tried to catch a glimpse but to no avail. A large contingent of my dad's extended family was gathering at our home for Thanksgiving, and I was helping him unload some folding chairs we had borrowed from the church.

When I stepped out of the car, the old man looked up and stared at us for what felt like several minutes. Baker either was caught off guard by my father's greeting or was suspicious, since the two of them had such an acrimonious relationship.

"I *guess.*" Baker smirked and then hesitated. "Happy Thanksgiving... to you too."

Trying to make small talk, my father asked if Vaunna was cooking dinner. Baker said she was out of town and he was alone for the holiday.

"I'm going to get a burger. I ain't much of a Thanksgiving person."

Baker looked in the other direction, then staggered across the lawn without making eye contact and opened the door to his beat-up car.

"Why don't you join us?" my father offered. "We have plenty of food."

He stepped onto Baker's lawn and motioned with his hand toward our front door. I couldn't believe what I was seeing. Members of my family didn't speak with Baker, let alone stand on his lawn, unless there was some type of conflict. Now my dad was inviting him to dinner. And not just any dinner—Thanksgiving dinner.

The old man sat down in his car and closed his dented door, which squeaked loudly. He tried to start the engine.

"Thanks," he said. "That's very nice of you, but I prefer a burger."

How rude. My dad really put himself out there, and the old man prefers a burger over my mom's cooking?

"I insist," my father countered. "You shouldn't be alone on Thanksgiving. We would love to have you."

My father stepped a few feet closer to Baker's car. He smiled, with the expression and body language of someone trying to convince a pit bull he was trustworthy.

For years I had thought of Baker as the consummate enemy. He was someone not just to ignore and avoid but to downright detest. *Why is my father persisting?* I wondered.

Wrestling with the thought for a minute, I started to realize what people meant when they spoke about the spirit of the holidays. My father was putting aside his differences and, in the spirit of Thanksgiving, genuinely reaching out to serve our neighbor.

"That's kind of you," Baker said. "Thank you…but really, I'm good with a burger."

He rolled up the driver's side window. The car sputtered and squealed. He revved the engine a few times, and a plume of exhaust spilled out of the tailpipe. The car with a thousand dents backfired, and Baker drove away slowly.

As I was grabbing the last folding chair from the Subaru about fifteen minutes later, I witnessed Baker's return. He waited in his car for a long time until I went inside my house.

From the front window, I watched him survey the landscape one last time from the driver's seat before exiting and walking briskly to his front door. His actions seemed to underscore his abiding desire to be left alone.

The aroma from a cornucopia of Thanksgiving fare was so thick in my home, you could almost see it hovering near the ceiling. My mother was putting the finishing touches on our feast as my father began to carve the turkey.

He put the first few pieces of the steaming white meat on one of our brown floral-patterned ceramic dinner plates, then spooned on potatoes, yams, green beans, and stuffing. Once the plate was overflowing with holiday fare, my father summoned me.

"Can you do something for me?"

From the tone, I knew it was not a question but a command, and before I could answer, he handed me the plate.

"Take this over to Baker."

I was stunned. I took a step back and hesitated.

"To Baker? Really, are you sure? Shouldn't someone else go with me?"

My mouth watered. I was temporarily distracted as I looked down at the steam rising from the mountain of hot spuds, complete with turkey gravy dripping down and immersing the meat, next to my grandmother's beloved stuffing, which was green from a copious amount of sage.

"No, just take it over, ring his doorbell, and hand him the plate. It's that easy." My dad turned and went back to work. He was engrossed in thought as he continued his fatherly duty of carving the carcass of our holiday fowl.

My mother nodded in agreement and then cut and handed me a large piece of strawberry rhubarb pie. "Also, it would be nice if you wish him a happy Thanksgiving," she said.

Taking the plate, I reluctantly ventured out into the yard. A few seconds later, I was about to step on Baker's lawn when I heard the old man's voice in my head:

Don't you dare come near my lawn. I don't care if your ball comes over here. If you step on my lawn, I'll...

I paused and changed directions, heading down my driveway and then tightrope-walking along the curb past the car with a thousand dents. I turned and headed up the Paxtons' driveway, then climbed the half dozen stairs to the porch. I had crossed into enemy territory.

Taking a deep breath, I tried to gather myself. The fear and uncertainty about what might happen gripped me like a vise. I paused for a few more seconds and then pressed the green doorbell, which was faded and cracked.

Waiting anxiously, I could hear Baker's muffled voice but couldn't make out what he was saying. By the time he wrestled open the door, he had stopped talking. Petrified, I just stood on his porch, absorbing his glare. It took me a minute to finally say something.

"Ah, um, ah...I brought you some food."

I tried to look calm and comfortable as the screen door slowly opened. Baker looked at me with one eye open, peering cautiously from behind the screen door.

"Okay, then..." he said.

Baker grabbed the plate and the door shut. In one fell swoop, the holiday meal was gone, and I was left standing in somewhat of a daze. It had happened so quickly, I couldn't quite process the situation.

"Haaa—happy Thanksgiving," I said, stumbling down the stairs and back to the sidewalk.

Although I had experienced a small dose of paranoia in making the delivery, it actually felt good. I looked back at Baker's front porch, and a smile spread across my face. I skipped home, my mood much lighter and more festive.

When I returned, my mother was setting the table and pouring ice water into glasses.

"How did it go?"

I looked away, attempting to avoid the conversation.

"Fine, I guess."

She stopped and turned toward me.

"What did he say, Christopher?"

I took a few steps toward the hall trying to escape her stare.

"Not much."

She wouldn't be deterred, and continued to quiz me. I stopped and groaned, rolling my eyes.

"Really, he said nothing, Mom."

She stepped toward me and touched my shoulder. "I'm sure it meant a lot to him. I'm proud of you for doing something nice for Baker. Maybe he will be a little nicer to you."

When we awoke the next morning, my six-year-old brother, Jeremy, found the brown ceramic plate I had delivered to Baker on our doorstep. It was clean, with a small handful of multicolored old-fashioned ribbon candy on it. Jeremy quickly popped one in his mouth and put the plate on the counter.

An hour later the phone rang, and my father answered.

"Thanks for the turkey dinner," I overheard Baker saying, while standing close to my father. "Sorry I was rude. I went to try to find a burger, and

183

nothing was open. I was sad to be alone on Thanksgiving. When your boy brought over the plate, I was surprised…. It meant a lot to me."

His voice was full of emotion, and he coughed to hide it before continuing.

"I am not the best neighbor…sorry. Hope you can forgive me. I…I can do better. I will try to be nicer to your boy. Okay, bye."

It was one of the few times Baker seemed to be sober. On these rare occasions, he was kind, contrite, even likable.

A few days later, I went to retrieve a football that had rolled onto Baker's lawn, which was covered with a thin crust of snow. The old man emerged in a drunken fit. He screamed and cussed, pointing at my footprints in the snow, claiming that they were evidence I had trespassed on his property.

"Boy, you—you good for *nothing* son-of-a…"

Clenching the football, I walked back toward the house.

Happy holidays, I thought.

CHAPTER 31

Blue Christmas

My newlywed wife, Laura, has already endured more than six months of constant disruptions and unexpected periods of loneliness. Come Christmas, she is still on a rollercoaster ride of emotion that seems like it will never end.

"I don't care who calls you," she tells me. "I don't care what has happened. Unless Elizabeth has been found, you are *not to answer the phone*. I need you to be present with my family—*this is their Christmas*."

Her words are as fiery as her brown eyes and long, curly red hair. Laura's parents have flown in for the holidays from Virginia, and because of scheduling conflicts and work schedules among her various siblings, they are all gathering at her brother's home in a suburb west of Salt Lake City for a Christmas dinner and celebration on December 23.

I have a poor track record with her family so far. While we've only seen them a few times since I started working with the Smarts, on each occasion, some issue or development has required me to step away.

The last time we got together with Laura's family, in October, I received a call from the media informing me that the body of a blonde fourteen-year-old girl had been found in a ditch near a Latter-day Saint ward house in Brigham City, one hour north of Salt Lake. The local television channels broke into prime-time programming shortly thereafter with the news that Elizabeth's body might have been found.

Fortunately, Ed was able to connect with law enforcement, and in less than fifteen minutes he learned they were confident it wasn't Elizabeth. I was able to relay this information to the media, which helped quell the hysteria. At the same time, the media still had a significant and broad interest in the body, since it hadn't been positively identified.

Laura understands the magnitude of the situation with the Smart family and tries to put on a good face. At the same time, I know the whole arrangement is difficult for her, and that I often disappoint. To make matters worse, her family has started asking how she is holding up with an absent husband, and if the demands of my job are having a significant impact on our marriage.

Trying to reassure Laura, I tell her I will be on my best behavior at Christmas dinner. I promise not to answer my phone.

Arriving at her brother Leland's home, I immediately work to engage with Laura's family. After visiting over some hors d'oeuvres and Mormon champagne, Martinelli's, we sit at the table and Laura's father says grace. I am touched when he includes Elizabeth and the rest of the Smart family in his prayer. We quickly fill our plates with turkey, honey-baked ham, funeral potatoes, green salad, and candied yams.

The conversation is light and the mood is festive; Christmas music plays in the background. Lost in the moment, I temporarily forget about the Smart family, then all of a sudden my phone vibrates.

With the precision of a surgeon, I slowly move the phone onto my knee and glance at the screen. It's Tom Smart. I send the call to voicemail. After Tom calls back two more times, I excuse myself to use the restroom. As I get up, Laura looks sternly at me as if she is trying to communicate, "Come on, you promised."

Shutting the bathroom door, which is near the living room, I turn on the water in the sink to help drown out the sound and dial Tom.

"Are you watching this?" he asks me.

Tom seems to be in a jovial mood, which temporarily makes me regret getting up from the table. I whisper that I am at my in-laws' Christmas party and on a very short leash. I ask what he's talking about.

"John Walsh is on *Larry King*. He just leaked everything about Mary Katherine—how she recently remembered it was a different guy who worked at the house who was in the room that night with Elizabeth. What happened to keeping this confidential?"

Ed calls on the other line and we merge the calls. I close the lid on the toilet and sit down. Ed is angry. It isn't just that John has leaked the information; it's the timing of it. In less than thirty-six hours it will be Christmas morning, and the immediate family's emotions are raw.

Tom and I reassure Ed that we have the situation under control. I tell Ed to focus on his family and not watch or read the news. Then Tom and I continue to strategize for a few minutes after Ed leaves the call. Needing to get back to Christmas dinner, I ask Tom to take good notes and update me later.

When I return to the table after about twenty minutes, the conversation suddenly stops. Leland snickers and stares me down.

"You were in there a long time. Is something not sitting well? Did it all come out okay?"

Leland continues to laugh. He's giving me a hard time because this is his nature, and because he is likely trying to throw me a lifeline by lightening the mood.

Laura is not amused though. She is silent on the ride home. When we arrive, she expresses her frustration and explains that the Smart case is taking a serious toll on her—and on our marriage. The conversation becomes somewhat heated. I tell her I'm going to quit working with the Smart family. It's not the first time I've said this, and it won't be the last. I spend the night in the basement, sleeping on our red sectional.

On Christmas Eve Day, I don't receive any calls from the media until around 10 a.m. Then the flood gates open, and I spend the next three hours fielding requests and conducting interviews on my front lawn. I prepared a response in advance, focused on three facts: There is credibility to what John Walsh has said on *Larry King Live*, the family is surprised it was shared, and they will be making an announcement with more details after January 1.

The approach is fortuitous. I will later learn that the Salt Lake City Police Department responded by saying that John is making the statements about Mary Katherine to promote his own TV shows, and that investigators had looked into the person mentioned and he isn't a suspect. According to them, Richard Ricci is still the prime suspect in the kidnapping.

During the past six months, with each interview, I have worked to define an objective and then create a proactive, positive message that was both applicable to the situation and, more importantly, would help propel the search and investigation forward. That morning, while waiting for the media to call, it occurs to me that Christmas might be the best opportunity for a break in the case. The spirit of the season has a way of softening hearts and compelling charitable acts. *Maybe this could work in favor of the Smarts?*

So I lean into this multiple times in each interview, saying: "There would be no greater Christmas miracle than to have Elizabeth home tomorrow, or at least know of her whereabouts."

The message sticks and makes its way into every story. But I don't realize its impact on me until the next morning.

Christmas 2002 is different for me; it is especially meaningful. Because of my deep care and concern for Ed, Lois, and Elizabeth's siblings as well as the extended Smart family, I can't help but think about and pray for them.

In hindsight, the experience that day reminds me a little of the two Christmas holidays I spent in South Korea as a missionary. Instead of being preoccupied by the busyness, gifts, and superficial aspects of December 25, I was focused on something more important, something that helped me constantly remember the true meaning of the day—forgetting oneself and serving others.

This Christmas Day in 2002, I wait and wait for a phone call to come. I envision hearing someone tell me, "Elizabeth has been found, and she's heading home to be with the family."

This type of reflection preoccupies me the entire day. I can't stop thinking about Elizabeth and her family.

As I'm brushing my teeth and getting ready for bed that night, I leave my phone on the nightstand. When I return, I see a missed call. I anxiously dial voicemail, thinking this might be the break in the case I've been waiting for. Instead, it's a robo call reminding me of a dentist appointment in a few days.

I sob—an ugly cry with mammoth tears. Laura holds me close, trying to assure me that everything is going to be okay.

CHAPTER 32

Betrayal

My voice held a mixture of rage and acute sadness. Fighting back tears from the passenger seat of my family's minivan, I dug my elbows into the armrest, elevated my body with frustration, then crashed back against the headrest.

"Mom, I am *quitting* the church. I will *never* go back. I don't want anything to do with those people."

At first, my mom mostly listened, trying to make eye contact while driving, her eyes volleying back and forth between my face and the road.

"I'm so sorry, Christopher. You have every right to be angry. You could easily justify leaving the church. You're fourteen and old enough to make that decision. I will support whatever you decide. I just want you to think about two things."

She pulled the car over in front of the Salt Palace and touched my shoulder. I looked out the window at the marquee to avoid making eye contact.

"Decisions that are made when we are highly emotional are usually not the best, so try to find some calm, and think through things," she said. "And second, it's not the people that are true; it's the gospel. Regardless, if it's in the church, at school, or with friends, people are imperfect, and you will always be disappointed if you expect otherwise."

Nearly half of the boys in my ward between the ages twelve and fourteen stopped coming to church. This was significant in the culture, since these boys had received the priesthood, starting a path to the church's most important rites of passage. The bishop was responsible for helping every young man in his congregation between the ages of twelve and eighteen progress through the various priesthood offices in preparation to serve a volunteer full-time two-year mission when he turned nineteen.

The Church of Jesus Christ of Latter-day Saints believes in, and is organized into, two priesthoods: the Aaronic, or lesser, priesthood, and the Melchizedek, or higher, priesthood. Latter-day Saints believe the priesthood is the power and authority to act in God's name. At twelve years old, boys are ordained to the Aaronic priesthood and to the office of deacon. They have the responsibility of attending weekly deacon's quorum meetings, serving in leadership roles within their quorum, passing the sacrament during weekly Sunday services, and collecting "fast offerings" to help the needy. They're called fast offerings because on the first Sunday of each month, members refrain from eating three meals, and donate the money they would have spent on food to aid the poor that reside in their ward and stake.

At age fourteen, boys are ordained to the office of teacher and have the responsibility of attending and serving in the quorum, as well as preparing the sacrament.

The final office in the Aaronic priesthood is that of priest, and boys are ordained to this office when they are sixteen years old. Priests assist the bishop, bless the sacrament, and have the authority to perform baptisms.

Advancement to each office requires being active in the church by attending weekly meetings, participating in service opportunities and other youth activities, and adhering to the commandments and standards of the church. This means no drugs, alcohol, tobacco, premarital sex (including even lesser immoral behaviors), or swearing. All members, not just priesthood holders, are also expected to be honest in their dealings with their fellow men and pay 10 percent of their income as tithing. It's a high bar.

Many who are less familiar with Mormonism believe the primary reason people adhere to these requirements is because they are born into the faith, but that isn't necessarily true. At some point in their life, most faithful Latter-day Saints have to navigate a difficult crossroads with respect to commitment, or battle through personal crises of faith. Without strong conviction, which usually comes through personal revelation—asking God and getting a divine answer regarding whether the church and gospel are true—members generally fall away from the epicenter of church activity.

If a young man is faithful and deemed worthy by a bishop and a stake president (who presides over several bishops and wards), he is ordained to the Melchizedek priesthood, and to the office of elder generally between his eighteenth and nineteenth birthday. In this capacity, a young man can receive his endowment—which involves making covenants, or promises, in the church's temples. These covenants are available to women as well and are based on principles of obedience, sacrifice, fidelity, and consecration. The choice to keep these covenants is signified by the wearing of a sacred undergarment. Young men who are set apart as elders can ordain others to the priesthood, under the direction of the bishop, and perform priesthood blessings of healing or comfort for others.

Holding the Melchizedek priesthood is an important step in church growth for a young man, because it is a prerequisite for serving a full-time mission, and later for getting married in the temple. Both of these milestones are distinctive and consequential for most young men in our faith, and also for their parents, who typically are highly focused on helping them to achieve these goals.

The boys in my teacher's quorum who had stopped attending church had done so for a variety of reasons. One was that the significant time commitment—including three hours of Sunday services along with a Wednesday-night activity—limited their ability to watch and play sports.

At our quorum meetings, we regularly talked about how we could help these boys. When I was called (assigned by the bishop) to be the teacher's quorum president, I was challenged to pray for, invite, and fellowship each of the boys who were no longer attending.

I took this to heart and looked for ways to expand my involvement with the boys, many of whom still played ward basketball and softball. Additionally, I strongly advocated in the monthly bishop's youth council meeting (which included each of the presidents in the Aaronic priesthood quorums as well as the presidents of young women's classes) for activities that would attract them.

Unfortunately, the other youth and many of the adult leaders didn't see my vision, and usually planned events like ice skating or a service activity, such as cleaning up an elderly congregation member's yard. While fun and positive for many kids, these activities were not of interest to my wayward quorum members. One month, I suggested attending a Utah Jazz game. I thought this was a surefire way to gather our lost sheep, but I was shot down. First problem? It was too expensive. Second, some argued that the activity wouldn't interest the girls, or the boys who were active in our youth group but didn't necessarily enjoy sports. Despite the initial rejection, I wasn't ready to give up.

The next month, I made a proposition that I thought was too good to refuse. I offered to *pay* for all the Jazz tickets out of my own paper route earnings. To my disbelief, this too was rebuffed. I was told there was a policy that prohibited me from paying.

At the next meeting, I got angry.

"You've challenged me to help these boys who aren't coming, but I don't have your support. I've told you they won't come to the activities that have been planned, and so far I've been right. If you want any chance of getting these boys to participate, you need to take my advice and go to a Jazz game. Otherwise let's stop pretending we care about them."

I stood up and realized I was shaking. As I was about to walk out of the room, the bishop told me to take a deep breath and sit down. He said I was right and that our next major activity would be going to a Jazz game. For the next two weeks, some of the youth and leaders complained about how I'd gotten my way, and sarcastically referred to the Jazz game as "Chris' activity."

On the night of the game, the youth were scheduled to meet at 6 p.m. at the church, to carpool to the arena with the leaders. I had a basketball game that afternoon against a school on the far side of the valley, and the bus to take us back to the school had arrived late. It was a few minutes before 6 p.m. when I returned home.

My mom suggested I change quickly, then she would give me a ride to the church. I told her how the Jazz game was being referred to as "Chris' activity" and there was no way they would leave me, especially since the boys who hadn't been attending church were planning to come.

I quickly showered, got dressed, grabbed a granola bar and a banana, and jumped into the minivan. When we arrived at the church at 6:12 p.m., no one was there. I scoured the parking lot and looked through the glass of the church doors. No one. I had been left. I wasn't *that* late, especially by Mormon Standard Time (that is, five to ten minutes later

Betrayal

than regular time). But there was no other explanation—they had gone without me. I was stunned, especially since no one had tried to call me or stop by my house.

My mom's response was that we should head downtown. She had a ten-dollar bill, enough to buy a ticket, and figured I could find the group. We made our way to the Salt Palace, and she pulled over, right in front of the arena. That was when the emotion of being left behind swelled, and I swore I would leave the church.

My mom and I spoke for the better part of an hour. I never got out of the minivan.

At school the next day, a couple of boys who were active in the church criticized me for not even showing up to "Chris' activity," and the wayward boys who had attended the game asked me what happened.

Over the next several days, I spent hours with my mom processing the situation and my emotions. I also spent time on my knees trying to reconcile the situation through prayer. I came to the realization that I had a lot to lose by holding a grudge and taking my proverbial ball and going home. I decided I needed to stay true to my convictions, forgive, and find a way to accept the imperfections of others.

I'm not sure, even many years later, that I've fully accomplished this, but I've experienced some growth and learned lots of valuable lessons while trying.

193

CHAPTER 33

48 Hours

Still experiencing melancholy from Elizabeth not being found on Christmas Day, I struggle to get up and get going the morning of December 26. The fact that a miracle didn't happen on what seemed like the most likely day of the year makes me feel as if she may never come home. I mope around the kitchen, sipping raspberry herbal tea and reading the newspaper, trying to escape my despondence, when my phone vibrates.

"How *could* you? After everything we have done for the Smart family… And with what we have invested in producing the special," Jane Clayson says. "How could you talk to John Walsh about this instead of us? Why didn't you at least let us know? You need to understand that this really put a damper on the holiday for all of us."

The indignation in her voice, as well as in those of the *48 Hours* producers in the background, is palpable. I let them continue to vent for several minutes before responding.

"We didn't know if the Smarts were *ever* going public with Mary Katherine's epiphany. In fact, Lois is the one person who didn't want the news communicated at all. Out of respect to her, we have sat on this information for more than three months. We spoke with John to get his perspective as the father of a missing and murdered child. He was supposed to keep everything *strictly* confidential. We're all upset that he leaked this on *Larry King*."

The response seems to do little to alleviate their frustration. The group suggests that the best solution is to allow *48 Hours* to exclusively release the sketch and details of Mary Katherine's epiphany. They make the case that the amount of interest and attention their primetime special would generate could be the catalyst for finding Elizabeth. In addition to offering the most compelling story as a result of the extensive time and resources *48 Hours* has invested in the story, they explain that the sketch and new details would receive significant attention both from what would be a highly rated broadcast and through efforts to promote the special on all of CBS's news programs, platforms, and in other venues. Jane and the producers propose flying to Salt Lake to do an interview with Mary Katherine in the next two days, then they will fast-track production to get the special on the air by the third week of January at the latest. While I understand the merits of their pitch, I'm not on board.

"No. If we do give you the exclusive, then we'll have to wait for three more weeks. And it will impact how the other media cover the story and the family. Your competitors will likely scrutinize or pan the development and it won't ultimately reach as large and diverse of an audience. We have to make this decision with Elizabeth's best interests in mind, which is why next week we will distribute an advisory and provide all the media outlets with equal access to cover the Smarts releasing the sketch and new information."

Jane, the producers, and I argue for another fifteen minutes until, in an effort to end the call, I inform the group that I have a meeting and need to go.

A few hours later, Jane calls me while I'm shoveling snow off my front walk. Later I will come to believe she was trying to help me understand the predicament she was in, as a result of unforeseen events and the incredible pressure both she and the producers were under. In the moment, I see it as another attack. I respond with irritation in my voice.

"The family's mission is not to make *you* look good or get ratings and accolades for *48 Hours*. We are trying to find a missing child. That's our sole purpose. I'm sorry if it doesn't fit with your agenda."

As I hang up the phone, I'm shivering from the cold, from frustration about the conversation with Jane, and from a dreary feeling that the challenges and obstacles the Smart family is enduring are never going to end.

I haven't informed Ed about the series of discussions with *48 Hours*, but I'm not surprised when he calls me later in the day and knows all the details. Jane has, of course, spoken with Lois, who is even more livid with John Walsh than Jane is.

This tug of war between Ed and Lois and the police has become more intense, with Jane and *48 Hours* now pulling on the rope too. Over the next few days, Ed, Lois, the extended Smart family, the *48 Hours* producers, and I have several conversations.

The extended Smart family and I stand firm on our position advocating for releasing the sketch and new information to all the media as soon as possible in the new year. I argue that *48 Hours* can take the details from the press conference and incorporate it into their special. We are adamant, especially since we believe this course of action is in Elizabeth's best interest.

On the flipside, the police don't want the sketch and more details to become public and, in addition to refusing to cooperate and provide these to *48 Hours*, they further make the case to the producers that detectives have thoroughly looked into Immanuel. The police affirm that he is no more of interest than scores of other people they have investigated and that Richard Ricci is still at the top of their list of suspects in Elizabeth's kidnapping.

After significant back-and-forth discussion, Ed and Lois agree to a compromise. They decide not to give the sketch and new information exclusively to *48 Hours*, but rather to allow Jane and the producers to have their last-ditch request for a few weeks to get their special on the air first. Then, a few days later, Ed plans on holding a press conference to release the sketch to the media at large.

The hour-long prime-time *48 Hours* airs on January 10 and is the most comprehensive story to date on the Smart case. Revered *60 Minutes* reporter Lesley Stahl introduces the story from a makeshift set in New York's Grand Central Station, then Jane in Salt Lake takes viewers on an inside journey of the family and investigation. The show focuses heavily on the theory of Richard Ricci being the most likely abductor. It plays up a new revelation that investigators now believe the window wasn't the point of entry on the night of the kidnapping, but that the cut screen was a ruse set up by the perpetrator, who likely knew where the Smarts hid their spare keys—and Ricci, as widely reported, was familiar.

When the 48 Hours episode airs, I am deluged with calls from angry journalists. They're upset because the children, especially Mary Katherine, are being interviewed, despite me telling them for months that this would never happen. I have to endure a quiver of arrows in the form of complaints and sharp criticism, from members of the media feeling punished for playing by the rules or telling me I lack credibility. Each journalist makes the case that the only antidote for breaking our promise is to allow *their* news organization to interview Mary Katherine inside the Smart home. My answer to these feeble attempts at one-upmanship is a diplomatic *no*.

Once the credits run on the 48 Hours special, I wonder if the biggest media challenges are behind me. Watching the end of the show with Laura, I ask rhetorically, "What could possibly top this?"

CHAPTER 34

The Fight

During the spring of my freshman year of high school, Baker's vile tone, angry demeanor, and profanity-laced threats escalated exponentially. I lost count of the times he threatened to shoot me. We were both getting older, which created a volatile combination: Baker was becoming increasingly cantankerous, and I was a more outspoken and defiant teenager.

I had become more adept at sneaking into ward houses, and occasionally into the high school gym, to play basketball. As a result, I shot hoops in the driveway only a fraction of the time. When I did play outside, it was as if Baker had bottled up his fury, twisted the cap on tight, and was waiting for me. He had a short fuse. And over the previous couple of years, his bombastic outbursts had become more animated, angry, and annoying.

On one particularly hot day the summer before my sophomore year, I attempted my first driveway shot. On the rebound, a stream of cold water came from nowhere. As I turned, the water hit me in the face. I couldn't close my eyes fast enough, and was overtaken by a stinging sensation that brought me to my knees.

"Serves you right…you bastard child," Baker growled above me. In an attempt to survey the situation, I stood up awkwardly, bumping into Baker.

"You want a piece of me?" Baker said. "I'll kick your—"

Before he could finish, I stumbled forward, still trying to clear the water from my eyes, and inadvertently crashed into the old man. Taking a few steps backward, Baker couldn't maintain his balance. He teetered on his heels before landing on the lawn. My unintended bump had provided the gas needed to finally ignite the inferno.

Baker flew into a rage unlike anything I had ever seen from him before. He cleared his throat loudly and then yelled something incoherent. Rubbing my eyes, I was desperate to regain my vision. My heart was beating uncontrollably.

I blinked and blinked as Baker's dingy green shirt came into focus. Then I saw the full outline of the old man's figure. It seemed as though he had been miraculously transformed. He no longer slouched, his muscles were more defined, and he seemed fast on his feet. He suddenly had the energy and physique of someone much younger.

He came out swinging.

We tussled, bobbing and weaving. The old man stepped toward me. I swerved to the side and then bounced back aggressively in his direction. He ducked and then quickly arose, throwing a right hook that glanced off my shoulder. Although I couldn't feel any pain, the impact inflamed me. My hands flailed in the direction of the old man. I closed my eyes, anticipating my knuckles colliding with his flesh. I didn't feel anything until I landed roughly on the pavement, scraping one of my knees. I had somehow missed hitting Baker.

Getting up quickly, I could finally see the old man clearly for the first time since the scuffle began. His superhuman strength seemed to be dissipating. He was breathing heavily, and I could smell the alcohol laced on every one of his winded expirations.

Baker suddenly went down right in front of me. He was mine for the kill.

I cocked my fist. My body tightened as I drew my arm back. The fast-twitch fibers of my biceps fired, exploding in a forward motion. Just as my fists were about to hit the point of no return, I heard my mother's voice as if she were right next to me:

"Be smart, Christopher. Use your head."

I had rolled my eyes at this phrase countless times over the previous fifteen years. I didn't always listen, but this time I heeded the message and aborted the punch, tripping awkwardly past the old man onto his lawn. I looked back toward my front door to see if my mom was near, but it was just Baker and me in his front yard. I wiped the sweat from my forehead and placed both hands on my knees to catch my breath as I sat down on the ground.

We stared each other down for what seemed like hours, although it was likely only a few minutes. Neither of us spoke. Baker finally got up on his feet, staggered left and then right, and nearly fell back to the ground. Gathering himself, he walked across the lawn, his pace quickening with every step. When Baker disappeared inside his house, my mind raced. My anxiety grew.

He's going to get a gun.

I scrambled to my feet and hurried inside the house to lie low. I didn't tell my parents what had occurred. I was both embarrassed and afraid of getting in trouble. At the same time, I concocted a story that convinced my sisters, Natalee and Amy, not to go in the front yard. When they tried to sneak away, I then told them a swarm of aggressive bees was outside. It stopped them in their tracks.

The realization that no one had seen what had happened, that it would be my word against Baker's, threw me into a frenzy. I was not a legal adult, but my six-foot, three-inch frame also wasn't a typical teenager's height. He could accuse me of some type of assault. I feared the worst, particularly my greatest nightmare: having my chance of playing high school basketball derailed. I felt extremely apprehensive for days.

In the years that followed, Baker and I kept our distance. While we never spoke of the fight, it was as if the two of us had agreed to a truce. I rarely played basketball in the driveway, and when I did, he never came outside.

I got my driver's license a few months after the incident, and my mom signed a loan for a car. I paid four thousand dollars for a twelve-year-old red Audi 5000 with black-tinted windows. Although the vehicle looked nice on the outside, it broke down frequently. I often parked it in the driveway, obstructing the hoop. More than once it sat there beneath the basketball standard for weeks, while I saved up the money to get it repaired.

When the Audi was working, I drove to a gym or the high school to play basketball. When it wasn't, I bummed a ride from one of my friends or teammates.

I saw Baker periodically, driving the car with a thousand dents, but I never waved or made eye contact. I had turned the page on our little incident, trying to forget about it and the old man—his belligerent tone and disquieting demeanor.

After graduating from high school, I enrolled at Westminster College, a private liberal arts school in Salt Lake City that had awarded me a partial journalism scholarship. Most of my friends were attending Brigham Young University or the University of Utah, where a large percentage of their peers shared the same faith, but I was seeking a different experience. I wanted to understand what it was like to be in the minority, at least from a religious standpoint. Despite being in the heart of Salt Lake City, Westminster offered diverse beliefs and perspectives, with literally only a handful of students and very few professors who were active in The Church of Jesus Christ of Latter-day Saints.

I couldn't afford both tuition and room and board, so I lived at home. Writing for the college's newspaper during my freshman year, I found myself in the crosshairs of an angry, crotchety soccer coach, who called my home often to yell and complain. He believed my coverage of the soccer team should always shine a positive light on him and his athletes. He took offense at anything that wasn't to his liking. It was a baptism by fire in practicing objectivity and adhering to journalistic standards and ethics.

One night after a lengthy and intense phone call with the soccer coach, my mother appeared.

"I'm sorry, I was eavesdropping and couldn't help myself. I'm so proud of how you handled things, Christopher. You didn't back down, and at the same time, you demonstrated strong diplomacy. Baker prepared you well."

I rubbed the back of my head. I was caught off guard by her comment, and it took me a minute to process what she had said.

"I guess he did," I replied. "I never thought something positive would come from living next door to Baker. Maybe I've been wrong."

This silver-lining sentiment, however, was fleeting.

Later that year, my parents purchased a larger home in a nearby neighborhood. We were moving. One of the benefits of membership in The Church of Jesus Christ of Latter-day Saints is access to movers who work for things like donuts and milkshakes. With help from this Mormon "moving company," which was actually the ward elder's quorum (the priesthood group of younger adults), we relocated most of the larger furniture and boxes to the new house. The next day, as my dad and I were cleaning up and loading the final random items into the U-Haul, he looked up at me.

"Chris, I bet Baker is celebrating right now. He's not going to miss us at all, especially you."

My dad then began to giggle as he wiped away the sweat from his brow. I wasn't going to let the comment pass without providing my two cents' worth.

"Maybe we should play basketball one last time as a going-away present."

Heading over to the bushes in front of our home, I found an old rubber basketball that had grown bald from years of wear. I dribbled a few times, turned, and took one last shot. It was a swish.

The ball rolled onto Baker's lawn. We pushed up the U-Haul's ramp and closed the large rolling door. I took one last look at my childhood home. Then we got in the truck and drove away.

CHAPTER 35

Bad PR

Ed cranes his neck sideways, moving his ear closer to my flip phone, trying to hear the other side of my conversation with a well-placed source at one of the news networks.

"I found out what's going on. You may want to sit down. This is going to make you really angry, Chris."

We stand underneath the ticker outside the News Corp building, looking onto Sixth Avenue. My phone is pressed so closely to my ear, it feels like a suction cup. The incessant honking horns, squealing brakes, and shrill sirens echoing in the background make it difficult for Ed to hear anything.

It has been almost four months since Mary Katherine's epiphany about Immanuel, the homeless drifter who she believes pulled a gun on Elizabeth in their bedroom during the early morning hours eight months ago. We haven't released the sketch or information yet. Most of this time was lost while trying to negotiate with police, getting the Smart family on the same page about releasing the information, doing damage control from John Walsh's December 23 appearance on *Larry King Live*, and waiting for the *48 Hours* special to air.

While Ed and I are disappointed and feel a little betrayed by John Walsh, Tom has a different perspective. He believes that if John hadn't leaked the details regarding Mary Katherine remembering Immanuel, *48 Hours* would have held back the special for another month until sweeps, and Lois might never have agreed to release the sketch. Angela, Cynthia, David, and most of the board agree with Tom. Later, many in the group will even say that providence might have played a role in the series of events surrounding John Walsh's unexpected comments.

Once the dust from *48 Hours* finally cleared, we planned to conduct a press conference to release the sketch and information surrounding Mary Katherine's epiphany early in the week of January 13. The Salt Lake City Police Department had other ideas, however, and applied a full-court press on the Smarts, doing everything it could to convince them not to release the new information.

The police called a meeting with Ed, Lois, the extended Smart family, and me, during which Detective Don Bell informed us that investigators had withheld some alarming details, namely that law enforcement had found bullet casings inside the white Jeep they believed Richard Ricci had used to abduct Elizabeth. Bell said this was one of several items that had led those in the know to have "99.9999 percent surety" that Ricci had abducted Elizabeth.

Ed stood up, pointing aggressively in Bell's direction. His face was flushed, and his shoulders quivered.

"Why, *why* did you withhold things from us? You told me *several* times that you had shared with us everything you knew. How can we trust anything you're saying?"

Angela stood and put her arm around Ed and rubbed his shoulder. Tom flashed a slight smile as he rubbed his chin and then calmly began talking.

"Okay, if it was Richard Ricci who abducted Elizabeth, which some in the FBI don't believe at all, there are several details that point to the fact he didn't act alone. What are you doing to find the other person the eyewitness said was *with* Ricci when he returned the Jeep?"

Tom had a knack for diffusing situations by asking thoughtful, pointed questions, especially when he wasn't the focus.

Bell tap-danced for the next fifteen minutes. He argued that he and the others in law enforcement always did their best to communicate as much as possible, but that they had to be judicious in what they shared. This protocol was in the best interest of the investigation, he said, and they never wanted to say anything that might create undue stress for the family.

Bell also claimed that the police department had found nothing to confirm that someone had aided Ricci. All the evidence pointed to the fact that Ricci had abducted Elizabeth and likely had committed the crime alone. Bell then made his pitch.

"We all need to be really careful here and think this through. Releasing information about Immanuel could be very detrimental in the long term. It could be embarrassing for Mary Katherine and could create lots of unforeseen challenges for all of us."

The possibility that it could negatively impact Mary Katherine worried Lois. While this concern wasn't inconsequential, the extended Smart family believed that Mary Katherine was the most credible witness, and we could shield her in the event that she was wrong. I also pointed out that the public was sympathetic toward Mary Katherine and understood her plight. It would take a lot to sway public opinion against her.

Over the next week, while Ed and Lois deliberated what to do, the board kicked into overdrive. The group had been meeting on Tuesday nights to review developments and collaborate on how to best help Ed and Lois and their children. Much of each meeting was spent playing detective, however—analyzing the evidence, discussing and debating different theories, and formulating questions for law enforcement.

Tom had fostered a relationship with a couple of FBI agents who believed the police department and other investigators were placing too much emphasis on Ricci—and as a result, were blind to other options. The agents were receptive to the board's questions and input, and in return provided insights and feedback that further fueled our fire.

After the meeting with Detective Bell, the board continued to apply pressure on Ed and Lois. Tom and David met with them, sometimes multiple times a day, to make the case for defying law enforcement and going public with the sketch. Other family members and friends reinforced the message during various meetings and conversations.

The turning point, according to Tom's book, was when David made the case to Lois that several FBI agents did not believe Richard Ricci had abducted Elizabeth, and when Tom argued that Ricci's fingerprints did not match those collected on Elizabeth's bedpost or the back door. Lois hadn't heard those details before, and they helped convince her to release the sketch.

Once Ed and Lois informed the police of their intentions, Detective Bell tried yet again to talk them out of it. He claimed the police had intel that Immanuel regularly worked the crowds panhandling at the twice-annual general conference for The Church of Jesus Christ of Latter-day Saints. The spring conference, in downtown Salt Lake City, was a couple of months away, and Bell feared that by going public the Smart family would send Immanuel underground and impact their chances of finding and questioning him at the conference.

This theory didn't deter the Smarts. In fact, it seemed odd that the police didn't believe Immanuel was a suspect but at the same time didn't want to scare him off. As a last resort to thwart our efforts, the police informed Ed they would not be present at or participate in the press conference.

A few days later, as we were making final preparations for the announcement, I could see that the stress of going forward without law enforcement was chipping away at Ed's steadiness. The veins in his neck bulged, his voice was an octave higher, and the dark circles under his eyes seemed more pronounced.

"I need a blessing. *Will someone* please give me a blessing?"

It was less than thirty minutes before the press conference, which had been billed in a media advisory as: "Smart Family to Release New Information Regarding Elizabeth's Abduction." The police were sticking to their guns and weren't participating. They agreed to provide the family with the sketch of Immanuel but hadn't delivered it yet, and the clock was ticking. This, too, was contributing to Ed's anxiety.

"I'm sorry," he said. "I can't remember the last time I was this nervous. I need something to calm me down. I need the Lord's help."

As mentioned, men in the church who hold the Melchizedek priesthood and are living by church standards can administer blessings to those in need.

Generally, priesthood blessings are for healing the sick and afflicted; however, they can be for comfort in the case of unique challenges or duress. They can also be given simply for guidance or inspiration. It's not uncommon for children to receive a priesthood blessing from their father on the night before the first day of school.

Ed took a seat on a brown metal folding chair. His brothers and other priesthood holders from the board, including me, stood around him in a circle, each placing our right hand on Ed's head and our other hand on the right shoulder of the man standing next to us. Everyone closed their eyes, and Dr. Smart began the blessing in customary fashion. He stated Ed's full name and then said, "In the name of Jesus Christ, and by the power of the holy Melchizedek priesthood, we lay our hands upon your head and give you a blessing..."

Dr. Smart asked for peace of mind and clarity in communication for his son, then paused briefly, likely seeking inspiration. Ed's eyes were moist and shut so tightly that his eyelids were wrinkled. His hands were folded in his lap, fingers interlocked and quivering slightly.

Opening my eyes briefly, I surveyed the room from the circle. I saw Tom, who sat on the periphery with Angela, Cynthia, and some of the other female members of the board. Tom was the only other person with his eyes open. He wasn't in the circle because he hadn't been active in the faith for a couple of decades. He had always been very respectful during prayers and blessings, which happened frequently during the search for Elizabeth. I'd always felt like Tom, despite his tough cowboy persona, was very spiritual in his own way.

Dr. Smart continued the blessing, imploring God to continue to uphold Ed and give him strength and resolve, especially in times when he was feeling insufficient. He then closed in the name of Jesus Christ.

There was a brief, silent pause, then Ed stood and hugged each man in the circle as well as everyone else in attendance.

I was touched by his humility and the courage it took to ask for a blessing. A calm, warm feeling filled the room. For a brief moment, I allowed myself to take it in. But as with most of the spiritual and emotional experiences during the search for Elizabeth, those seconds of respite and reflection could not last long. I had to put my game face back on and go back to work.

At two o'clock, the police still hadn't arrived. The media had already gathered in front of the church and were waiting, so I stepped out and explained that we were running a few minutes late and would be out shortly. Ed and I huddled and determined that the best approach was to explain Mary Katherine's epiphany and refer the media to the police to get the sketch. If anyone asked why the police weren't attending, or why they hadn't provided the sketch, our response would be to diplomatically say, "We don't know. You would need to ask them."

As Ed started his remarks, an unmarked police car drove into the parking lot. I walk around the perimeter of the press conference and met Detective Fred Louis. When I expressed how grateful we were to see him, he quickly downplayed the situation.

"I need to be clear. I'm not here to participate. I'm just quickly dropping off the sketch."

I walked with him to where some of the family members were standing behind Ed. Detective Louis stopped and looked up. The skin on his forehead tightened, and his face was stoic. Deep in thought, he seemed calm and at the same time perplexed. After a few seconds, he stepped toward the podium and opened a manila envelope with the sketch. The detective waited for Ed to finish his thoughts, and then said a few words to the media. He remained at the podium standing next to Ed.

Detective Louis' kindness and calm demeanor were exactly what Ed needed in the moment. With the detective standing by his side, Ed seemed more at ease relaying Mary Katherine's story and pleading for the public's help in finding Immanuel. At the end of his remarks, Ed also announced a ten-thousand-dollar reward for anyone who could exonerate Ricci.

After the press conference, Ed and I flew to New York to do interviews with the morning shows. We knew the routine well. We arrived on the last flight of the day and checked into our hotel after midnight.

I settled down to try to sleep, knowing that in only a few hours my phone would start ringing, and I'd have to take calls from producers to confirm details and logistics, all while getting ready. I would then meet Ed in the lobby to briefly prep before a driver arrived to take us to the first studio.

The next morning, however, turned out to be anything but routine.

When I answered the first call early that morning, I was still lying in bed half asleep. A producer explained that they'd overbooked guests, and unfortunately, Ed was the odd man out. The info went in one ear, but by the time it came out the other, I had fallen back asleep.

I'm not sure how long I'd been sleeping when a producer from another show called to inform me they had to cancel the interview. This time I was awake enough to press the producer for an answer. He told me he didn't know. He was simply the messenger.

A half hour later, as I was about to leave the room, I received *another* call declining the interview. The producer gave me a far-fetched excuse about needing more time for a feature story by one of the anchors. Supposedly, their story had ended up being much longer than they anticipated.

When we arrived at Fox News for the only interview that hadn't been canceled yet, a producer met us at the front desk of the News Corp building and said they had to bump Ed's interview for breaking news. We watched the broadcast of *Fox and Friends* outside on the monitors while I made phone calls. The breaking news never aired.

We will soon learn that even the local media largely glossed over the Immanuel development. The *Tribune* didn't publish the sketch and, along with the *Deseret News*, included the stories in the metro section instead of on the front page, as had been customary with every major development since Elizabeth disappeared. The local newscasts aired coverage of the press conference at the end of what is known as the B block, which is where soft news runs before the anchors break for the weather. The stories focused on the reward for exonerating Ricci, and mentioned Mary Katherine's epiphany largely as an afterthought.

Upon leaving Fox News, we stand under the ticker of the News Corp building, fenced in by the commotion of New York City. I'm relieved to reach a trusted source at one of the other networks. Despite his recommendation to "sit down," there are no chairs or benches available—nowhere to get off our feet in an attempt to cushion this latest blow.

My source on the other end of the line takes a deep breath before continuing.

"The Salt Lake Police Department told us to be very careful with this Immanuel thing, that the sketch is an attempt by the Smarts' PR agency to get Elizabeth's story back in the news. They said they checked this guy out and don't believe he was involved. I'm sorry to say this, Chris, but the producers are stepping back and playing it safe."

It's a bitter pill to swallow, as I try to process why the police would go to such lengths to sabotage the announcement. Being used as a pawn to discredit this news is infuriating. I feel like I'm living out a John Grisham novel.

Ed and I start walking back toward the hotel, but when we arrive at the revolving doors, we don't stop; we keep on walking. A few hours later, we find ourselves standing in front of an antiques store, strategizing: How can we get the public to take the Immanuel development seriously, especially when the media is avoiding us?

We talk while we walk through the antiques shop. Then we stroll through another shop, and then another, buying nothing—just talking late into the afternoon. As the sun slips behind the many skyscrapers, we realize we have walked at least ten miles and have patronized dozens of antiques stores.

We determine that our best option is John Walsh. Although his leaking of the initial news about Mary Katherine's epiphany was disappointing, Ed and I know he is a genuinely good person who wants to help. I call John and tell him about my conversation with the network source. He doesn't flinch. He isn't surprised.

A few days later, I welcome a correspondent and crew from *America's Most Wanted* into my living room. We're still avoiding interviews at the Smart home, and none of the other board members' residences were available, so I improvised. When Laura comes home early from a business trip, she is surprised to see large trucks outside, a crew on the front porch, and our furniture rearranged, with bright lights and screens behind the couch. When one of the neighbors watching from the sidewalk asks her what's going on, Laura responds, "I can only guess."

The following Saturday, *America's Most Wanted* leads with the Immanuel story, and that moment is the beginning of the end. A week later, a woman contacts the show and informs them that the mysterious man in the sketch is her brother, Brian David Mitchell. She says he has a checkered past and is capable of the abduction.

The development receives moderate coverage locally, but *America's Most Wanted* knows this lead is significant, so the team doubles down on the coverage and John Walsh decides to come to Salt Lake to interview Ed.

This time I give Laura a heads-up, and the night before the interview, she nonchalantly mentions it to one of our neighbors. Word travels fast through the grapevine. A small crowd gathers outside our home to watch as trucks pull up with lights, video cameras, and other gear to transform the living room into a makeshift set again.

An hour later, they cheer when John Walsh gets out of a Lincoln Town Car and walks up the driveway to the front door. John stops and waves. Inside the house, he and Ed embrace.

"Ed, it's so good to see you. I want you to know that I haven't and will *never* give up on you and Elizabeth, and neither will the viewers of

America's Most Wanted. We are going to find this dirtbag and bring him to justice."

The energy of this interview is different from any I have witnessed in the past. It feels more hopeful and less pensive. Ed and John converse like old friends, and optimism abounds.

That Saturday's story on *America's Most Wanted* is the longest yet. Another follow-up will air one week later.

John Walsh is listening when no one else will. He believes the Smarts and has stepped in willingly when it seems like everyone else in the media has deserted the family. John is a hero for providing the credibility the story and family so desperately need at this most critical juncture in the search for Elizabeth.

And, most importantly, John's efforts will help lead to an outcome few families of abducted children, including his own, will ever experience.

CHAPTER 36

Remember Baker

Baker stood stoically behind his screen door, staring me down. "What do you want?" the old man asked. He was caught off guard and didn't know how to react to my unexpected visit.

"Baker, it's nice to see you too. You haven't lost a step…. I'm leaving tomorrow and I wanted to say goodbye."

He seemed stunned and was quiet for a minute before he opened the door. "Say goodbye to *me*?… Well, come on in then."

Shortly after my family moved away from my childhood home, I decided to serve a full-time church mission and was assigned to live and work in South Korea for two years. The afternoon before I was to depart, I was feeling sentimental and drove through the old neighborhood.

On a whim, I pulled over, parked the car, walked up the driveway, and knocked on Baker's door.

As I entered his living room, I experienced an aroma of coffee and Bengay that reminded me of my grandparents' home. Baker was sober. He was thoughtful, considerate, even charming. After making small talk, he shifted the conversation to a somber topic.

"Did you hear about Ron?"

Ron Ballard, Baker's best friend and home teacher from the ward, had collapsed a few months earlier while on his morning walk. Despite immediate medical assistance, efforts to revive him had been unsuccessful. Ron was fifty-seven years young when he died.

"Yes, Baker. I am so sorry. He was a good man. Ron really admired you. He told me several times how much you meant to him."

I looked into Baker's eyes, which were moist.

"Oh, I didn't do nothin' for him. Ron did everything for me. He was the best neighbor any of us could have ever had. Things just haven't been the same without him."

He tried to conceal his emotion and collect himself.

"And Ruth?" Baker continued.

Ruth Hitler also had passed away, earlier that same year, 1992. She'd fought a long, hard battle with brain cancer, and for the previous several years, we'd rarely seen her outside.

Before I could respond that I'd still been living next door when Ruth passed, Baker continued: "She was an amazing woman. Just like Ron, she was the best neighbor you could ever hope for. I don't think she liked me much. I said something years ago that I've always regretted, and it hurt Ruth. I kept my distance from her and her family ever since. I hope she forgave me."

Baker turned his head and discreetly wiped away a tear with his palm.

"I'm sure she did, Baker. Ruth wasn't the type of person who would hold a grudge. She loved everyone, including you."

We reminisced about Ruth, Ron, the garage, Chris's Crawlers, the countless times my basketball had rolled into his yard, the sprinkler. We laughed. We connected. Baker and I nearly became emotional a few times as we reflected on the events of the past sixteen years.

While I'd anticipated only a short visit, Baker was engaging and contrite, and I was so absorbed in our conversation that I stayed for several hours. It was as if time were standing still.

Baker told stories from World War II. He explained in great detail and with such emotion what it had been like to land on Omaha Beach on D-Day that for a brief moment, it was as if I were there with him in June 1944 on the northern coast of occupied France.

I could feel the cold water, smell the ocean, hear the explosions, and see the bodies tossed in the surf. There were planes and paratroopers overhead and a barrage of artillery whistling toward us from what seemed like every direction.

Baker leaned forward and told me he wanted to show me something. Disappearing briefly, he returned with a heavily worn cardboard box. He pulled out several old photographs, including one of him with General George S. Patton. Shortly after arriving in France, Baker told me, he was assigned to Patton's Third Army. The old man claimed he and Patton were two peas in a pod and that he'd gotten most of his cantankerous personality from the general.

"But, hey, as mean as I am, I ain't nothin' compared to Patton. He was the orneriest son of a bitch you could ever meet."

Baker pulled out an impressive collection of Nazi flags, leaflets, and propaganda pieces he had collected while invading various towns. I was engrossed by every story, every image, every artifact, every detail.

Suddenly, his disposition shifted. He grew increasingly agitated. The muscles on his wrinkled face were contracted. Closing his eyes, he began to explain what it had been like to operate a giant artillery gun, recoiling as he imitated the sound of the shells exploding from the barrel. Then he started sobbing.

"Do you have any idea...the horror of killing another human being?"

My senses were heightened. I could feel a strange twang in my stomach. There was an awkward, visceral pause. I was speechless.

Baker explained how he had been put on watch and had been sitting atop an enormous gun when several enemy soldiers came out from the shadows.

"I didn't hesitate. I fired. And I watched as they fell and suffered. No one should ever have to see what I saw. No one should have to live knowing they were the cause of such sadness to those mothers who had to bury those boys."

I exhaled heavily, closed my eyes, and did everything I could not to cry.

"Baker, you can't blame yourself. It's not your fault. You were fighting for our freedom." My voice crumbled. I couldn't contain my emotions. I was crying so hard that I could no longer talk. Baker picked up the slack.

"From that day forward, I had extreme shell shock. I could feel the guns exploding. I could hear the bullets. I could see the men. I could hear their screams. I could see them breathing their last breaths. It wouldn't go away, and I have experienced this hell every single day since."

We both fell silent again for a moment, trying to process and contain our emotions.

"Baker, I am so sorry."

I looked at the old man, hoping that my body language would convey my sympathy, gratitude, and sorrow—things I just couldn't begin to express with words.

He quickly changed the subject.

"What happened with the high school basketball team? It didn't look from the box scores in the newspaper that you played very much."

I was surprised that Baker had even known I was on the team.

"It was a rough experience. I gave it everything I had. But it didn't turn out like I had hoped. It was nothing like what you went through. It was disappointing, but I can't complain."

Baker told me he had been an all-state basketball player, the biggest star in southern Utah, and how he'd aspired to play in college. He also had been a champion boxer. As he humbly recounted his personal sports history, I marveled that his athletic prospects had been practically endless.

Then the war came and changed his life. It stole his dreams. It robbed him of almost everything.

"I need to apologize to you, Chris. I was so jealous. Every day I would watch you shooting hoops. You had everything I had lost. You worked hard. You were always out there."

He paused as more tears streamed down his worn crimson cheeks.

"Not only was I jealous, but the bouncing of the ball really got to me. I could hear the shells exploding. My stomach would churn. My bones would ache. I would try to distract myself. I would turn on the TV. I'd go downstairs. I'd pour a drink. I knew it wasn't your fault. But by the time I was outside, I wasn't myself. I was so mean. I was rotten. I am *sorry*. You didn't deserve none of this."

I was completely taken aback by his comments. I'd had no idea Baker had been suffering in this way. I also couldn't comprehend that this same man I had loathed for so long was apologizing to me. Never in my wildest dreams could I have imagined this.

"It's okay, Baker. I forgive you. I hope you will forgive me...for all the times when I was disrespectful."

I rubbed my eyes with my index finger, trying to keep a small amount of composure.

"Of course I do, Chris. But you don't need to apologize. It was my fault."

Several hours later, when I couldn't stay any longer, I was at a loss for how to say a final goodbye. As Baker walked me to the door, I put out my hand. Instead of shaking, however, we both embraced. His acutely arthritic fingers pressed against my shirt, grabbing me tightly.

"Thank you, Chris. You have no idea how much this means to me."

I stood for several long seconds, taking in the experience, before I found the composure to speak.

"You have no idea how much it means to me too. Take care of yourself, old man. I'll see you in two years."

CHAPTER 37

Only the Good Die Young

The city bus sputtered as it veered off the paved highway, traveling slowly down a graded dirt road. I watched through the window as old women wearing ornate silk pants worked the rice paddies and plowed the fields by hand. As we came to a stop, one of them pointed at me and said something indiscernible in an animated tone. I was the novelty here in South Korea, perhaps the first foreigner they had ever seen.

The road twisted and turned through the lush, bucolic countryside, becoming increasingly steeper as we journeyed downhill into what seemed a monstrous abyss.

I stared out the window, deep in thought, barely noticing the heat from the air that seeped through the floor and the cracks around the windows. My stomach grumbled audibly. It was working overtime to adjust to the motion sickness and the spicy kimchi stew I had devoured for both breakfast and lunch.

The transition to Korea had been significantly more difficult than I anticipated. Having never lived away from home, I was experiencing bouts of anxiety and extreme homesickness. These struggles were exacerbated by the rigors of being a missionary for The Church of Jesus Christ of Latter-day Saints—fourteen-hour workdays, six-and-a-half days of the week, were the norm.

During the weekly half-day break—called preparation day, or P-Day— we were expected to do our laundry, shop for groceries, get haircuts, and take care of other errands. Occasionally, we had a few hours for taking a nap, or touring cultural sites.

Many missionaries considered the mission rules to be even more stringent than the work regimen: no dating, movies, television, nonreligious music, or secular books. Missionaries worked in pairs and were required to be with their assigned companion 24/7. We weren't allowed to contact family and friends, aside from writing letters on P-Day, and were permitted to call home only twice annually, on Christmas and Mother's Day.

I never seemed to have enough time to catch my breath. I was physically and mentally exhausted from the work, which included trying to learn a new language and culture, largely by immersion.

While Korea is densely populated, I initially served in rural cities and often worked with people in remote areas. It wasn't uncommon to travel roads for what seemed like hours by city bus, traversing terrain for which an SUV seemed better equipped.

Leaning against the window, I felt somewhat lost and out of place. I daydreamed about being back home, attending college and hanging out with my girlfriend, whom I had been dating for more than a year prior to leaving for Korea.

The decision to serve on a mission wasn't easy for me. When I was growing up, The Church of Jesus Christ of Latter-day Saints expected that all worthy male members would serve for two years beginning at age nineteen (the age was reduced to eighteen in 2012). Approximately 90 percent of the active Latter-day Saint boys in my high school filled out their paperwork and received a call to serve on their own dime in one of a multitude of locales, from Idaho to Africa. No one had any say in where they went; the destination was left to the inspiration of the church's missionary department.

Most of my friends had left on their missions within a few weeks of their nineteenth birthday. I had lagged behind, wanting to finish a full year of college and travel with my grandmother over the summer to visit her father's hometown in Italy. This had worried many of the church's faithful, including my girlfriend's father, who had delivered blank mission application papers to my house more than once.

My freshman year of college had been fruitful. I created a part-time position in the school's public relations department while also making a name for myself on campus, writing for the student newspaper. I had positioned myself to be the editor in chief by my junior year. Everything had been falling into place.

For a male, the social ramifications of not honorably completing a two-year mission loomed large. It was ingrained in most girls in the culture that they should marry an RM (returned missionary). Many young women were reluctant to seriously date someone who hadn't completed a mission. Even outside the realms of courtship and marriage, not being an RM carried a stigma. Not serving a mission often informed how church members viewed the young man's faith and personal choices.

But it wasn't necessarily the immense pressure that fueled my decision to serve a mission. I had prayed about it and felt strongly it was the right thing to do, and as hard as it was to leave everything behind, I knew I had to follow my heart and the inspiration I had received.

During the final hour of our ride deep into the Korean countryside, there were no houses, buildings, or other signs of civilization. If someone had told me I was in Outer Mongolia, I might have believed them.

Finally, a small hamlet of about a half dozen homes appeared. The bus driver indicated we were nearing the stop. Visitors to this agrarian community were rare, and foreigners even more so, which is why I was catching the attention of nearly everyone who lived there.

From a distance, the locals watched my every move.

The woman we had come to visit ran down the path. She uttered something to her neighbors, likely letting them know she had invited us, because they seemed to let their guard down a little.

When my native-Korean companion and I arrived at the entrance to the woman's modest home, a half dozen dogs on long chains barked angrily at us. They weren't pets but rather the family's livelihood—they would be sold at the market. Dog meat was a delicacy in rural Korea.

The home was small, with a traditional ceramic Asian pitched roof, and was heated by burning giant round charcoal cylinders under the floor. We were enthusiastically greeted by the woman's three teenage daughters, who attended our church and were surprised we would travel so far to their family's home.

The purpose of the visit was to help with several projects and to provide some emotional support. The woman's husband, the girls' father, had died tragically in a farming accident a few months earlier. His grave, which looked like a giant grassy baseball pitcher's mound, was on the far end of the property.

While we had come to work, the mother wanted to talk. She insisted on us sitting down, and then skinned a large Asian pear with a paring knife, cutting the peel in a circular motion that created what looked like a large, coiled snake.

After drinking a cup of plum tea, she began to talk rapidly. While I could only understand a small portion of the words she spoke, her thick rural accent was unmistakable. I tried to follow the conversation. It was obvious she was talking about her late husband.

The grief was tangible.

The girls tried to console their mother by holding her hand and patting her back and shoulders. One of the girls grabbed a book of family pictures. She opened it and reminisced about happier times, explaining what their father had meant to the family and how grateful they were for the little they had.

After about a half hour, the girls grew fatigued. They'd had enough mourning for one afternoon and wanted to lighten the mood by playing UNO. I pulled the card game from my red hard-shell briefcase. After a round or two, my companion and I helped move some items into a shed outside and assisted with a handful of odd jobs.

The woman struggled to accept the service and begged us the entire time to come back in the house and play cards. She said that she and the girls could do the work later, and that the best thing we could do was entertain her daughters with UNO.

While we played, the woman cooked a simple vegetarian soup made from a brown root that grows wild in the countryside. After dinner, my companion and I played one final hand, and then we had to leave to catch the last bus. We bowed deeply and thanked the family. The woman grabbed my arm and cried as she expressed her appreciation for the visit.

"*Annyeonghi gaseyo*," we said as we departed, which translates to "stay in peace."

From the moment my companion and I had arrived at their home, I had been fixated on their loss and how incredibly painful it seemed even months later. As the bus rattled back through the dark countryside on the journey back to the apartment, I was overcome with melancholy. I had never felt so far from home, so sad, and so alone.

Back at the apartment, I was too tired to brush my teeth and change into sweats. Instead, I went face-first into my "yo," an inch-thick pad on the floor that served as a bed. I fell asleep wearing my white shirt, black name tag, and necktie.

In a dream, I found myself observing a vivid scene from afar. My mom was driving the family minivan down Parleys Canyon into the Salt Lake Valley. She was taking the connector to Interstate 215, a few miles from our home, when a semitruck veered into westbound traffic, hitting her head-on.

The car was obliterated. Smoke and pieces of debris flew over the cliff toward Suicide Rock.

My mom was gone.

I awoke screaming, in a cold sweat, and crying uncontrollably. The dream had been so real. I had never experienced anything like it. I quickly found my phone card. I didn't think twice about breaking the mission rules. I dialed the number.

My mom answered, and I said hi and then couldn't get a word out.

"Christopher, are you okay? Are you *okay*? What's going on?"

Her worried tone was so familiar, it was as if I could see her leaning forward, her forehead creased with concern.

"I'm okay. I just…" I couldn't utter a full sentence. Tears stung my acne-plagued cheeks.

"Let me…catch my…breath. I'll explain."

After a few minutes, I told her about the dream and about my experience the prior evening with the grieving family. She consoled me in the way only a mother can. Despite her being more than six thousand miles away, her voice and words were analeptic.

I calmed down a little, and we spoke for another half hour. Since I'd arrived in Korea, my family and I normally communicated by mail, and it took a week or two for letters to arrive home. This meant it would take two to four weeks to get a response to anything I sent.

Toward the end of the call, my mom hesitated. There was an abrupt silence.

"Since…since I picked up the phone, I have been debating whether or not I should tell you something. I know this is going to upset you, but it will be worse if I withhold it."

There was another pause. She swallowed and struggled at first to form the words.

"Ba-Baker…Baker passed away this morning. He had a heart attack. It was sudden and unexpected. I'm really sorry."

Tears rained down my face like a Korean monsoon. The emotional storm that had subsided for a few minutes now returned with increased intensity.

"It's okay. It's okay, Christopher. You made peace with him. You probably thought your entire life that you would never cry the day he died… but he meant so much to you, and he has taught you more than you may ever realize."

My sniffling became so loud that my mom stopped for a moment, perhaps hoping the silence might provide a small degree of solace.

"When he wasn't drinking, he was the kindest, sweetest person. You saw that when you visited him. Vaunna told me several times just how much it meant to Baker that you made time for him on your last day at home."

My hands were pale, and my shoulders shook. I had never been in shock. I lay down on the cold yellow linoleum floor with the receiver at my ear and tried to take a deep breath. After a few minutes, I regained my composure and sat up.

I tried to picture Baker in my mind's eye. It seemed as though he had never aged. In my thoughts, Baker was the same angry old man he'd been the first time I saw him while chasing that errant bouncy ball onto his lawn when I was three years old. My mom informed me that Baker had been relatively young, dying at the age of seventy-two.

I thought nonstop about Baker for the next several days. Although the trauma surrounding learning of his death would trigger panic attacks that I would have to endure for more than a year of my remaining missionary service, my memories of Baker were always profound and positive.

While I don't recall receiving an obituary or hearing anything about the funeral service, I didn't forget Baker. When I returned from Korea in the late summer of 1994, one of the first things I did was drive through the old neighborhood. I parked my car across the street from Baker's house. This time I didn't get out. Instead, I sat alone.

CHAPTER 38

Alive

"I'm not supposed to be calling you...I was ordered by the police not to talk to anyone, not even Lois."

Ed's cracking, high-pitched voice causes me to stop multitasking. I've been trying to draft messaging while listening to Tom, who is sitting across my desk from me, playing a recording of his call the previous evening with two *Salt Lake Tribune* reporters.

"Ed, then why are you calling me?"

My tone is intense, with a slight dose of sarcasm, to try to diffuse some of the pressure I am feeling.

It's a few minutes before noon. Six hours earlier, I was caught off guard when I stopped to grab the *Tribune* at the end of my driveway. I was taking my in-laws, who had been visiting from Virginia, to catch an early flight. As I climbed back into the car, I quickly glanced at the over-the-fold headline to see the words "Smarts Frustrated with Police Progress," but I didn't have the opportunity to read the full story until I was parked in front of the terminal.

The *Tribune* article was an extensive interview with Tom, who expressed stinging frustration with the Salt Lake City Police Department. The story detailed mistakes, missteps, and several instances when the police had been disingenuous with the family.

Despite numerous journalists trying to bait the Smarts into criticizing law enforcement for more than nine months, the family had deliberately taken the high road and knew that any type of public rebuke of the police would divert focus and resources from finding Elizabeth.

Before returning home from the airport twenty-five minutes later, I would hear from several East Coast media, including the *New York Times*, and all three network morning shows. There is an irony to the media's response. This new story has very little to do with actually finding Elizabeth, yet the conflict and drama of the Smarts finally criticizing law enforcement are of significant importance. This sudden attention is in stark contrast to the sparse interest and coverage that seemed to be an afterthought a few weeks ago when the family released the sketch of Brian David Mitchell—the very detail that would eventually lead to Elizabeth's rescue.

The media's big question for me that morning is if Ed and Lois are in lockstep with Tom in their disdain for law enforcement. I explain that I haven't had an opportunity to talk with anyone in the family yet; that there will be some type of response, likely a press briefing, by late morning or early afternoon; and that I will circle back with details when they're available.

Because of the waning interest in the case in the weeks leading up to the *Tribune* story, I've gone back to working almost full time on agency clients. The board also has cut our stipend in half, to a couple of thousand dollars a month (we've been receiving this to help cover our costs after volunteering for the first six weeks after Elizabeth was abducted), and has hinted that March would likely be the last month our services would be needed. This isn't necessarily because the board is running out of money or doesn't want to pay. The larger issue is that the case is still taking a significant personal toll on everyone in the family and their inner circle.

Most of the women in the group can't justify the emotional price their immediate families are paying to continue the effort, when the prospects of even finding Elizabeth's body seem bleak. In fact, Lois has rarely been participating in board meetings or discussions after saying a very personal goodbye to Elizabeth.

A couple of months after the abduction, Lois could not go on any longer with the thought that someone was holding her daughter captive. In order to have the strength and focus to attend to the needs of her other five children, she bravely let go. Early one morning, Lois put on Elizabeth's boots, spurs, gloves, and cowboy hat; saddled up a horse; and along with

Dr. Smart rode up the trail to one of Elizabeth's favorite locations—Moffit Peak, deep in the Uinta mountains.

She paused, peered out at the mountain vista, and began to cry. Lois then removed from her vest the light blue circular pin that had Elizabeth's picture on it and the words "Pray for Me," and deposited it into the earth. After more tears and retrospection, she got back on the horse and headed back home, fully focused as a mother of her surviving children. Lois would recount in her book with Ed that she "had to put on a protective coat of armor to safeguard [her] family—and that coat needed to be big enough to fit all of [them] inside. I need[ed] to see to it that whoever had taken Elizabeth from us didn't succeed in taking all of us.... I wanted to believe with every ounce of my heart that Elizabeth was still alive and that she'd one day come home. I could not let this destroy our family."

While the women on the board had been advocating for scaling back efforts, the men weren't as willing to change directions; in fact, most were defiantly opposed to the notion. A few weeks ago, when Ed and I traveled to New York to do an interview on a show Phil Donahue was launching on MSNBC, there was a knock on my hotel room door well after midnight.

Through the peephole, I could see a somewhat blurry version of Ed. He looked pale. His blonde hair was ruffled. His eyes were crimson.

"Did I wake you?" he asked as I opened the door. "I'm sorry. I can't sleep. I really need to talk."

He came in and took a seat in the swivel chair at the desk.

"Chris, you may think I'm crazy by what I am about to tell you. Maybe I *am* crazy. A lot of people think I am. But it doesn't matter. The only thing that matters is finding Elizabeth."

He paused and began to tear up.

Being caught off guard and sleep-deprived, I was somewhat at a loss for what to say, but I knew Ed needed to be validated.

"It's okay, Ed. I got you. You...you aren't crazy. You're doing everything you can."

He sat forward in his chair and looked at me inquisitively.

"Am I doing everything I can? Am I? Are we doing everything we *can*? That's the reason I came to talk with you, Chris. Call me crazy, but I know Elizabeth is *alive*.... She is out there. She is waiting for us to rescue her. I just know it.... I *know* she is alive."

A chill reverberated through my body. A bead of sweat formed on my back. It was as if I were a wallflower in a Baptist congregation, counting the minutes until the service was over, and then the Holy Spirit unexpectedly hit me so hard that I was compelled to stand up and shout, "Hallelujah!"

"No. you're not crazy, Ed. I *believe* you."

We were both silent for several minutes before I continued: "We're here, aren't we? You traveled across the country to do *The Phil Donahue Show*. You took two days out of your schedule to participate in a cable show that only a handful of people even knows exists."

Although Ed was battling feelings of weakness and inadequacy, I honestly couldn't think of anyone I had ever met who was more committed to an important cause, or of anything more he could be doing.

We spent the next several hours reviewing and analyzing the investigation, the media outlets we were currently working with, and our efforts to lobby Congress for the National Amber Alert. Ed informed me that Tom "might be crazy too" and had been riding TRAX, Salt Lake City's light-rail system, around the city for hours each day after someone reported on the search center hotline that they believed they had seen Mitchell with two robed women on public transit.

Tom recalls in his book that in March, "Detective Tom" and his monomania were back. He wasn't eating much, and slept only when he took an Ambien. Tom also had the unshakable thought that Elizabeth was alive, and was committed to doing everything possible to find her.

After dropping my in-laws off at the airport early that March morning, I returned home briefly, then headed out to meet with a client at a resort in Midway, a quaint Utah town, settled by Mormon immigrants from Switzerland, nestled in the mountains an hour east of Salt Lake City. I was on the phone the entire drive, fielding calls from family members and media.

My phone continued to buzz at the resort as I tried to collaborate with the client on strategy for the summer season. Ed and Tom called me several times in a row, so I excused myself and stepped out for the better part of fifteen minutes. When I returned, the client held up a copy of the *Tribune*.

"I'm guessing this is what you're dealing with. It's totally fine. Take care of the Smart family. Let's reschedule for next week."

I departed and continued to try to navigate the battle within the extended Smart family, a conflict that seemed to escalate with every update I received. Initially, Lois was incensed that Tom would speak for her publicly and express a position she didn't necessarily agree with. It triggered her emotionally, since it was contrary to her extended family's long-held position regarding law enforcement.

Lois' three sisters and five brothers, the Francoms, had been actively involved in the early days following Elizabeth's abduction, working alongside the extended Smart family to help run the search center. Lois' brother Dave even initially had served as one of the primary family spokespersons. The Francoms seemed to believe strongly in respecting authority, and were often turned off by the extended Smart family's, especially Tom's, cynical and cavalier attitude toward the Salt Lake City Police Department.

After a few weeks, the Francoms decided to go in a different direction. They moved to an office in Holladay, a suburb fifteen minutes from downtown Salt Lake, where they assisted with telecommunications equipment for the search center hotline and other duties. I hadn't seen them at the Arlington Hills ward house since.

Ed was caught in the middle of an escalating feud between Lois and Tom. He would call every fifteen minutes to provide me with an update, then would briefly vent before getting pulled back into the ruckus. The battle had reached a breaking point around ten o'clock in the morning, when Ed and Lois received a call from the police.

"Lois is beside herself," Ed explained. "The police are beyond angry and said the article has done more damage to the investigation than we can comprehend. A detective told me they will only be communicating with us on a need-to-know basis moving forward. The crazy thing is, I don't totally disagree with what Tom said, especially about the police not putting enough emphasis on Brian David Mitchell."

Ed and I collaborated and determined that our best approach would be a press conference, at which Tom would apologize and walk back some of his comments. Ed would clarify his position, express his appreciation of law enforcement, and then emphasize the importance of finding Mitchell. In theory, the approach was solid; the challenge would be getting Ed and Tom to stay on message.

When I arrived at my company's offices at around noon, Tom's daughter Sierra, who had completed her internship and been hired as a public relations coordinator, informed me her dad was waiting. He was almost an hour early.

"Chris, you wouldn't believe how bad I let them have it last night," Tom told me. "I know this has caused a lot of turmoil, but Lois will get over it. Someone had to say these things. The truth hurts."

He grimaced and pulled out a micro tape recorder. Tom pressed Play and started the hour-long tape of the interview. "Watch me make Vigh and Cantera look like complete idiots." Michael Vigh and Kevin Cantera were the *Tribune's* reporters covering the abduction.

I cringed listening to the dialogue.

Vigh and Cantera went easy on Tom in the article. This could be so much worse, I nearly muttered.

That's when my tarnished silver flip phone vibrated on the desk with Ed's call.

"Ed, so why are you defying law enforcement's orders by calling me?"

"I'm afraid I'm going to have to miss our meeting, and I know we have a lot of work to do to prepare for the press conference. I…I was told to go to the Sandy City Police Department. Not to stop. Not to talk to anyone, not even Lois. I'm sorry. I'll try to get to your office as soon as I can. Do you think we can postpone the press conference?"

I tell Ed not to worry about the media and to call me as soon as he knows what this is about. After I hang up, Tom asks me if he heard the conversation right. My response is two words: "Jason Burnette."

"Jason Burnette? What? Chris, who is that?" Tom looks puzzled and continues to quiz me as I scroll through the contacts on my phone.

A few years before the abduction, I was working one afternoon in the office when an alert for an email with the subject line "Is that you No. 44?" popped up on my computer monitor.

Jason Burnette, one of my high school basketball teammates, was recruiting me to play on his city league team. It was an easy decision; the league was exactly what I needed to stay in shape.

In addition to getting together for weekly basketball games, we started going to lunch. Then double dates commenced when he started seeing a new girl. When they decided to get married, several months later, Laura and I were one of a handful of guests invited to their intimate wedding at a bed-and-breakfast in southern Utah. Jason was a detective with the Sandy City Police Department. His wife, Michelle, was the department's public information officer. Ironically, we had tickets to see a production of the musical *Big River* together at Hale Centre Theatre that very night.

I quickly find Jason's cell number and call it. Voicemail.

I try his office line. Voicemail.

I try his home number. Voicemail.

I page him and then try his cell number again. This routine continues frantically for several minutes. Finally, he picks up; his voice is curt.

"What in the *heck* do you want? *Stop* calling me. I would answer my phone if I was available to talk."

While I have been overly persistent, Jason's tone and demeanor come as a surprise.

"Jason, I'm sorry. I know something is going on with Ed Smart. If you can tell me anything, I would be forever grateful."

"*I can't...*"

I hear a click. He has hung up on me. This is completely uncharacteristic of Jason, who has always had a fun-loving, laid-back personality.

I grip my forehead, then cover and rub my eyes. When I finally look up, I see that Sierra has joined Tom sitting across from me. Tom looks me point blank in the eyes.

"Who were you talking to? *Who* is Jason Burnette?"

Tom is growing frustrated that I haven't stopped to explain. Before I can answer, my phone rings again.

"I am so sorry, Chris," Jason says. "I was in a meeting and your calls were interrupting things. We've brought in an indigent teenager who we think is Elizabeth Smart. We're waiting for Ed to come and identify her."

I try to swallow. My throat constricts. Sierra gasps and nearly collapses as she steps away from her position perched next to Tom, the two of them straining to listen in on the call.

"Where did they find the body, Jason?" I hold back tears, doing my best to stay professional.

"What *body*? She's sitting in the room next to me. She's alive. We don't know why it's taking Ed so long to get here."

Tom embraces Sierra tightly as she sobs.

I thank Jason and ask him to call me with updates. Then we dial Ed. He immediately answers. He's frantic.

"I don't know anything yet. I'm pacing in the parking lot. I'm too afraid to go into the station."

"Ed, they have Elizabeth. She is alive. She is waiting for you."

There is no response. The line goes dead.

I find the resolution plan I developed when the body of the blonde fourteen-year-old girl was found near Brigham City last October. Tom and I begin executing the plan. After Tom confirms Elizabeth's rescue with his main FBI source, I delegate the task of informing each family and board member of Elizabeth's rescue to him. I have something more important to do.

I dial Laura's number. She doesn't believe me at first, and then when she realizes I'm being serious about Elizabeth's rescue, we both become emotional.

"We did this together, Laura. I may have been on the front line, but it wouldn't have been possible without your support, sacrifice, and amazing counsel. I love you..."

We talk for several minutes about how it seemed like this would never end, especially in such a miraculous fashion. After hanging up with Laura, I sit down on the floor in my office. It will be another forty-five minutes before the news breaks. I try to catch my breath and gather myself, aware of something that few others know: A tsunami is about to hit Salt Lake City.

CHAPTER 39

The Day After

Trying to collect myself, I pop open a Diet Coke. The hypnotic sound of the carbonated bubbles, penetrating the aluminum tab, provides a short-lived reprieve.

It's a little after midnight, fewer than twelve hours since the phone call with Ed that Elizabeth is alive and is waiting for him inside the police station. My mind sprints in multiple directions. I'm reliving events in vivid detail while trying to tackle several complicated issues. I am euphoric yet overcome by the challenge of helping to tell Elizabeth's story.

There are difficult questions to address, given the extent of the physical and sexual abuse Elizabeth has endured. Why didn't she try to escape? Is she sympathetic to her captors? Is she pregnant? How does the family feel about a political commentator using the words "crybaby" and "moron" to describe the reaction by Ed and his siblings to the rescue and then mocking Elizabeth for being raped?

Additionally, there is the issue of polygamy. Despite Brian David Mitchell's beliefs and practices being isolated, extremist, and contrary to those of The Church of Jesus Christ of Latter-day Saints, the role that Mormonism and its history might have played in Elizabeth's abduction is a prominent theme in the national dialogue. The media organizations want me to defend or provide greater context surrounding the history of the church and polygamy, as it relates to the abhorrent behavior of Mitchell and his wife, Wanda Barzee.

I will continue to diplomatically balk at these questions. The story, from the Smarts' perspective, is about a brave girl who has survived and outwitted a sick pedophile and his accomplice. My focus is on positioning Elizabeth and her family as survivors, and leveraging her rescue to push for passage of the National Amber Alert. It's not to try to explain or justify the possible motives of her abductors.

However, throughout the night I will think through all the possible questions that might be posed, including why Elizabeth's abduction happened and how her environment contributed to it. I know that polygamy once again will rear its ugly head. While it won't be in the family's best interests to address these questions, I'll work through the answers on my own to make sure I'm thoroughly considering all the possible angles and scenarios.

As in the case of Ron and Dan Lafferty's murdering their sister-in-law, Brenda, and her fifteen-month-old daughter, Erica, in 1984, the root of Elizabeth's abduction isn't religious extremism or polygamy. Instead, this is a convenient excuse. Mitchell is a perverse, mentally ill man who employed all forms of manipulation to fulfill his selfish desires. He is reported to have sexually abused girls long before he adopted his so-called Mormon fanaticism.

For more than a century, religious extremism—including as practiced by factious groups, especially those practicing polygamy—have often been incorrectly associated with The Church of Jesus Christ of Latter-Day Saints, which disavowed the practice in 1890. Despite the efforts of church leaders and members (which, as of 2022, number almost seventeen million worldwide) to disassociate themselves from these splinter groups (an estimated thirty to forty thousand people), the public and media continue to mistakenly connect them directly and indirectly to the church.

This can be attributed to several factors, including that bizarre high-profile criminals with ties to Utah—such as Mitchell, the Laffertys, Warren Jeffs, and Ervil LeBaron—have used their "religion" as a salacious façade to try to justify, explain, or defend their heinous behavior.

For example, in 1984, the media called the Laffertys' crimes religious killings, but according to a 2022 *Deseret News* story, Utah court records indicate something very different. Ron Lafferty was using his so-called revelations as an excuse to kill Brenda, but prosecutors strongly argued that his motive was in fact seeking revenge on Brenda for encouraging his ex-wife, Diana, to divorce him a year earlier.

Elizabeth underscores this argument in her book *My Story*, writing that Mitchell "simply used culture and language of religion to manipulate people in order to get what he wanted.... He was his number-one priority, followed by sex, drugs, and alcohol, but he used religion in all of those aspects to justify."

Even in total, the number of religious zealots with beliefs and practices tied to a distorted view of the history or doctrine of The Church of Jesus Christ of Latter-day Saints is very minimal. Of those individuals, only a very small fraction have committed crimes under the banner of self-centered radicalism.

Their stories, coupled with a loose, distorted, and often poorly researched connection to church history or doctrine, make for compelling and commercially successful articles, books, movies, TV shows, on-demand docuseries, and plays, but those works do little to accurately represent a robust and growing faith that journalists have touted as "the most American religion."

In truth, these stories have very little to do with the modern Church of Jesus Christ of Latter-day Saints, which in the past 130 years has evolved beyond its polygamist past. But to paraphrase church founder Joseph Smith, no man knows our history. Historians continue to debate and reevaluate the church's earliest accounts and the justifications for polygamy, but those reasons cannot be boiled down to simple perversion, revenge, power, or insanity. The answer is much more complicated.

Knowing this type of mischaracterization of polygamy will be unavoidable is especially disheartening. While my culture, religion, history, and people, like most others, are not without their warts, idiosyncrasies, and sins, it always leaves me feeling a little wounded when we're misrepresented, stereotyped, or written off.

I recognize that we are not the only members of a religious group who feel this way, and I'm afraid this trend of mischaracterizing religions is not going to change anytime soon, especially given the tribalism in our country today. While that's not an optimistic take on society, I am encouraged and inspired by the resolve of countless people from various backgrounds, religions, and cultures who are genuinely good and who are working in their families, churches, and communities to be more understanding, kind, inclusive, and loving of neighbors and associates who are different from themselves.

As I type into the night working on response messaging, coherent thoughts become more and more elusive; it seems as if fewer and fewer neurons are firing in the soft tissue between my ears. During the early-morning hours of March 13, 2003, as I contemplate the challenges and issues at hand, I briefly think back to when I helped Annabelle on her classroom legal defense almost twenty years earlier. In a similar manner, my sleep-deprived brain races to solve the impossible, with the hypnotic rhythm of typing in the background providing an innate sense of comfort. My default is to continue typing on my computer and working to solve the problem, even when the circumstances and challenges are well beyond my ability.

The only difference between the eleven-year-old boy and my current self is Diet Coke. My mental elixir. I take a sip, reset, and get back to work.

A couple of hours later, as I drive past the Arlington Hills ward en route to the Smart home, I see so many satellite trucks, cameras, lights, and crews that it looks like the pre-game show for the Super Bowl or the red carpet at the Academy Awards. The scene is in stark contrast to a few days ago, when some journalists were complaining about having to cover the story because of its "sensational" nature versus it being "real" news.

When I arrive, Ed walks down the steps and gets into my car. He is dressed in a tan suit with a yellow tie. I notice a large cold sore forming on his lower lip. He's giddy at first, but as I drive down Kristianna Circle, his demeanor slowly changes.

"Pull over, Chris. I need to talk before we go down there."

I put the car in park as Ed continues.

"You can't begin to imagine the terrible things that man, well actually both of them, did to Elizabeth."

He pauses. His eyes bulge. The wrinkles on his forehead grow deeper.

"Chris, I only heard a small portion of what happened, and it literally makes me want to throw up. I am so happy Elizabeth is home, but I never thought about having to deal with all of this."

He confides in me several of the details that Elizabeth shared with him that evening—details I never wanted to know and wish I never heard. Yet, at the same time, they provide me with a unique perspective into what Ed is feeling, what he is trying to process.

"I'm speechless, Ed. That's *horrific…absolutely horrific.*"

My body tightens. My heart races. Trying to conceal a wave of nervous energy, I put my hands over my mouth and exhale loudly. I don't believe Ed notices though, as he is fidgeting and pointing angrily.

"Ed, it's imperative that you vent to me about these things and not show this level of anger publicly. Focus on the miracle of Elizabeth being home, not these two psychopaths and what they have put her through. If anything, channel this fury into the fight to get Congress to pass the National Amber Alert."

He nods in agreement. We spend the next fifteen minutes simulating interviews and preparing Ed to answer hard questions. He seems to relax a little during the short drive to the Shriners hospital (across the street from the Arlington Hills ward), where the network morning shows have set up makeshift studios and have flown in their top journalism talent on private jets.

After a couple of hours of interviews, we break away and walk down to the church for a press conference. The shutters from scores of cameras fire in rapid motion; a crush of journalists yell questions; talent agents try to hand me proposals and business cards, wanting to buy the family's story. Many people have gathered at the perimeter of the property as well, including ward members and search center officials. Countless strangers are present too, many of whom were likely volunteer searchers who feel an intense connection to Elizabeth and the Smart family.

Once we navigate through the chaos, Ed steps forward and addresses the crowd.

"It's real. I can't begin to tell you how happy I am. What an absolute miracle and answer to prayers this has been."

Ed's level of jubilation is on par with the reaction of Utah Jazz fans when John Stockton hit a miraculous three-pointer to send the team to the NBA finals a few years ago. Ed thrusts his arms victoriously into the air.

After he talks for a few minutes about how Elizabeth is doing, his mood and demeanor unexpectedly shift. I know he is thinking about Mitchell and Barzee and the unmentionable things they did to Elizabeth. I brace for the worst.

"…if nothing comes out of this other than to send a big message to Washington and Jim Sensenbrenner: If you're out there, *I'm talking to you.* You are the reason the Amber Alert has not gone through, and I'm calling on you, and I'm calling on Congress, and I'm calling on them to pass the Amber Alert *now*. Children cannot afford you fumbling around. The blood of those children is on *someone's head*."

Ed shudders. His eyes are large, and his tone is almost vile, as he yells as if Sensenbrenner, the House Judiciary Committee chairman, is in front of him. Sensenbrenner has been holding up the legislation, which passed the Senate, by adding more controversial and partisan judiciary measures. Despite our multiple attempts over several months, Representative Sensenbrenner has refused to meet with the Smart family. Now Ed is using his bully pulpit to send him a message and make Congress act on the National Amber Alert.

While some will consider Ed's diatribe a little dramatic and over the top, I am relieved he didn't attack Mitchell and Barzee.

Following the press conference, the extended Smart and Francom families, search center board members, and other close friends congregate in the overflow of the Arlington Hills ward chapel. Dr. Smart, who drove with his wife, Dorotha, through the night from Palm Springs, California, after receiving word of Elizabeth's rescue, addresses the group.

"We have experienced a miracle. This has occurred because of the faith and works of everyone in this room and countless people from around the world. I want to thank each of you. I love you. I know God lives..."

As Dr. Smart is finishing his remarks, the door on the west side of the chapel swings open.

Wearing a black turtleneck, red blazer, dark skirt, and high heels, Jane Clayson is beaming as she walks toward Lois with her arms outstretched. Her disposition is that of a child blowing out candles on her seventh birthday.

Jane remarks that covering the Smart family has been one of the highlights of her career and that she's so happy for everyone. The fact that Jane has slipped past the security volunteers outside the church doors and is the only reporter in the room, as well as the only person outside of the family or inner circle, makes the moment feel not quite right. But saying something doesn't feel right either, so I stand quietly, waiting for the attention to shift back to Dr. Smart and the family members.

Suddenly, Dorotha Smart steps in front of Jane, pointing a finger in her face.

"Who do you think you are? I can't believe the nerve marching in here..."

The fiery matriarch of the family is not about to let things go.

"Elizabeth continued to be abused while we all waited for your silly show to air. She could have been killed. You should be ashamed of yourself. Ashamed..."

Before Dorotha finishes, Jane gasps, begins crying audibly, and dashes out of the room. Tom quickly follows, calling after her.

The door closes.

I feel bad for Jane because of the sharpness of the exchange that has just occurred. While it's true that Ed and Lois initially held up releasing the sketch of Mitchell by a couple of weeks to accommodate *48 Hours*, this delay pales in comparison to the police who impeded its release for more than four months.

Jane returns fifteen minutes later. She is visibly chastened and apologizes. It will take me a long time to realize the pressure Jane has been under, and how she has been misled by the police, who gave her significant time, access, and compelling reasons to keep the focus on Richard Ricci. I will also realize that Jane's dogged attempts to build a relationship and work with Lois are common journalistic practices. It is a reporter's job to use every angle, advantage, and connection to get the story.

Years later, Jane will bravely share some of her personal challenges in the book *Silent Souls Weeping*, which is about mental health and the Latter-day Saint culture. Seeing her in this light makes me realize I have been guilty of the very thing I try to fight against. At times, I judge, vilify, and listen only to what I want to hear. But I continue to relearn this lesson, that our lives are much more complicated and deeper than depicted on the surface level—and, most important, that every story has more than one perspective.

CHAPTER 40

The Vet

As I step into the lights, the fluorescent filaments are jarring. It's as if I'm sitting in an optometrist's chair and without notice, a bright flash pierces my retina, causing my dilated pupils to recoil. All I can see are auras ricocheting in the distance, like a stone skimming on water. While I struggle to regain my vision, the baritone voice of a news anchorman asking me a question a few feet in front of me is crystal clear.

"You have lived this night and day for more than nine months. What does tonight mean to you?"

It's a few days after Elizabeth was rescued. Mayor Rocky Anderson has organized a public celebration at Liberty Park, a prominent open space near downtown Salt Lake City. The purpose of the event is to thank law enforcement, the thousands of volunteers who searched for Elizabeth, and the people who called the police when they recognized Elizabeth walking on a sidewalk in Sandy, Utah. It is also an opportunity for the community to come together and rejoice in Elizabeth's miraculous return.

The event has the air and energy of a presidential victory party. The mayor, John Walsh, and members of the Smart family address an enthusiastic crowd of thousands. Thurl Bailey, a former Utah Jazz basketball star who ironically is now a jazz musician, and a convert to The Church of Jesus Christ of Latter-day Saints, performs.

As the program is winding down, I am invited to be interviewed live on a makeshift news set with Mark Koelbel and Shauna Lake, anchors with the local CBS affiliate. As I step out from the shadows onto the risers, the large bright lights catch me off guard.

Squinting, I answer the warm-up question about what the event means to me. Slowly my sight begins to adjust. I start to make out silhouettes of people gathering. I have participated in hundreds of interviews, many live, but none with a crowd this large.

"What went into Elizabeth's decision to stay home tonight?" Koelbel asks.

There had been pressure for Elizabeth to attend the event, but we determined it was too soon for her to make a public appearance. Instead, I worked with her to write a note, which was then superimposed over a photo Tom had taken of her holding William the day before. The image was enlarged to create a large poster that served as a significant visual in front of the podium.

"When I sat down with Elizabeth this morning, I was struck by how mature she is, and how genuinely grateful she is for everyone who helped her get home…"

Before I can finish my thought, something distracts me.

A balding man with a long scruffy beard, blue sweatshirt, jeans, and a dark green jacket paces nervously in the foreground. His demeanor and presence are an anomaly, despite there being a sea of diverse people milling around the park.

I become so fixated on this individual that my mind goes on autopilot. I don't recall answering the last few questions. I manage to thank Koelbel and Lake, then walk off the riser onto the grass.

The man takes a few steps toward me, then cowers, puts his head down, and starts to walk away. I am perplexed and slightly unnerved, but at the same time, I feel a strange sense of needing to connect with him. I walk closer and put my hand out.

"Hi, I'm Chris. Thanks so much for coming."

I try to appear welcoming, but beneath the smile on my face, I'm feeling cautious.

The mysterious man stops and doesn't shake my hand. Instead, he begins to retreat. But he pauses awkwardly and then changes direction, stepping gingerly back toward me.

"Wa…wi…will you please pass…pass along a message to *Elizabeth*?"

His voice is a raspy mumble. His face is stoic. He avoids making eye contact.

"Ta...ta...tell her that, ah, her...her courage was so inspiring that it brought me here tonight. I...I haven't been in public since coming back from Vietnam."

His expression melts into emotion as he seems to be losing composure. He looks away.

"Of course, I will tell her. Elizabeth will appreciate hearing this."

The veteran's head turns back, and his blurry blue eyes dart at me as I also become a little emotional.

We converse for some time. The man loosens up a little but never seems comfortable. He tells me that being around so many people at the park is overwhelming, but that it's bearable since everyone and everything are so happy. He then quickly changes the subject, wanting to know where I was when I heard the news about Elizabeth's rescue. I relay the experience with my friend at the Sandy City Police Department and how we were able to inform Ed outside the station. The man is amazed by the story and then tells me how he was washing dishes in his kitchen when he heard the news on the radio, and how he sobbed, knowing Elizabeth was safe.

Tears well in his eyes and stream down his face as he tells me the details. He periodically stops and turns away, trying to regain his composure.

"It's okay. You're so brave to come to the park and tell me your story. You remind me a lot of a World War II hero who lived next door to me growing up. Like you, he paid an incredible price for our freedom. I want you to know how much I appreciate your sacrifice."

Before I can finish, someone taps me on the shoulder. A reporter with a cameraman in tow requests a quick interview. I agree and ask them to set up and give me a minute.

When I look back, the Vietnam veteran is starting to walk away. I step toward him. He hesitates and then looks me in the eyes.

The sentiment from Baker's living room almost a decade earlier floods my thoughts: *You have no idea how much this means to me.*

As he is about to depart, I begin to extend my hand. Not unlike the old man, the veteran brushes past; we embrace.

Epilogue

During my junior year at Skyline High School, I was shocked and devastated when I was cut from the basketball team. After a week of practicing with another school and preparing to transfer, I changed my mind at the last minute. I had an affinity for writing and didn't want to lose my position as sports editor of the *Skyline Horizon*, the student newspaper, so I sucked up my pride and went back to school. That day, the basketball coach sought me out and asked me to return to the team. While I was scrawny—six foot four and barely 160 pounds—I outworked and outplayed the larger, more talented players, and this dynamic helped to increase the intensity of the team practices.

That year, I gave everything I had in practice but rarely saw any action on the varsity team. As a result, at the end of the regular season, I didn't have the required playing time necessary to letter. I also knew, however, that there was an easy solution. Utah high school rules stipulated that anyone who played in the state basketball tournament qualified to letter. The tournament had a double elimination format. My team lost one game by more than twenty points and won another by almost thirty points. In both games, the coach almost emptied the bench, putting everyone in except for me.

Unfortunately, there was no *Rudy* moment. No one aside from my father even noticed. The team and fans didn't lobby the coach or start a chant to put me in the game. My dad was so upset when it happened the second time, he had to be restrained by two other parents, and I had to help calm him down almost thirty minutes later.

The next year, I lettered by default, simply because I made the team as a senior. I refused to acknowledge the honor. I threw away the certificate and rebuffed my parents' repeated attempts to purchase a letterman's jacket for me. While this setback motivated me to work harder, I held a grudge and harbored hard feelings toward the coaches for several decades. With time, I realized I was the only one hurt by not wearing a letterman's jacket and proudly recognizing my hard work and achievement.

Shortly after Elizabeth was rescued, a very generous client arranged for Laura and me to take the Smarts to Hawaii for a week. The client recognized that the family needed to escape Salt Lake City and have some time together to unwind and reconnect.

On the trip, the Smarts attracted attention everywhere we went, from the time we departed Salt Lake International Airport until we returned. While this wasn't unexpected, given the miraculous story and the amount of attention it had received, what surprised me most was that no one seemed to recognize Elizabeth.

In the ten days since she had been rescued, Elizabeth's appearance had changed. With sleep, exercise, and proper nutrition, she appeared like a more mature version of the girl from the photos and videos that had been flashed across the news while she was missing. She looked much less like the weathered, puffy-cheeked teenager from the handful of images that had been released since she had returned home.

Nearly everyone who approached Ed and Lois on the trip didn't recognize Elizabeth, and asked them how she was doing. This usually happened while Elizabeth was standing right in front of them. On a kayaking expedition, the guide even privately asked me who was taking care of Elizabeth while the family was away. When I explained she was in the boat behind us, the guide did a double take and said, "Really? That's her?"

This was a blessing that provided the perfect cover. Elizabeth could work to acclimate back into normal life without being recognized everywhere.

As we were waiting to board the return flight from Hawaii, Ed received a call. The family had reached a settlement with the *National Enquirer* regarding its story about the family sex ring. An announcement was going to be made a couple of hours after our red-eye flight returned. And the announcement would reignite some of the frenzied interest in the story.

The *Enquirer*, as part of the settlement, would do something that no legitimate news organization would ever consider: divulge its sources for the story. These sources were none other than *Salt Lake Tribune* reporters Michael Vigh and Kevin Cantera, who had been paid ten thousand dollars each by American Media, Inc.

These were the two men who had written numerous stories citing unnamed sources that initially created speculation that the kidnapping had been an inside job, and later published articles that supported the Salt Lake City Police Department's position that Richard Ricci had been responsible for Elizabeth's abduction. Over the next week, both Vigh and Cantera would be fired and the *Tribune*'s popular and long-tenured editor in chief, Jay Shelledy, would resign.

After helping the Smarts navigate the situation, I turned my attention to the passage of the National Amber Alert. Even after the rescue, Ed hadn't stopped lobbying and had brought Elizabeth into the effort, writing letters that were read on the floor of Congress. When the legislation finally passed on April 21, 2003, the White House called.

Unlike with the Conference on Missing, Exploited, and Runaway Children, the White House and President Bush wanted the Smarts to come to Washington, DC, and be in the Rose Garden when he signed the legislation into law.

I went back and forth with the White House regarding the Smarts' participation. Before I would even discuss options, I wanted to know why the Smarts initially hadn't been invited to the conference in October. The White House wouldn't provide specific details but more or less told me there had been bad intel regarding the family. (I have always surmised that the exclusion had been a result of intelligence gathered from local law enforcement, but I don't know for sure.)

The White House had first contacted me about the president wanting the Smart family, especially Elizabeth, to participate in the ceremony fewer than forty-eight hours before the event. Negotiations were fierce. The White House adamantly wanted Elizabeth front and center, standing next to the president, when he signed the legislation. I stalled, knowing this would compromise Elizabeth's newfound anonymity. At the same time, Ed told me that Elizabeth really wanted to meet the president.

The White House said if Elizabeth wasn't willing to publicly participate in the ceremony, they wouldn't fly the Smarts to Washington. As diplomatically as possible, I told them the Smarts were okay with not being a part of the signing, and wished them well.

An hour later, a key staff member from Senator Orrin Hatch's office called and informed me they had been asked by a high-ranking White House official to broker a deal. I made the pitch that Ed and Lois were willing to be in the Rose Garden ceremony, but that Elizabeth would only meet privately with the president beforehand. There would be no photography; however, the president was welcome to talk about meeting Elizabeth in his remarks. We negotiated over several phone calls. Finally, with fewer than four hours before the last flight to Washington, the White House caved and agreed.

As I was packing, I called Ed to tell him the good news but was blindsided by a new twist.

"Chris, Lois doesn't want you to go with us. She feels like you're managing us too much and wants the world to see how beautiful Elizabeth is and how well she is doing."

This was out of character. While I didn't interface much with Lois, she had always been cordial and complimentary. She had never voiced any feedback, complaints, or harsh words.

I paused and took a breath. My voice shook with emotion. I was doing everything I could to contain myself and not yell.

"I either represent you and your family, or I don't. While I disagree with putting Elizabeth out there, I respect and can work with Lois' decision regarding what is best for your daughter. If Lois doesn't want me there though, then it's probably time to make a change. I either need a commitment moving forward or it would be best for me to go back to focusing on my work at the agency."

Ed hesitated and asked me to give him a few minutes. He wanted to try to reason with Lois before accepting my resignation. When he called me back a short time later, I knew the answer from the tone of his voice. Ed said it just wasn't going to work for Lois, apologized, and thanked me for my service to the family.

Hanging up the phone, I was lightheaded. I could feel my heart pounding and couldn't speak. All of the emotions from the past eleven months, many of which had been pent up, began gushing like water through a broken dam. Laura sensed something was wrong from the other room. She came rushing into the home office and held me while I sobbed for hours.

I stayed home from the office the next day. I turned on the live coverage of the Rose Garden event but couldn't stomach watching it. I changed the channel. Fortunately, the Cubs were playing a day game.

Later that afternoon, my business partners, Mike Grass and Missy Larsen, dropped by and gave me a bronze statue of a girl doing a handstand. There was a note from the sculptor, Dennis Smith, expressing that while it might seem as if my efforts had not properly been recognized, they'd made a difference for Elizabeth and countless other missing children, for which he was grateful. I still get emotional thinking about the experience. The statue is one of my most cherished treasures.

I would be lying if I said I wasn't deeply hurt by the separation from the Smart family, and that hurt lasted for quite a while. I also knew, however, that Ed and Lois had been through more than almost anyone could comprehend. I would come to recognize that the break from the pressure, stress, and demands of the assignment was a good thing for me, and probably divine. It was essential to moving forward, strengthening my relationship with Laura, starting a family, and building a business.

Back in 2003, I knew I had an important decision to make though. I could be bitter and avoid the Smart family, or I could try to forgive. While the former would have been justified, I knew from experience I would be the one who would lose—and I didn't want the Smarts to become another letterman's jacket.

So Ed, Lois, the children, and the extended members of the Smart family and I maintained a strong friendship. I attended many weddings, mission farewells, homecomings, rodeos, and the funeral of Dr. Smart. I was always welcomed as a member of the family.

When Brian David Mitchell and Wanda Barzee came up for trial in 2010, Ed asked me to help consult on the media strategy and response. I jumped at the opportunity and worked on site during the verdict and sentencing, helping Elizabeth to leverage those opportunities to bring attention to and help other children who were missing or had survived sexual abuse.

Following the sentencing of Mitchell to life in prison in 2011, Elizabeth asked me to continue working with her, to help position her as a child advocate. Witnessing Elizabeth behind the scenes and seeing how genuine and sincere she has been in working to help others over the past eleven years has been one of the most rewarding experiences of my career.

Outside of her advocacy work, I have helped Elizabeth with the news of her engagement, planned and executed her surprise wedding in Hawaii, assisted with announcements of the birth of her children, and helped her navigate the heartbreaking news of Ed and Lois' divorce.

The various experiences over the past twenty years have been enriching. They also have helped prepare me for new work opportunities and opened numerous doors beyond Elizabeth and the Smart family. I have been blessed to help almost three hundred companies, nonprofit organizations, individuals, and families respond to a myriad of crisis situations. Many of my efforts have involved helping and collaborating with people in their darkest hours and witnessing the strength and resilience of the human spirit and the family unit.

I have applied lessons learned while managing the Smart kidnapping and scores of other family crises to develop a free public relations website, FamilySpokesperson.org, which offers tools, templates, and other resources for everyday people who find themselves in the public eye. When Elizabeth went missing, the Smart family was blessed with tremendous resources and connections that aren't typically available to most people. FamilySpokesperson.org is a small effort to help bridge that gap (from a communications standpoint) for all families. It is my hope that one day there might be a nonprofit organization that works nationally to provide pro bono public relations consultations and response assistance to families in crisis.

It's been said that time expands our understanding and appreciation. I can attest to the truth of this from the countless hours I have spent reminiscing, researching, and writing down my memories.

In the grueling but miraculous journey of finding Elizabeth, I experienced the very best of humanity, including people from different backgrounds putting aside their differences and coming together with one common purpose. I witnessed the organization and precision of Elizabeth's ward and stake as they helped one of their own. And I was touched and forever changed by the courage, faith, and insatiable drive of the Smart family to do whatever it took to rescue Elizabeth.

With Baker, I experienced an unusual and charged relationship that fortunately, before it was too late, became a friendship that I still treasure. I also came to appreciate the incredible price that many of our brave servicemen and servicewomen have paid (and that many still are paying) by enduring a lifetime of agony from the deep mental and physical wounds of war.

And growing up in the culture of The Church of Jesus Christ of Latter-day Saints, I have been blessed experiencing the joy that comes from serving others. I have learned to be less judgmental, knowing that most people, including myself, while flawed and imperfect, are trying to do their best. And I have learned the tremendous peace and benefits that come from staying true to my convictions.

Overall, I have come to realize that the most challenging experiences in life serve to teach us truths we can't learn on the paths of least resistance. They prepare us to tackle future obstacles and opportunities. Many hard things in my childhood uniquely prepared me to handle the rigor and stress of the Smart case. And much of the wisdom I gleaned from working with Elizabeth and the Smart family has prepared me for today's adventures.

Through it all, I have discovered that the people and things we often dismiss because they are different, difficult, or don't perfectly align with our beliefs and perceptions offer the most valuable lessons.

It is part of the human experience for individuals, cultures, and adversity to be underappreciated, but if we shine a light long enough on them, we will see that there is beauty, texture, and purpose in every soul, situation, and struggle.

Acknowledgments

Similar to my experience during the search for Elizabeth Smart, writing this book involved the help, inspiration, and support of a diverse group of people, for whom I will always be grateful.

Thank you, Roger Thompson, former president of the Rotary Club of Salt Lake City, for asking me at the last minute to deliver a tribute on Veterans Day 2019. My five-minute talk about growing up next door to Baker Paxton, coming to understand and appreciate his tremendous struggle and unheralded sacrifice, was the start of a journey toward writing this book. I am also grateful to my fellow Rotarians for their kind response and encouragement to write Baker's story.

Thank you, Marion Roach Smith, for your incredible instruction, feedback, and passion for this book. The structure, focus, and writing would not be as strong without your guidance and mentorship. I also appreciate my fellow master class students, Eric Meade, Jill Kerr, Steve Newman, Amy McHugh, and Diane Yoder, for your help, insights, feedback, and perspective. Specifically, you made a significant contribution to this book by helping me see my religious culture from the outside and encouraging and inspiring me to write about it.

Thank you, Brilliant Miller, for your friendship and the opportunity to contribute to your book, *Behind the Drive: 99 Inspiring Stories from the Life of an American Entrepreneur*, and to Linda Luchetti for connecting us and for supporting me on this project, as well as several others. This experience helped me to find my voice and gave me confidence that I could one day tackle a book of my own.

Thank you to my amazing teachers and mentors, Dana Tumpowsky, Fred Fogo, Susan Gunter, Susan Cotler, Tom Steinke, Ty Harrison, Nancy

Panos Schmitt, Ray Ownbey, Mike Korologos, Bob Hunter, Jeff Hasen, Joy Kohnken, Shannon Michael, Fred Rollins, Nan Chalat Noaker, Jeri Cartwright, Clarann Jacobs, Bliss Roberts, Dale Fueling, Gerry Fowles, Shauna Johnson, Susan Glenn, Charlotte McDonald, Paul Romney, Betsy Drake, Gladys Buxton, Pauline Vogel, Winnifred Jardine, Marilyn Poulson, Jack Marzo, Robert Hodgson, Judy Dykman, Gene Bechthold, Martha Felt, Merilee Barton, Kelly Hindley, Carrie Gaykowski, Barry Scholl, Lorin Ronnow, and several more I know I am missing. Thank you for believing in me and taking the time to help foster my love of learning and writing.

Thank you Mike Grass, Missy Larsen, Karen Hale, Nate McDonald, and the other members of the Elizabeth Smart Search Center communication team, for all your unheralded and behind-the-scenes work during the search and rescue.

Thank you to the members of the immediate and extended Smart family and the other members of the Elizabeth Search Center Board, especially Ted and Kathy Wilson and Phil and Suann Adams. Your trust, friendship, and collaboration during the search meant so much. The experience of working with you was life changing and something I will always cherish.

Thank you to all the journalists and television personalities I have had the pleasure of working with during the search and rescue, and in the years that have followed. I'm grateful for the friendship I share with several of you twenty years later. The incomplete list includes: Steve Cohen, Santina Leuci, Barbara Walters, Robin Roberts, Diane Sawyer, George Stephanopoulos, Chris Cuomo, Jim Vojtec, Jim DuBreuil, John Walsh, Jamie Kotkin Hammer, Rick Segall, Audrey Wood, Susan Zirinsky, Gayle King, Nancy Kramer, Jane Clayson, Harry Smith, Larry King, Nadine Shambulyat, Sarah Schnare, Ben Winslow, William Shatner, Jill Chappell, Wolf Blitzer, Anderson Cooper, Meredith Vieira, Shephard Smith, Sean Hannity, Gretchen Carlson, Greta Van Susteren, Geraldo Rivera, Craig Rivera, Hoda Kotb, Elizabeth Vargus, Debbie Dujanovic, Nicea DeGering, Heidi Hatch, Scott McCane, Lee Benson, Pat Reavy, Jennifer Napier-Pearce, Alexandra Jewett, Jennifer Dobner, Cristina Flores, Holly Wayment, Heather Simonsen, Fields Mosely, Max Roth, Dan Rascon, Mark Koelbel, Shauna Lake, Bob Evans, Shelley Osterloh, Stacy Butler, Rod Decker, Ann Curry, Katie Couric, Matt Lauer, Savannah Guthrie,

Kathy Lee Gifford, Soledad O'Brien, David Bloom, Connie Chung, Ashleigh Banfield, Lisa Ling, Dan Abrams, James Nelson, Maggie Haberman, Jeane MacIntosh, Phil Donohue, Linda Fantin, Patty Henetz, Ray Grass, Patrick McMahon, Maryam Ayromlou, Ron Ralston, Carol McKinney, Dina Long, Charmayne Lewis, Shellie Smith, Jim Mietus, Peter Ornstein, Jeff Brooks, Sandy Reisgraf, Derek Jensen, Buddy Blankenfeld, Chris Jones, Brian Mullahy, Mary Nickels, Ron Bird, Tim Hughes, Tom Barberi, Grant Nielsen, Amanda Dixon, Doug Wright, Kevin Peraino, Lindsay Smith, Kevin Walters, Nina Zacuto, Ron Hill, Lee Davidson, McKay Coppins, Elizabeth Waller, Reed Cowan, Ruth Todd, Kim Johnson, Jeff Allred, Michael Brandy, Cathy Free, and many others (those whom I have missed, please forgive me).

A special thank you to my therapist, Holly Willard, for your amazing support, perspective, and collaboration. I went back into counseling (after a two-year absence) when I started the first iteration of this book and needed help in processing many of the experiences I write about and in navigating the roller coaster of emotions as well as the stress and strain that accompanies a project of this magnitude. I am a huge proponent of counseling and believe that everyone, regardless of your situation, can benefit from having a caring, personal consultant. I am grateful to many talented therapists over the years, including Clair Mellenthin, Dr. Julie Hanks, Dr. John Lund, and Gary Glenn, who have played an important role in my life's journey.

Thank you to my agent, Michael Smallbone. You have been a tremendous advisor and friend throughout this process. I'm so grateful you were able to help me secure a relationship with the perfect publisher for this book. I also really appreciate your candor, honesty, integrity, and desire to always do the right thing.

Thank you to Post Hill Press for believing in me. Thank you Anthony Ziccardi for taking a chance on me and for your insights and collaboration. Thank you Madeline Sturgeon for all of your amazing work and help through all the ups and downs of the process. I also appreciate the support from Michael Wilson, Alana Mills, Rachel Hoge, Melissa Smith, and the entire editorial, publicity, and production teams. Thank you, Elena Vega and Mary Cantor, for your amazing copy editing. Your attention to detail, perspective, and suggestions are second to none.

Acknowledgments

Thank you to my good friends who provided insights and feedback on the concept, structure, and several aspects of the book. This includes Steve Cohen, James and Maria Garrett, Laura Klarman, Leigh Gibson, Greg Hopkins, Leland Bresock, Donna Angel, Jody Genessy, Nicole Stansbury, and Jenny Miller.

Thank you, Scott Eggers, for your creativity and amazing work in designing the book cover as well as for your steady example and friendship.

Thank you to my bishop, Sean O'Brien, who was inspired to ask me to deliver the Christmas address to my church congregation in 2021, and to the Olympus First Ward for your reaction and kind words. At the time, I had been struggling for more than three months with this book and was ready to give up. While the talk did not include any of the subject matter from this book, it provided an opportunity for me to employ some of the storytelling techniques I had learned and the response I received gave me the needed confidence and motivation to move forward.

Thank you to my personal editor and friend, Catherine Arveseth. You not only did an amazing job cleaning up and making my writing sing, but pushed me to explore, analyze, and expand several key areas of the book. You were also instrumental in helping provide additional context surrounding the culture and history of The Church of Jesus Christ of Latter-day Saints, which added a lot to my story. I am so grateful for all of your hard work, hustle, and attention to detail.

Thank you, Elizabeth Smart. It has been an amazing ride and I am so grateful for everything I have learned from you and for many of the crazy experiences we have had together. (Sorry about the blinding eyeful of whiteness surfing mishap I just learned about!) I am so grateful for your support of this book. When I called and told you about it, your immediate encouragement and willingness to help meant the world to me. Your response after reading the manuscript brought me to tears.

Thank you, Jeremy, Natalee, and Amy. You're the best sibs. I appreciate everything you have done and still do for me.

Thank you, Dad, for providing me with incredible opportunities and pursuits as I was growing up. Working alongside you in the trenches catching crawlers, throwing newspapers, and aerating lawns taught me so much. Some of my fondest memories are from the Jazz and Cubs games we attended, as a result of the money we earned together from your side hustles.

Thank you, Mom, for everything. You never gave up on me when others did, including that time a first-grade teacher told you, with me present, that I was helpless and would never amount to anything. I am eternally grateful for your persistence in helping me as I struggled mightily to learn to read and grasp the basics. I appreciate your inspiration and for passing along your love of writing, which has become a lifelong passion for me. Some of my fondest memories are sitting by your side as a teenager and learning from you during those late-night sessions, typing away on the Franklin typewriter.

Thank you, Harrison, Carter, Grayson, and Willa. I appreciate your support, your encouragement, and the sacrifices you have made to help me bring this book to life. Along with your mom, you are the greatest blessings in my life. I will always love you no matter what.

And finally, a special thank you to Laura, my wife, companion, and love of my life. This book would not have been possible without your vision, input, sacrifice, and support. You were there for me and provided incredible inspiration, feedback, and direction at each critical juncture along the journey. I am especially grateful for all you endured while Elizabeth was missing and for your willingness to relive several of those experiences, feelings, and emotions as we collaborated on the book. I will be forever grateful for you and your contribution. I love you.

About the Author

Chris Thomas is a writer, speaker, and communication professional. He is best known for his work as the Smart family publicist during the nine-and-a-half months Elizabeth was missing. In this capacity, he fielded more than ten thousand calls from journalists, served as a family spokesperson by completing hundreds of interviews, helped coordinate the Smart's lobbying efforts for the national Amber Alert, and managed a crush of media when Elizabeth was rescued. John Walsh of America's Most Wanted said that Thomas deserves most of the credit for keeping the public and family focused on finding Elizabeth.

Thomas also managed the trial and sentencing of Elizabeth's abductors, helped position her as a leading child advocate, and managed Elizabeth's engagement, her surprise wedding, the birth of her children, and the divorce of her parents.

In addition to Elizabeth, Thomas has managed more than three hundred crises for companies, nonprofits, government organizations, and families. He earned a bachelor's degree in communication from Westminster College.

For a book club discussion guide, pictures, commentary, and more, visit
www.ChrisThomasWriter.com